Critical theory and the English teacher

The English teacher must be aware that the very identity of English as a subject for study in secondary schools is open to doubt. It is becoming increasingly clear that the values and beliefs which have formed traditional English tend to devalue or at least exclude the experience of most students. At the same time, the tools of critical theory have been used in higher education to make the subject still more rarefied and distant from everyday experience.

In this radical exploration, Nick Peim, himself a practising English teacher, shows how the insights of discourse theory, psychoanalysis, semiotics and deconstruction can be used on the material of modern culture as well as on literature, traditionally defined, on the practices of writing and in oral work. Throughout, he writes in a style which even those with no background in critical theory will find approachable, and backs his arguments with practical classroom examples.

Nick Peim is Head of English at Beauchamp College, Leicester

Teaching Secondary English
General Editor: Peter King

This series provides a focus for a variety of aims and teaching styles in contemporary English teaching. It is designed both for new teachers who want a simple guide to good practice, and for more experienced teachers who may want to revitalize their own teaching by considering alternative ideas and methods.

Also available in this series:

Encouraging talk
Lewis Knowles

Encouraging writing
Robert Protherough

Teaching the basic skills in English
Don Smedley

Using computers in English
A practical guide
Phil Moore

My language, our language
Meeting special needs in English 11–16
Bernadette Walsh

Starting English teaching
Robert Jeffcoate

Critical theory and the English teacher
Transforming the subject

Nick Peim

London and New York

First Published 1993
by Routledge
11 New Fetter Lane, London EC4P 4EE

Simultaneously published in the USA and Canada
by Routledge
29 West 35th Street, New York, NY 10001

© 1993 Nick Peim

Typeset in 10/12 point Times by
Ponting–Green Publishing Services, Chesham, Bucks

Printed and bound in Great Britain by
Mackays of Chatham plc, Chatham, Kent

British Library Cataloguing in Publication Data

A catalogue record for this book is available from the
British Library.

*Library of Congress Cataloging in Publication Data has been
applied for.*

ISBN 0–415–05751–5   ISBN 0–415–05752–3 (pbk)

To the memory of Mikolaj, Catherine and Timothy

Contents

List of examples

List of figures and tables

FIGURES

TABLES

General Editor's preface

The imposition of a National Curriculum in English at secondary level has forced into the open opposing forces striving to gain power over the curriculum. Without going into any of the political, ideological or educational arguments which have erupted onto the English curriculum landscape through the push of these forces, it is necessary to stress that far from providing the definitive answer to the question 'What is English?', the National Curriculum has made the question even more insistent. The anger over the 1992 review of the English National Curriculum and the furore over the SATs debacle have only fuelled a debate which cannot in the least be said to be theoretical as it underpins (or undermines) the pedagogical ground on which every English teacher stands.

Harrassed English teachers might be forgiven in 1992 for crying, 'a pox on both your houses', in the face of ignorant interference from politicians on the one hand, and on the other the continuing demand for a reworking of English as a kind of cultural studies from the literary radicals within some university departments and parts of the National Association of Teachers of English. They can be forgiven, but nevertheless they must be urged not to give in to the temptation to curse both sides and turn away to seek some imagined peaceful place of straightforward teaching. For there is no such place. The most practical matters of our teaching strategy and pupils' learning experiences depend upon our view of the nature of our subject, its content and its processes. This is why in this book Nick Peim addresses both theory and practice together.

This is not a book to be dismissed as of value only to those English teachers who are already sympathetic to the ascendency of literary theory in English study over the last fifteen years. Those whose view is that English at school level should have nothing to do with literary theory will find this a book as informed by practical thinking about teaching and learning as they would hope to see. Nick Peim is not just asking questions about the nature of English; he is actually showing how the answers to these questions lead to particular classroom strategies. It is a practical book arising from the work of a practising teacher. It is practice that is yet not pragmatism, but rather action born of reflection upon the content and processes of the subject.

It is seductively easy at the present time for an English teacher to take the view that her job is just to teach the kids and to come to terms with the confusing demands of a National Curriculum and steer through the chaos of its implementation. And of course, this latter is something that must be done. However, it is dangerous at times of crisis to believe that the immediate struggle is all that can take your attention if you are to survive. Frequently, the means to survive are available only to those who can fight with a mind cleared by grasping a principled, conceptually organized position. There are many political forces currently at work which appear to wish to de-skill the teaching profession, to reduce the teacher to a technician carrying out the commands of those who determine what is to be taught. Teachers who refuse to think about the nature of their subject will make it easy for such forces to overcome the profession. This book can help any English teacher to fight back.

What Nick Peim does in this book is to provide such a means for survival by looking at the central core of the English curriculum and vigorously questioning such matters as: the concept of reading and the definition of literacy; the nature of the secondary canon; categories of writing; speech and identity. He opens up the nature of the discourse within which we express what English is and through which we do what English we do. In asking his questions he finds means to answer them through employing some of the insights provided by advances in recent literary theory (which have themselves led to a changing view of the nature of literature as a study) to change our view of what secondary English can do. The continuum between literary theory within higher education and the secondary English curriculum is not a matter of teaching new knowledge in school (it is not akin to new discoveries in science being so important that they have to be prescribed in the school curriculum), but of reviewing our very concept of English and the relationship between English as a study and the social context out of which it comes.

This book is part of the Teaching Secondary English series published originally by Methuen and now by Routledge. The books in this series are intended to give practical guidance in the various areas of the English curriculum. Each area is treated in a separate volume in order to gain the necessary space in which to discuss it at some length. The aim of the series is twofold: to describe good practice by exploring the approaches and activities reflected in the daily work of an English teacher in the comprehensive school; and to give a practical lead to teachers who wish to try out for themselves a wider repertoire of teaching skills and ways of organizing syllabuses and lessons. Taken as a whole, the series does not press upon the reader a ready-made philosophy, but attempts to provide a map of the English teaching landscape in which the separate volumes highlight individual features of the terrain.

At first glance it may seem that this particular book is at odds with this description of the series in that it does press upon the reader a particular philosophy. And it is true that this volume is explicit and insistent about its particular approach to English. However, it does share with the other volumes a concern for how English shall be taught in the classroom, and Nick Peim presents his philosophy in pertinently practical terms. The philosophy Peim advocates does not lie behind other volumes in this series, although the practical approaches described in other volumes would not be outlawed in Nick Peim's kind of classroom, but it seems fitting that a series which has been published over the last decade should end with a volume that exhibits some of the radical thinking of that decade and which provides the possible basis for good practice in the next ten years.

In the last decade, particularly since the publication of Peter Widdowson's *Re-reading English* (Methuen, 1982), we have become familiar with the cry of 'crisis in English!' headlines in the quality newspapers towards the end of the 1980s. We have had stories attacking changes in the content of English degrees, with claims that students are required to read works of literary theory at the expense of novels and poetry. From the McCabe affair at Cambridge in the late 1970s to the fuss in some quarters of the press concerning the appointment of Terry Eagleton, a known Marxist and literary theorist, to one of the most highly regarded professorships in English at Oxford, these stories have frequently been told as dramas about the supposed dark influences of radically motivated literary theorists strangling the old literary canons in a deadly grip. Similarly, in the last two years some of the press have spotted similar sinister forces of radical influence behind the way in which those who have wished to preserve the broad approach to secondary English in the 1970s and 1980s, have fought off attempts to reinterpret the English National Curriculum in the narrowest definitions of literacy and literature. Setting such journalistic simplifications aside, it is true that what has emerged is a wider fight for influence and power over the whole English curriculum, and in such a fight the secondary teachers themselves must be armed with the ability to analyse conceptually their subject and to understand the nature of the discourse in which the subject is argued over. Nick Peim's book enables all English teachers to understand their position in that fight and the importance of the battle. It helps give them the power to contribute to changing their subject, not by indulging in polemic, but by reasoned action within their own classroom practices.

Peter King
Series Editor
March 1993.

Acknowledgements

The writing of this book was a largely solitary affair; but I owe several debts of thanks to people who had an influence in its production – of one kind or another, but who can't be held responsible for any of its faults. Peter King was a helpful and patient editor. Helen Nixon made useful comments on an early draft of Chapter 2. I thank Annette Patterson and Bronwyn Mellor who both read a late draft of the whole book and made encouragingly positive comments. The English department at Beauchamp College have been a constant source of institutional support. I owe thanks also to the management of Beauchamp College for giving a little precious time for a project that had no immediate or obvious returns. Paul Moran, Adrian Stokes and Imelda Whelehan, members of a local theory group, provided a rich context for the exchange of ideas and knowledge – as well as considerable friendship. Paul Moran was also a (remarkable) colleague who has done more than anyone else to advance my grasp of all things theoretical and their impact on the subject, English. Discussions with Paul played their part in the production of this book, but have also played another part in taking my thinking well beyond it. I am also indebted to the members of the national 'Theory in English Teaching' group, too many to mention by name, for sustaining an interest in the idea of changing the subject. If I single out Alastair West, it is for engaging my interest a long time ago in the politics of English teaching.

My greatest debt of thanks is to Domini for her many kinds of support, friendship and more. I must thank Lizzie, Katy, Louise and James for their various, powerful kinds of sustenance, too, and for their useful and good-humoured scepticism for a project that seemed very remote from their concerns.

The End of Something (from *The Essential Hemingway*, 1977) is reproduced with the permission of HarperCollins.

Introduction

This book seeks to ask questions – and to make some proposals – about the identity and functioning of English in the secondary school curriculum. This interrogation is conducted from a point of view informed by what has been called theory. The kind of theory advocated here, though, is not simply literary; it seeks also to address the social, the cultural and the institutional being of English, aiming to establish a critique founded on the idea of an alternative practice. The project I've attempted is to re-examine the fundamental practices of English: to re-examine the practices of reading, writing and oracy in schooling – in the light of a theoretically informed rereading of what they are and how they work in existing, routine and institutionalized practices. Proposing different activities and a different orientation in classroom practice, the aim is also to examine some of the issues concerning the institutional identity of the subject.

The particular model of theory I've adopted is generally, if loosely, referred to as post-structuralism. Post-structuralism here is conceived of as a body of theory addressing textual and linguistic cultural practices in a completely decentring, and deconstructive manner. Post-structuralist theory renders it impossible to claim that any signifying events, texts or practices can guarantee or fix their own meanings on their own. Post-structuralism is not, though, just a nihilistic theory of the absolute relativity of meaning. Post-structuralist theory also indicates how signifying events, texts and practices do get given fixed meanings within social practices and contexts; these contexts being institutions of reading and meaning. Post-structuralism, as construed here, addresses aspects of language and textuality as they inhere in particular social forms, refusing to address some mythical, essential, textual being that might be referred to as the spirit, or the value or quality of the text. There are no doubt other kinds of theory that will make similar points about language, texts, meanings and contexts. And there are, no doubt, other ways of using – or of not using – post-structuralist theory that would contest my readings of the various aspects of theory and the theoretical issues I've dealt with here.

Post-structuralist theory may be used to question all the familiar and habitual assumptions of English, everything that has been taken for granted as the general currency of the institutional being of English. This includes ideas – like author, response, meaning and creativity, for example – that attribute specific, limited meaning and value to particular texts. It also demands examination of institutionalized practices of teaching and assessment – all the beliefs in practice of the subject, the different perspectives and terms it puts to work, effectively deconstructing, problematizing the ready-made assumptions and practices that give the subject its recognizable, characteristic content.

Post-structuralism demands an awareness of the social, cultural conditions of meaning, of the dynamic interactions between texts and their contexts, the cultural practices and habits that determine the nature and directions of the process of meaning. Institutions – as organizing contexts – are centrally significant in terms of holding meanings in place, promoting specific meanings, enabling and disqualifying meanings. Institutions here include institutionalized reading practices, for example. Post-structuralist theory, then, enables analysis to go beyond the immediate encounter of reader and text to examine the institutional practices that position readers and texts, and to come to an awareness of the culturally powerful, readily available systems and possibilities of meaning. Post-structuralism also has the most powerful available descriptions of the individual subject of language and meaning – as a mobile entity enmeshed in cultural formations. This radically changes our understanding of reading and meaning processes: it also has implications for our understanding of cultural processes more generally.

In general, post-structuralism is likely to be sceptical of the claim of any single system of knowledge – like literature, for example – to comprehensive explanatory power, universal value or truth. Post-structuralism would insist on the necessary recognition that our knowledge and understanding of *anything* is inseparable from the business of representation (language – signs, texts, discourses, institutions). Post-structuralism would tend to insist that knowledge and understanding are always *positioned* – and that the identity and meaning of things shifts radically given different perspectives and cultural contexts. Post-structuralism is a multi-directional thing, a mobile theory of texts, language, the subject, subjectivity. It draws on different kinds of knowledge: for example, linguistics, philosophy and psychoanalysis.

Post-structuralism has, in turn, been influential in the fields of feminism, political and social theory, history and archaeology, as well as geography, art theory and many other forms of knowledge.

Post-structuralist theory isn't a singular and strictly delimited thing, of course. What's offered as 'theory' in this book is *one* version of post-structuralist theory that I've attempted at times to link with sociological and comparative sociolinguistic perspectives. What post-structuralism is is necessarily difficult to define and is likely to refer to different things in different contexts. In certain contexts post-structuralism would be closely associated with or even equated with post-modernism, post-colonialism. The terms post-modern and post-colonial are used variously to describe a way of seeing things and/or a particular state of things in the contemporary world. There are some who might say that post-structuralism really begins with Marx, Freud and Nietzsche. Others might say that Heidegger is really the source. Some might describe post-structuralism as the culmination of a counter-trend running through the history of western thought, whereas others might well dismiss the whole matter as a faddish distraction. Some would attach great, global importance to it, others pointing out its particular Frenchness, indicating the greater significance of the German tradition. What post-structuralism means, then, is subject to different interpretations and different uses. Post-structuralism may, for example, be used to find new ways of reading the canonical texts of English literature; it may also be used to call into question the whole idea of the authority of the canon of English literature, looking rather at how it has been constructed as a specific discourse within specific institutional contexts and for specific institutional purposes. In the present context, I've chosen to direct a certain limited reading of post-structuralist theory to the identity of subject English.

The principal names classically associated with post-structuralism are – arguably – Derrida, Foucault, Lacan and Lyotard, though there are a host of subsidiary writers that might be cited. There are problems, however, with any attempt to insist on attribution to singularly identified names or positions. Although associated with certain names, the ideas generated by post-structuralism can be found in many different aspects and accounts of the theory. These accounts may be considered as strictly secondary, but only on a reading ascribing original meaning to the original texts and their authors. This would be a thoroughly un-post-structuralist procedure, though no doubt it has become a norm in certain academic contexts. The very idea that there could be a singular and generally known version of the post-structuralist theory would run counter to all the implications of the theory itself. It would, in effect, be impossible also to attribute these ideas and the uses they've been put to here, to particular and specifically traceable sources. Post-structuralism tends to operate against totalizing theories of meaning or knowledge. Although specific aspects of it have been associated with certain proper names, the bearers of those names can't be held to account for all its many manifestations. Nor can the various things post-structuralism has become be traced back to specific and single sources. To refer to those names is to acknowledge the idea of the author as authority: to engage in a specific academic language game that demands these rules of reference be obeyed. In academic discourses there is a vested interest in maintaining these established forms of reference, with their connotations of an initiate, exclusive knowledge. Indeed, academic professional identity may depend on it. However, deconstruction, for example, may exist – may even thrive – completely independently of the name of Derrida.

None of these kinds of theory are of any particular value in themselves. In the context of the teaching of English they are worth pursuing in so far as they offer a way of looking again at the familiar forms of things, at the habits of practice, at assumptions. Theory can give a new hold on old practices and can make the established and familiar appear not quite so acceptable and proper. As part of the same movement away from established prejudices of thinking, theory can open up new spaces for new practices and directions. The theory I've adopted is useful to the extent that it makes the connections between language practices, educational practices and social forms inescapable. In other words, useful in that it addresses the politics of the subject – power and ideology at work in specific ideas and institutional practices.

The elements of theory I've proposed are certainly not essential. There may well be other ways of unhinging the established identity of the subject and of proposing different models and practices by doing so. No doubt there are. Deconstruction is not the exclusive property of post-structuralism. This might be expressed another way, by saying that the meaning of theory is changed by the uses it is put to and the contexts it works in, just as much as the kind of theory at work may determine practices. An important point to make here is that the very meaning of theory is changed by the uses you put it to. Theory itself doesn't necessarily guarantee a position dedicated to some kind of radical shift in the order of things.

The position expressed here claims that the identity of English has been and is founded on premises and practices that are no longer really viable. My argument is against English – against its current practices and the values they represent – proposing a newly defined field of ideas and activities.

Even though it may continue, doggedly, to make special claims for itself – special claims about its unique role in education – English takes up its place in the curriculum, being continuous with the systematic discrimination that is most crudely realized in exam procedures. It works against the majority of its students. English does this while proposing quite specific values and beliefs – about literacy, about the individual and about the world. These values and beliefs tend in general to devalue, or at least to exclude, the cultural experiences of most of its subjects, or students. Although often representing itself either as dealing in universal truths, or as being liberally open to all, English in schools as we know it is an ideologically loaded business. There is no English – no real, essential English – outside of its institutional practice. The institutions of English are many and varied and include, for example, the institution of the school, the institution of the teaching profession, the institution of examination processes, as well as institutionalized ideas about literacy and learning.

It is the contention of this book, then, that certain philosophical and sociological knowledges make it impossible to avoid confronting the ideologically loaded nature of English. Just as the philosophical critique of the founding ideas of the subject exposes its ideological inflection, so the sociology of the subject deconstructs the pretensions of English to independent existence. The very being of English is defined by the general institutional functions of education. It does not reside in some ethereal, in some mythical space uncontaminated by the material conditions of its world. The content and the style of English are vulnerable to a drastically deconstructive, philosophical and sociological analysis – an analysis deconstructive of any pretensions English may have to simplicity, to being objective or neutral or natural, or to having anything beyond a strictly institutional existence.

The general critique of educational practice as naturalized systematic discrimination – offered by what might be referred to as a deconstructive sociology – has fatal implications for the special claims English has made for itself in terms of models of cultural heritage and personal growth, and those other institutional practices of correction and discrimination that have more silently dominated it – versions of language and culture as proper heritage. These accounts of English – along with some of their more recently proposed potential successors – have lacked the terms of reference to address, on the one hand, the consistent history of English as 'reproduction', and the fractured and contradictory operations of the subject in practice. Liberal ideas held by the advocates of creativity have never been interested in situating the subject within the context of its history as institutionalized discourse. That is what has made them completely consistent with conservative ideology.

Looking critically at the theoretical base of English, subjecting the subject's institutional practices to sociological knowledge, deconstructing the rhetoric of the subject's official and established identity, it is impossible to avoid confronting the politics of the subject and the subject as a kind of politics: involving a politics of culture and a politics of institutional educational practice. Politics here refers to material and ideological effects. Theory may offer a kind of thinking enabling the institutional identity of the subject and its ideological inflection to be probed. The point here is not to do away with ideology nor to escape the confines of the institution – neither would be possible – but to address both: to continue to address both in all the discourses and practices of all aspects of the subject. Subject English has always tended to deny – in its beliefs and rhetorics – that it has any relation to the political. Theory promises the possibility of opening the subject to its political being. The introduction of the question of theory is a necessary condition for political change.

Theory of whatever kind, though, is not necessarily and unambiguously a force for positive change, nor for change at all. It is perfectly possible to use post-structuralist theory simply to add new perspectives to old practices and positions: in higher education this is evidently the way that theory has worked: effectively to rejuvenate a flagging subject, tired of its own forms of thought, its uncertain field of knowledge and its worn out debates. If academic theory has purveyed itself to English teachers – among many others – as abstruse and irrelevant, then that's academic theory for you, and is not the condition for the existence of theory itself. Phenomenologically speaking, there is no theory-in-itself. Theory, though, may be simply construed – or constructed – to mean the process of questioning and making explicit fundamental principles and may be the condition for a more consciously and self-consciously aware practice. Theory in this sense may still appear difficult and alienating because it addresses what commonsense, routine habits of thought in English (in this case) would otherwise pass over in silence. To go beyond common sense may mean, for example, overreaching the bounds of common sense habits of expression – common sense being the mute acceptance of the routine assumptions that keep things safe from the mobility of critical thought.

It's certainly conceivable that in the rigourous context of schooling, theory – as interrogative critique – is much more likely to diagnose the subject's complicity with modes of thinking and institutional practices that are based on social discrimination. English in schooling represents a significant social practice, on a mass scale. It is also more likely to provide a new idea altogether of a 'foundation' from which to produce the conditions for a completely different basis for the subject's operation. The dual movement of critique and reformulation – as a continuous process – is the potentiality that theory offers to English in schools as a means of dealing with its present, compromised position. A project of redefinition answering to this description would be very different from academic theory in higher education.

The kind of cultural analysis – a thoroughly critical analysis – of English that a theoretically informed reading of the politics of the subject enables, renders English as we know it unviable, except as it can be practised in thoroughly bad faith. The implications of post-structuralist, sociological and sociolinguistic theory throw into doubt all the language practices of English, including all those practices associated with creativity, with self-expression, as well as those that emphasise social aspects of language, like correctness or appropriateness, for example. Comparative sociolinguistics problematizes the assessment of language and constitutes an aspect of theory making, for example, assessment criteria unable to conceal their political function. Any comparative theory of culture also means that literature – an idea that has been important in English in various forms – is not at all a sustainable category. Among the problems of literature highlighted by this kind of theory, it should only be necessary to mention that no one really knows what it is – the problem of definition, in the first place, and, secondly, the problem of value – no one really knows what it stands for. A culturally critical analysis of the idea of literature – and its associated ideas – will find that it has stood for a kind of discourse which is more suited to some people than others; that it is really an empty category that's been used to further the processes of social distinction as they operate in education.

The position of English in relation to language and literature is thoroughly anomalous. English has saddled itself with ideas and practices that are very strictly limited and limiting. The thoroughly negative direction of this critique could, however, become positive. The realization of a general field of language and textuality systematically excluded from English represents greatly extended possibilities. I'm proposing here – albeit partially – that this more inclusive field be addressed, a field of language and textuality in which questions of power and ideology, for example, could not be ignored.

The practices of a subject addressing language and textuality in a far more broad sense than any ever dreamed of by English would necessarily address the textual politics of subjects and institutions. It's difficult to see how these political issues could be anything other than central and explicit. To reconfigure English so that it addresses language and textual practices in general – in the media, in institutions, in everyday social exchanges – to do all this seems to me essential to rescue the subject from the hollowness of its fundamental founding categories – stories, poems, Shakespeare, personal response or themes – and from the narrow range of concerns they imply. Unfortunately, this doesn't mean that the grading system will go away. The general case made by the sociology of education remains to be answered. But the sociology of subject identities – unmasking the pretensions of English to be based on some natural order of things – may be confronted by a different definition of the field of literacy than has been occupied by English. This may mean teaching explicitly and sociologically against the institutional operations of inequality; to show how forms, categories and processes of schooling, for example, are loaded in favour of dominant power groups; to show how identities are inscribed according to these forms, categories and processes, as well as refusing to pretend that matters of language and literacy can be taught without reference to social forms. To reconstruct English in this way, means addressing issues of inequality and cultural identity: it also means addressing more fully and more centrally issues of race, class and gender, issues in relation to culture and democracy, concerning, among other things, language differences and power, what it means to be literate – for while these issues are excluded from the central preoccupations of the subject, they must remain marginalized and the learning of language and literacy must therefore be distorted.

What you've then got may no longer be English as we know it; but then again, who cares? In other words, in whose interests is English – in its present forms – maintained?

In certain contexts, in recent times, recognition that English is political has become something of a truism. What this means precisely in terms of the will to change the definition and practice of the subject is a difficult and complex issue. These complexities can only be dealt with bluntly here, based on the following line of argument. The subject English has historically been implicated in models of practice based on ideas of cultural heritage, on a culture of correction, on a liberal culture of individual creativity, on a model of multiculturalism or on a model of the transmission of cultural capital. All of these models are rendered clearly untenable by post-modern conditions – as well as by post-structuralist descriptions – of cultural exchange. Under these conditions, transnational cultural products, produced and distributed in transnational institutional conditions, come into reading contexts that are very specifically local. These conditions bear no relation to the models that structure English. These conditions make necessary a rethinking of how the political is tied in with the processes and effects of change. In terms of an address of the established forms of knowledge known as subjects, this means that specifically educational questions merge into considerations of political, economic and social systems. An important issue here would be the very nature of ethnicity and how it relates to powerful meaning systems. The school, and how it mediates forms of knowledge, would be one point from which to begin such an analysis.

The practice and the meaning of the subject in the arena of state education is a significant issue. At least the explicit emergence of the question of theory has offered the possibility of breaking out of the historic limits of the subject. This brings within the horizon not only a perception of the material and ideological conditions of its being: it also makes possible the conditions for change.

The problems of definition facing any cultural politics in relation to the idea of literacy are issues that are only touched on here. What's offered is a position taken and the beginnings of an attempt to institute a deconstructive practice of a subject dealing with language and literacy within the arena of state education. The project touches upon – without extensively dealing with – important matters arising from any engagement with signifying systems. The relations between institutions and audiences; questions about ethnicity – local, national and transnational; official, dominant, subordinate and all sorts of popular cultures, as well as matters of a more explicitly political slant: questions about all these issues are certainly raised by the kind of project for deconstructing English I've proposed here. In the end questions are also raised about what might be meant by key terms such as democracy and equality, and how these terms might be conceived of as quite different from their present general uses.

1   The habits of English

AN EVERYDAY TALE OF ENGLISH FOLK

Reading stories in the name of English is routine in many senses. In schools it happens every day. In thousands of classrooms in schools across the nation, teachers – English teachers, teachers of English – read stories to their classes. So commonplace an activity forms an apparently natural part of what has been called 'bread and butter English' to the point where English might well seem unimaginable without it. Whatever the brand of English being espoused (and it has recently been officially conceded that there are many brands of English), reading stories constitutes something central, essential – even quint-essential – about English. The central place accorded to this activity in the universal education system could be expressed as the core of the core – often conceived of as a kind of spiritual essence at the heart of English, itself at the heart of, even *the* heart itself – of the national curriculum. Reading stories is one of the great universal activities of English, and English is one of the core subjects, if not the core subject, of national education. Reading is obviously and explicitly at the centre of practical, theoretical and ideological concerns in education. Questions about reading, differences in relation to reading, engage signifi-cant cultural and political tensions. Reading stories must be caught up in this arena of differences.

Throughout the primary and secondary school, the essential features of the scene may be envisaged. In its ideal form we may imagine the teacher giving an engaging – but not actively or overtly leading – rendering of the story in fine, modulating tones. The class listens or follows attentively as the story works its magic on the uniformly enchanted group. Somehow the students' responses begin to stir. A discussion or writing may follow. Issues will have been raised, responses formulated and developed. At the end of the process everyone will be the richer for the encounter. In its idealized and conventional description the reading of stories is often represented as just such an uncomplicated and essentially self-contained process. There is – in a very important sense – no need to justify the activity. Its value is held to be self-evident – a truth universally acknowledged. It just seems to be obvious, common sense that stories should be central to the English curriculum, that their reading should produce positive, enriching effects and that stories constitute an essential stage on the royal road to literacy – as well as promoting the humanly desirable qualities of empathy, awareness, and knowledge of the world beyond.

An interrogative approach to the business of reading stories in English might aim to examine critically the common-sense and commonly held assumptions that sustain the perceived meaning and value of stories in English, and that inform attitudes to reading and textual communication generally. The idea is to question the centrality of stories, to enquire into what stories are and how they function, and – in doing so – to begin to challenge assumptions about what English is: why it takes the particular forms it does, why it promotes certain ideas and activities; also to begin to propose that there may be alternatives to current practices, and that there may be very good reasons why alternatives should be considered.

The approach offered here uses ideas from 'theory' to question the common-sense assumptions that tend to operate in the uses of stories in education and in the reading of stories more generally. The intention, though, is to avoid the – often alienating – language of high-level theory and to borrow terms and procedures from 'common sense' in order to exercise a critique of established reading practices. Starting from a single example it is possible to begin to approach the well-established, common-sense position on stories. The kind of questioning procedure used in what follows is perfectly plausible in classroom practice. Carefully prepared questions themselves, asked with sufficient persistence, can be enough to begin the process of unmasking the theories of English and constructing new ideas, new models.

QUESTIONS: STORIES IN EDUCATION?

Some form of critical analysis of dominant practices might begin by asking a few questions to raise and identify issues – in this case about the role of stories in education. It is important to establish, one way or another, that common-sense readings and common-sense versions of the business of reading are bound up with an ideology of knowledge – a system of ideas, often explicit or unspoken, but regulating what can and should be thought. The apparently simple, innocent, everyday event of reading stories carries with it, in fact, powerful ideas and assumptions, in the first place, about the nature of the text, the communication process, appropriate responses to the text, to this kind of text. Beyond this, reading stories also will tend to reinforce certain kinds of culturally stereotypical ideas about identity, about reality, about meaning – fundamental issues of social life. And the more sophisticated the text, very often, the more sophisticated will be the means of reinforcing these stereotypes or myths. That this should be done – via reading stories – on the mass scale of public education seems to be a phenomenon worth exploring.

Some preparatory exploration of ideas and assumptions about reading stories may be gleaned readily and quickly by asking for some five-minute written responses to three questions asked of the class – in this case a group of year ten students (secondary fourth years). These questions may be used to provide a context for work on stories to take place. In most practices of English it's likely that the questions asked here will not be asked and the issues they might raise will be excluded from the daily working of the curriculum. The questions below are merely brief examples of what could be a more extended group project to examine beliefs and attitudes about stories.

1 What are stories?
2 What are stories for?
3 What is the place of stories in education?

Responses to question 1 have included the following:

'Stories are tales that have happened or are made up for people's benefit and enjoyment.'

'Stories are telling something. Getting a message across about something.'

'Stories are a way of putting down events on paper. They can be fictional or non-fiction. They can be an account of what's happened or just from the imagination.'

'Stories are pieces of communication which relate a situation, sometimes fiction, sometimes true.'

Some representative responses to question 2:

'Stories help people to find out and learn new things.'

'Stories are for anyone. They give people ideas about things that could happen or instances that will come about in the future.'

'Stories can be used for many things – to put a point across, to educate, to provide enjoyment and to set you thinking in a different way.'

Responses to question 3:

'Stories are a way of learning things and help you to understand things.'

'Stories are very educational and tell people what could happen, ways of speech, how to act. People learn from them.'

'Stories can be used in education in many ways. I think they are useful for expanding the way you think (in older children) and for learning (in young children).'

It is evident that, although not always coherent and consistent, these responses indicate that stories have certain effects or properties relevant to the purposes of education: stories are informative, mind-expanding, an aid to understanding. Stories convey meanings, they communicate, they convey messages – for benefit and/or enjoyment. This brief survey can do no more than identify views already held by the group. These may simply be identified at first – perhaps by listing some of them anonymously on a printed sheet or on the board – and then perhaps put to the test in the reading of the story and what follows.

WHY CHANGE STORIES?

Why interfere with an already established practice that seems to offer so many beneficial effects? It seems brutal to attack so innocent an activity as reading stories with a heavy bombardment of theoretical questions. Brutal and futile, perhaps. Why attempt to disrupt what's now apparently firmly in place? If stories are somewhere at the foundation of English, doesn't their 'deconstruction' somehow imply the destruction of English itself? And why should anyone want to contemplate that apparently anarchistic prospect? Why bother? What's the point? What's at stake? These are big and important questions, essential to the present project. They can only be answered by careful examination and argument.

It's part of the argument of this book to assert that using ideas gleaned from theory with students is, in practice, a potentially very positive move. Even if this means no more than giving students access to certain kinds of questioning processes, it will be a development beyond what's conventionally and commonly held to be English. A whole new field of study may, in fact, be opened up: a field of study concerned with texts and meanings more generally, for example, locating stories within a wider cultural context or seeking to understand how ideas like 'fiction', 'story', 'truth', 'reality' and 'history' operate in the general circulation of meanings constituting our cultural life in all its aspects. Perhaps this kind of project might appear too ambitiously grandiose – especially in the context of the secondary comprehensive school. But simply beginning with any of the most cherished practices of English in a questioning, probing – or theoretical – way may yield endlessly productive results.

The End of Something

In the old days Hortons Bay was a lumbering town. No one who lived in it was out of sound of the big saws in the mill by the lake. Then one year there were no more logs to make lumber. The lumber schooners came into the bay and were loaded with the cut of the mill that stood stacked in the yard. All the piles of lumber were carried away. The big mill building had all its machinery that was removable taken out and hoisted on board one of the schooners by the men who had worked in the mill. The schooner moved out of the bay towards the open lake carrying the two great saws, the travelling carriage that hurled the logs against the revolving, circular saws and all the rollers, wheels, belts, and iron pile on a hull-deep load of lumber. Its open hold covered with canvas and lashed tight, the sails of the schooner filled and it moved out into the open lake, carrying with it everything that had made the mill a mill and Hortons Bay, a town.

The one-story bunk-house, the eating-house, the company store, the mill office, the big mill itself stood deserted in the acres of sawdust that covered the swampy meadow by the shore of the bay.

Then years later there was nothing left of the mill except the broken white limestone of its foundations showing through the swampy second growth as Nick and Marjorie rowed along the shore. They were trolling along the edge of the channel-bank where the bottom dropped off suddenly from sandy shallows to twelve feet of dark water. They were trolling on their way to the point to set night lines for rainbow trout.

'There's our old ruin, Nick,' Marjorie said.

Nick, rowing, looked at the white stone in the green trees.

'There it is,' he said. 'Can you remember when it was a mill?' Marjorie asked.

'I can just remember,' Nick said. 'It seems more like a castle,' Marjorie said.

. . .

'You don't have to talk silly,' Marjorie said; 'what's really the matter?'

'I don't know.'

'Of course you know.'

'No I don't.'

'Go on and say it.'

Nick looked at the moon, coming up over the hills.

'It isn't fun any more.'

He was afraid to look at Marjorie. Then he looked at her. She sat there with her back towards him. He looked at her back. 'It isn't fun any more. Not any of it.'

She didn't say anything. He went on. 'I feel as though everything was gone to hell inside of me. I don't know, Marge. I don't know what to say.'

He looked at her back.

'Isn't love any fun?' Marjorie said.

'No,' Nick said. Marjorie stood up. Nick stood there, his head in his hands.

'I'm going to take the boat,' Marjorie called to him. 'You can walk back around the point.'

'All right,' Nick said. 'I'll push the boat off for you.'

'You don't need to,' she said. She was afloat in the boat on the water with the moonlight on it. Nick went back and lay down with his face in the blanket by the fire. He could hear Marjorie rowing on the water.

He lay there for a long time. He lay there while he heard Bill coming into the clearing, walking around through the woods. He felt Bill coming up to the fire. Bill didn't touch him, either.

'Did she go all right?' Bill said. 'Oh, yes,' Nick said, lying, his face on the blankets.

'Have a scene?'

'No, there wasn't any scene.'

'How do you feel?'

'Oh, go away, Bill! Go away for a while.'

Bill selected a sandwich from the lunch basket and walked over to have a look at the rods.

(Hemingway 1977)

In the imaginary everyday English classroom, what kinds of activities might follow from the reading of this story? An enlightened teacher might simply give the story time to settle in, as it were, and, after due pause, might ask the great open question: What did you make of that? There's nothing, apparently, leading in this, nothing directing anyone's responses, nothing inhibiting any particular reactions. This kind of open question, inviting open responses is central to what might be called liberal humanist practice. It imagines each student as an auto-nomous 'subject', bearing valued personal opinions, each with unique, individual responses ready to hatch from its open encounter with the story. The question is a mere prompting, a formality designating an open invitation to express yourself, even to find and to know yourself through and in the story. It closes nothing off and asks with perfect openness for no particular kind of reaction. It neither guides nor inhibits. And yet we know in relation to this question that certain kinds of response will either not be proffered or, if proffered, will not be allowed. We know the limits and the constraints that operate. And we know that these limits and constraints exist independently of the teacher, the story, the class; even, to some extent, of the question. So, for example, the simple response: 'It's boring' – which may very well be quite appropriate – would be a response as difficult to manoeuvre as, for example: 'It's stupid' or 'It doesn't make sense' or other responses of an equally curt but more trenchant nature that would require the intrusion of teacher's authority into the reading and responding situa-tion. These kinds of response are all in effect discounted. But it isn't just these – perhaps disreputable – responses; a whole host of other responses, entire ways of looking at the story or of reading it are very likely to be discounted, too, by the already established procedures of reading and responding at work. If these procedures, for some reason or other, are not at work, they must be taught.

THE ESTABLISHED CATEGORIES OF RESPONSE

An obliging, well-read-to, well-trained class, though, might begin to proffer a whole range of immediate responses to the original open question: What did you make of that? Theory might suggest that these responses will be expressed around a group of familiar categories, all of them, theory would also suggest, constructed completely independently of the text itself. These categories, or ideas, would be, for instance:

character	plot/development
place	time
theme	coherence
meaning	author
reader	personal response
presence	reality
significance	life
empathy	

Why are these particular ideas dominant over others? Working with students on stories and ideas about stories it's perfectly possible to pursue this enquiry further and to interrogate each of these categories and their interdependence. Take, for example, the idea of coherence. The idea of coherence assumes that the text is completely (or at least largely) coherent – that all the bits are connected in some necessary way with one another, that there is a logical sequence, from the beginning, through the middle bits, to the end, and that at the end the story is complete: so that in the case of *The End of Something* it is important that Hortons Bay is 'described' at the beginning, and there must be some essential and unifying connection between Hortons Bay, Marjorie's silence and the sandwich at the end. Some kind of development will be assumed to have taken place, perhaps consisting of events and changes of some significance. Indeed, the events and/or changes would have to be of some significance, because to concede that they might be of no significance, or of indeterminate significance, would tend to render the whole exercise – story reading, that is – meaningless or incoherent. The idea of meaning itself is pretty essential, also, to a conventional approach to story reading.

THE IDEA OF MEANING

It takes no intimidating theoretical vocabulary to begin to ask awkward questions about meaning in relation to *The End of Something* (or any other story or text). A few well aimed questions, formulated without recourse to arcane terminology will do.

Is the text identical with its meaning?
Where is the meaning of the text?
Where does the meaning of the text come from?
Is there more than one meaning to the text?

The pursuit of these questions can easily lead to intense difficulties with conventional ways of reading stories. The idea of meaning does seem – somehow – to be essential. To do without it would seem to suggest a fall into abysmal nihilism, incoherence and meaninglessness. And of course this applies to most social and cultural activities, not just to reading stories. So how can this heavy investment in meaning be squared with its apparently fragile being. Where *is* the meaning of *The End of Something*? A conventional reading might define the meaning as not necessarily being specific, as a moral to a fable would be – something like, 'Girls, don't go fishing at night with taciturn boys.' A conventional reading might refer instead to the subtle interplay of themes, like: things coming to an end, communication problems, adolescent love, male and female friendship and love, and so on. According to this kind of reading, meaning hovers playfully in and through all of these. But the conventional reading can't deny that the themes it identifies as significant – as giving meaning to the text – are themes the *reading* decides are significant. The text doesn't announce its own themes.

It's easy to subvert the theme-identifying business in this case by proposing an alternative set of themes, absurd perhaps, but equally conjoined (or not) to the text as the others. It's possible to imagine readings of this story identifying themes such as night fishing technique, old style lumber mills, ecology, human disregard for the rights and feelings of animals (fish), the end of the world, and so on. It's also possible to imagine readings informed from completely different, and perhaps more seriously subversive, perspectives – so that themes could be identified as homosexual identity and love (what do we assume about the sexual orientations of the 'characters'?), the industrial revolution, monopoly capitalism and the end of community, and so on. Whatever theme or set of themes is chosen, it is not, to repeat, chosen by the text itself. So what determines the choice? An act of decision must be taken, and yet that is not at all how conventional reading practices assume the process works. And, it has to be conceded, conscious decision-making is unlikely to occur in the imaginary, everyday English classroom. The reason for this is simple: the decisions have already been made; they have been long established as an orthodoxy, a very powerful orthodoxy extending well beyond the walls of that classroom. It is, in fact, an ideological orthodoxy at work – an orthodoxy that informs ideas about character, identity, meaning, reality and other very important issues central to the cultural politics of the era.

The most apparently obvious categories are, at times, the ones that can seem most bizarre. Take, for instance, the idea of place. Simple questions can make this category seem quite problematical, if we grant the reading the kind of status given to conventional reading practices. This may begin with: Where is Hortons Bay? Is it in the story? Or is the story in it? Or just near it? What kind of place is it? Is it a fictional place with only fictional identity granted to it by this story? – in which case the only existence it has is as determined by what's given in and by the story. Or is it a real place that has been put into a fictional context? Well, what kind of place is it? The story tells us something about what was once there but is there no more, but does little to inform us about what is there now. And for the moment, we only have the story to go on. What can 'there now' mean, though, since we're reading a story and the everyday operations of time don't apply? 'Now' doesn't simply mean now, for we are in the realms of story time. Hortons Bay, the starting point of the story, seems to be curiously absent from it, and is certainly not present (now) in it in any clearly comprehensible way – unless, that is, these kinds of textual questions are refused, suppressed, or completely banished through long years of reading training.

The idea of character – so familiar and so deeply entrenched – is similarly bizarre. The character of Nick, for instance, must be singularly elusive. What qualities and actions are ascribed to Nick in order to make up a definition of character? He knows about fishing? He knows Marjorie and Bill? He 'is' (strange word here) in Hortons Bay, wherever that 'is' or isn't? He seems upset? It seems as though he and Marjorie had a (kind of?) relationship, somehow, but not clearly, connected with love – well, she seemed to think there was love in it? It also seems as though he wants to end this relationship. For reasons unknown. He seems upset. He has a friend called Bill. He doesn't seem to like Bill, or does he? Maybe he likes Bill more than he likes Marjorie. Maybe that's how it is with boys and girls, if that's what they are. The idea of character, though, will discount that kind of procedure and invite us to make assumptions that will render the story coherent and sensible (even if it isn't). The idea of character will define Nick more lucidly and will be at pains to make sense of his enigma and, ironically, will then turn around and insist to us that stories are for making sense of experience. The idea of character will tell us things we could otherwise never know, will encourage us to imagine Nick in other settings – perhaps looking back as an older man on the end of his relationship with Marjorie – in short, it will furnish an identity, or possible identities, for Nick out of the small change of cultural signs. So many uncertainties, half-hints and uncorroborated clues have to be pieced together. The idea of character will also propose that there is a limit on the possibilities of identities for Nick, though it will never, ever demonstrate what that limit is.

The character of Nick? What does the idea mean, though? The word character implies personhood – identity which is complex, full and present in the story; but this idea of character, in this case to begin with, must be a falsehood. There are so many things we know nothing about. These gaps in the text are as vital to its ideological workings as the signs and clues we are given. (But this is as true of Heathcliff, Hamlet or Hercule Poirot; and is, incidentally, also true of the Royal Family, Marilyn Monroe or Kylie Minogue). For these gaps are the very places where cultural assumptions, checks, definitions, prejudices, forms of knowledge and so on reign supreme. It's these – assumptions, checks, definitions – that construct identity, rather than anything belonging to or intrinsic in either the name of that identity (as in the case of Nick) or even the bearer of the name of that identity (as in the case of Marilyn Monroe).

Consider just a few of the (important) things we don't know about Nick. We don't know his age. We don't know his state of physical or mental health. We don't know his race (though it will be most frequently assumed – entirely without justification – that he is 'white Caucasian'). We know nothing about his background, his class, his parents' occupations, whether or not he has brothers or sisters. We don't know what he does for a living. We don't know what kinds of clothes he wears, or wants to wear, what kind of music he likes, television programmes he watches, era he lives in. We don't know about his sexual orientation either, and though it might perhaps be thought strange to consider it, how can the ending avert this question.

As for Bill? Bill's no more than the ghost of a shadow, a presence dismissed as soon as summoned, banished into the darkness which gives no features, makes all assumption. Yet his sudden appearance and disappearance at the end seems to promise so many interpretative possibilities. The name, 'Bill', appears in the text. According to the ideas of meaning and coherence, it must be significant. Reading practices will rescue Bill from the vacuous limbo he inhabits and will flesh him out with a function, a meaning, a contrasting position, even, perhaps, with the fullness of a character.

The idea of character and personhood – an idea hardly ever challenged by reading practices – is highly questionable. What is a name, though? Theoretically speaking, writing – whether the name of an object or a person – represents the person's presence. The person isn't present in the name, clearly. So the name stands in the place of the person or the object. The name is like a metaphor, a substitute term for someone or something. The name – any name – is, in fact, a metaphor because, of course, it can't be the thing itself, but can only refer to it or point to it or stand in its place by being different from it. Our thinking about subjectivity, however, is strictly constrained to identify very closely the name and the thing (the person, the subject). A rose by any other name might well smell as sweet; but try to think of Hamlet or a close relative by any other name and the trick's not quite so easy to pull off. In stories name itself tends to imply character even where – as with Nick, and more extremely with Bill, in *The End of Something* – there's precious little defined character to go on. It's important to remember in this context that, when invited to experience or express 'empathy' for a fictional name or identity, empathy is likely to be visited upon just such metaphors of possibilities, filled in by cultural stereotypes, promoted by certain kinds of limited reading practices. The invitation to express empathy with a character, with the name in a book, with a textual function, is quite as sensible, in this sense, as the invitation to express empathy for Bill's sandwich in *The End of Something*. What can be the meaning and value of this kind of exercise?

To begin to conclude this brief exploration of perhaps 'other' ways of looking at this tiny fragment of what constitutes English – *The End of Something* and the forms of reading it's likely to be subject to – there might be some point in examining briefly the remaining ideas on stories identified earlier, ideas that are very important in the thought of English as a whole: presence, author, reader, meaning, reality. It might be objected, of course, that at least some of these are not ideas at all; they are palpable things. Authors and readers really do exist. And of course this is true; but they don't exist independently of the ideas that identify them, give them shape and form in the discourses of English and in other discourses.

Presence might seem an odd idea to pick out in relation to a critique of the dominant forms of reading practices. And yet presence is an essential element in a complex of ideas, including ideas about the author, the meaning, and ideas about the fundamental nature and status of the text generally. This kind of presence allows the text to have a stable status: there are, it's assumed, things that are actually and simply in it, including, very often, the mind of the author. The presence of this mind is asserted in phrases formulated along the following lines: 'In Hamlet's soliloquies Shakespeare asserts the existential crisis . . .' or 'Through Pip's progress Dickens exposes the social values of his own times . . .' These kinds of statement establish the idea of the author's consciousness permeating the text, so that the reader may believe s/he has direct access – via the text – to that consciousness or mind. So in this sense at least, the idea of presence, not always explicitly, but quite persistently, asserts the idea of a controlling, guiding, though perhaps hidden, presence of mind – an intelligence that guarantees the coherence of the text as well as an acting as a kind of authenticating stamp that guarantees the worth of the text. So use of the term 'Dickens' as an author's name in relation to a text would, perhaps, grant the text certain particular Dickensian qualities that would be bound to be there.

But the idea of presence isn't only important to the idea of the author. It is significant in relation to the whole notion of how the text is read, how it holds meaning and what kind of thing it is. Certain things will be held to be present in the text, even though, as explained above, they may only be referred to through use of signs in language, and in that sense cannot be present, but must logically be absent, though referred to. The signifier in no way guarantees the presence of the signified. So what does that do for Bill's sandwich, for instance, in *The End of Something*. Is the sandwich *in* the text? If it is, it's not really a real sandwich but a word that signifies a sandwich, whether there's a real sandwich or not. So it's not a sandwich, but the representation of a sandwich. But which sandwich is it a representation of? Bill's sandwich? But, it's a text, a fiction: there may be no Bill, no 'real' sandwich. So, the sandwich is just the *idea* of a sandwich? What kind of a sandwich is that, though? Clearly, we'd have to rely on our own perspective on sandwiches to help us to solve that question, and there can be no chance that we can produce a correct reading of the sandwich – since the sandwich remains no more than the idea of the sandwich. The sandwich in this story remains trapped in the ethereal realm of the signifier. It's an *empty* sandwich and can only be filled by an endless attempt to define it substantively – something the text doesn't do, can't do. No process of detection could recover its true identity.

Of course, the sandwich is a trivial example, but the same kind of 'deconstructive' thinking can be applied to any of the things that are thought to be present in the text. All the things in the text, according to conventional reading practices, are there in an uncomplicated kind of way, and even though the text may be given the status of fiction, their presence will be represented as unproblematic. It might be difficult, though, to decide what things actually are in the text. In what sense is Hortons Bay in the text? What about Nick and Marjorie's 'relationship'? Is that in the text? What about Nick's relationship with Bill? It seems to be implied by the text, but there again, on what the text gives, its flowering seems perhaps imminent with the demise of Nick and Marjorie's, if that's what it is. But we can't be sure. All these things that we might take innocently as features of the text that are in the text, are clearly *ideas*. These ideas have to be produced in and by the reading of the text. The reading of the text itself is determined by the reading practices which promote that kind of reading and inform that particular reading. According to this kind of thinking, reading texts is a more ideologically loaded business than may previously have been considered, not so much in terms of the texts that are being read, but in terms of the reading practices that are used to read them. Because if the things we thought were present in the text, to give meaning to the text are not necessarily or simply present in the text, then the status of the text as an ordering of things, as a stable entity, as a representation of things that are, must be at least reconsidered, if not relinquished. It's here that we touch upon some of the most complex and far-reaching implications of bringing theory to bear on common-sense, conventional habits of thought concerning language, meaning, texts and all of the fundamental, founding ideas of English and its activities.

To return: What, then, is the meaning of the text – in this case, of *The End of Something*? Where does it reside and how can it be decided? If you ask this kind of question of a class of secondary fourth years, one common response you are likely to get is that the author knows the meaning and that the meaning of the text lies with the author. This clearly poses problems, though, if the author happens to be dead – and unfortunately, so many of them are. Well, even then, the author knew what the meaning was when s/he wrote it. That's the real meaning. But the idea of the authenticating author as spirit controlling the meaning of the text fails in so many ways, as indicated above. It fails to take into account the effects of writing; it fails to understand the intertextual nature of texts and it supposes that there is some kind of correct, or accurate, reading possible – a reading encompassing some core of meaning, some essential message, often conceived of as a kind of ineffable spirit hovering through, behind, around the text. On the other hand, given the evaporation of the author in the text as writing, it might be asserted that the meaning is given in the words on the page, and that, given sufficient time and the right kind of reader(s), a reading could be produced which would be generally acceptable as something approximating to the meaning of the text. We could agree, it's thought, on reasonable interpretations and discount the outlandish and freakish.

REFLECTIONS ON MEANINGS AND TEXTS

None of these positions, though, can take into account the full range of possible variant readings, readings that may vary according to the cultural experience, class, gender, race, age, beliefs and so on of the readers, their particular contextual siting and the institutional conditions of the reading in question – as well as the historical moment of the reading. There was relatively recently a great deal of debate, especially among feminist and black writers in the USA, about the 'meaning' of the film and the book of *The Color Purple*; for example, accounts varying from those valorizing them as liberating to others going so far as to condemn them as neo-Nazi. It's difficult to see how the author could resolve the issue in this case (since we assume the author would be party to the dispute), and also difficult to see how a consensus might emerge from two such mutually exclusive readings. One approach though, frequently used and very handy in dissolving such issues is to appeal to the reader as absolute arbiter of meaning. The reader decides the meaning. Everyone is entitled to their own opinion. Everyone is an individual. Everyone is free to choose how to respond to, how to judge and what to think of a book, film or story. This is the individualist position and is at the heart of what gets called liberal humanism. It celebrates the freedom and individuality of the free individual. It is the kind of thinking expressed in the idea of the open question. In terms of reading practices, it intends to mean that every one is free to respond how they want. But, perhaps sadly, things aren't quite as easy as that. The analysis at the beginning of this section intended to show that readings are always already constrained by dominant reading practices. The individual's responses don't come from some inner, private, strictly personal core, but are programmed in advance by a whole range of cultural practices that enmesh reading. And we know also that powerful institutions are also constantly, if sometimes silently, at work to establish what are proper responses, what are not, what can be said, what can't, and what should be said. One of the most powerful of these institutions is the school.

There's always been general agreement that meaning is a pretty slippery business, so that a multitude of interpretations of Hamlet and his antics has been seen most frequently as a sign of the text's complex richness and as confirmation of Shakepeare's genius. It would be less acceptable, though, to propose a reading of *Hamlet* denying the prince his individual character, his personhood or his right to act, react and develop through the progress of the play. To propose that Hamlet is merely a signifier in a mobile chain of signifiers, a cultural sign, promoted by an industry, seems to be a violation, an attack on the established truth of the prince, the real and complex Hamlet who lurks within the words of the text. To propose that Heathcliff, to take another example, is at times represented in *Wuthering Heights*, the novel, as black and sometimes not, similarly seems to violate the integrity of the text. There's textual evidence to support this contradiction, but conventional reading practices, addicted to the idea of consistent representation of developing characters, cannot manage it, and so, of course, suppress it. While variations in meaning have been allowed, variations in ideas about what constitutes textual values and identities have not. And the same kind of limitation applies generally to a conventional 'liberal humanist', common-sense understanding of the relation between stories and reality.

QUESTIONS: THEIR IMPLICATIONS FOR ENGLISH

Stories must, it seems, have some relation to the real, otherwise they'd be no more than a load of empty – stories! So some stories will tend to be classified simply as realist – as might *The End of Something*. Other stories may not be realist, but may be realistic – in that they deal with certain important, real truths about the real world. Some stories might be blatantly unreal, but may then be symbolically real and deal with a different level of reality. And so on, all conforming to the tune that there is a knowable 'real' existing unambiguously and independently of the texts, forms of writing and knowledge that describe it. This 'real' can be known, tested and perceived in relation to these texts. Again, with these points we come upon some of the most significant issues in theory, issues tending always to get suppressed in common-sense readings. And this isn't because common sense knows best, intuitively, experientially, but because common sense denies, suppresses, discounts the kind of questioning that would open these issues out for scrutiny. Common sense, being powerfully pervasive and ideologically dominant, can afford not to engage in any argument with alternatives.

We're still left with the question that the year ten students at the beginning tried to answer: What are stories? To pursue that question is to begin to theorize the story. A beginning could be made with a reading of *The End of Something* based on the kind of questioning I've tried to propose here, centred on some of the more familiar ideas brought to bear upon the reading of stories in English and more generally in cultural practices. Another sequence of questions could be addressed to the identity of this story in relation to its place in the limitless network of stories we are caught up in: What kind of story is it? What different kinds of story are there? and so on, so that the reading of the story could be put into the context of an examination of the ways we commonly categorize, define and delimit stories and their meanings. This would open out onto a vast field of enquiry encompassing ideas about different discourses, assumptions that are made about their different statuses and their different functions. A whole new line of questioning could thus begin, none of it beyond the scope of fourth and fifth year secondary students to explore. The development of this questioning would tend to advance critical understanding of important issues concerning literacy, writing and meaning.

The questions I've attempted so sketchily to explore throughout this introduction are questions that open out onto the whole discourse within which the practices of English reside. Many of these questions are theoretical, that is to say, philosophical. They usually begin from the question of identity, the initial question of philosophical investigation: What is ... ? This question may introduce critical enquiry discontented with the unexamined certainties of 'common sense', probing beyond the apparently simple and obvious. It's a critical way of thinking about issues and topics that are often taken for granted.

THEORY AND STORIES

To 'theorize' English means to make clear the theories – or models – that are already at work in the existing practices of the subject. It will seem an oddity of theory, perhaps, to insist that stories do not speak for themselves. It goes against the grain of common sense to claim that stories, in general, are already 'read' before they get read. Or to claim that what a story has to say is decided more by the theories and practices of reading it is embedded in, than by the story itself or even by the reader. This oddness, however, is quite simply a product of the power of the theories about stories that are already at work in English and elsewhere. These theories are so well established that they appear to have the clear and uncomplicated status of truth. They are the ruling theories of reading practices in and across many media. So secure is their domination of the business of reading that other theories, other approaches are experienced as alien and, in their alien languages, an affront to common sense, to its clear truth and self-evident naturalness. It seems obvious, for example, that stories are about characters, events, objects, places, and set in particular times – and that they mean something.

What theory aims to do is to challenge the self-evidence of these terms, of this thinking: to make explicit the fact that they themselves constitute but one theory of reading, a theory which, quite strictly, controls ideas, responses and habits of thought. The kind of theory I want to advocate, and want to attempt to demonstrate in practice, aims to both expose the theories that are latent in common-sense practices of English and to suggest other theoretical perspectives offering a more critical questioning of the ideas in English and, by doing so to open new fields of study. This involves an intensive questioning of English and its most cherished assumptions. The interrogation, though, is not merely iconoclastic, not purely destructive, but seeks to explore the cultural, social and political network of the subject. Although such an approach works, initially, by exposure, it also proposes new models, new modes of thinking and produces a new field of knowledge that encompasses the cultural, social and political practices of the many manifestations of reading, writing and talking – the field of language and textuality.

It is the case that literary theory has got itself a bad name through its academic haughtiness and its modish, coterie status. It's also clearly paradoxical that for all its claims to be 'radical', it has been hopelessly aligned with academic elitism and exclusivity. No doubt it has thus succeeded in alienating much of the English teaching profession. But this needn't be the case. I hope to demonstrate how the kind of work with narrative described above can provide the basis for interesting work with any aspect of literature. And I hope to go beyond that to explain how 'deconstructive' thinking about stories can extend into a more ambitious project. This project will entail an extension of what has been English into a kind of cultural studies – a broader, more properly relevant field of study, dealing with issues in the whole, complex, intertextual network of discourses that enmesh any given text, whether it's *The End of Something*, a pair of Levis, *Othello* or 'Neighbours'.

QUESTIONING ASPECTS OF THE IDENTITY OF THE SUBJECT

To reappraise the body of practices and thought that encompasses English in its present form in schools entails interrogating much that's taken for granted. Exam syllabus contents, criteria of assessment, marking procedures: why do these take the forms that they do? What institutional attitudes determine the limits of this subject? How is it decided what English is and what isn't English? What is good English? What is poor English? Why are certain things – texts, activities, ideas, attitudes, habits of thought – held to be central to the proper purposes of English, and why are others held to be marginal? Why are some ideas and practices systematically excluded or degraded?

Reading and the idea of literacy

All of the time-honoured practices of English perhaps stand in need of having their assumptions violated. What thinking, what theories, are at work in the choice of time-honoured texts, in the established approaches, in the criteria that operate in judging appropriate responses to texts? How does English define literacy? What measures are taken in English towards the promotion of reading in schools? What positive attitudes are propounded and what constraints are imposed on the reading of students in secondary schools? What status is granted to the idea of fiction, what ideas prevail about the significance of books; what ideas are there at work about authors, readers and authority? How can we account for the absence of certain kinds of text from the discourse of English? How far is it possible to determine the boundaries of the subject, even according to its currently dominant forms in schools?

Writing

These questions do not need to simply constitute a critical study of existing English. They are bound to produce new material: new texts for study, new combinations of texts, new attitudes towards textuality and its significance in the cultural forms of our times. To put the subject radically into question, to refuse its conventional identity, is bound to involve producing other forms and ideas and practices. Writing, for example, would no longer necessarily be limited to written exercises done in the classroom. Writing could be put under scrutiny while it is being done in some new ways on new topics in the classroom. What is writing? What would a taxonomy of writing look like? What different kinds of writing are there in different contexts? How does writing work? What kind of sign system is it? What is a message in writing? What is ordering? What is syntax, structure? To what extent is writing creative, and to what extent is writing an external technology? Why is the idea of creative writing important in conventional English? What is the elusive connection between writing and meaning? To examine written texts, to produce written texts in relation to thinking about the idea of the integrity of the written text, the limits of the written text: why have these activities not been part of English? Why has the central role of metaphor in writing been neglected, so that metaphor has become a kind of special effect of specific kinds of writing? What does rhetoric mean, and why has its importance not been acknowledged in English? Why have these aspects of language and writing in the cultural practices of communication been neglected by English?

Oral English

Why is oral work conceived of and constrained in its present forms? Why not explore more systematically the operations of institutional talk? Why not do some theoretical work with talk? What kinds of knowledge might be involved in a teaching involving oracy? Why not examine the powerful idea of talking as a kind of writing – scripted speech – analysing the forms and conventions of daily dialogue? Why not examine the relations between speech, discourse and power? Oral work in English might very productively move beyond its present restrictive limits. Why are students not involved more in questioning the assumptions involved in social and educational assessments made on speech? How can there be oral English grades? What are the political implications of this? Is English still systematically complicit with unacceptable forms of social distinction, social denigration and exclusion?

The present forms of English cannot encompass the range of these questions. To meet them effectively, and to reappraise the grounds of current practices in English, entails a twofold process: first, analysing assumptions at work in current practice, and second, producing new forms of practice to displace the current. To embark on this process means to engage positively in changing the subject.

2　Theory and the politics of English

THE ASSUMPTIONS OF ENGLISH

It's obvious perhaps but always worth reiterating that English has been structured by various beliefs embedded in practice throughout its history. In this sense there is always theory at work in the subject. Official ideas – official theory – in relation to what English is and what its practice should be are explicitly expressed in public documents like examination criteria, *The Kingman Inquiry* (1988), 'The Cox Report' (1988 and 1989), *English 5–16* (DES 1985), and so on. Not that these documents necessarily represent the beliefs or reflect the practice of all English teachers, or of all forms of English teaching; rather they represent the authorized version of the subject, produced by various institutions that have some stake in its constitution. The beliefs of practising teachers of the subject may constitute a different body of theory – one that accords to varying degrees with official theory.

Indeed, some of the content of official documents has been opposed by representatives of the more progressive versions of English – versions that might be said to represent a dominant definition of the subject as expressed, for example, in NATE (The National Association for the Teaching of English) publications and in various forms of the practice of English. Arguments between representatives of the more conservative models of the subject and the more liberal versions tend to be expressed around issues like grammar versus use and expression, around ideas about language development, sometimes about Literature versus literature (or stories and poems), about correctness versus creativity, and about the best forms for deciding grades. All of these issues, and the arguments conducted around them, tend to neglect the problem of the identity of the subject, English, and tend also to neglect the politics of literacy – of reading, writing and speaking practices within the context of English in education – as well as the political implications of examining and grading.

All of the various beliefs expressed in public documents and the practices that go with them – as well as any other versions and practices of English – entail models, or theories, of language. These models or theories might not always be explicitly formulated, and may well be, philosophically, contradictory. They may to varying degrees express the main concerns of practising English teachers, but within the arena of English generally they operate with binding force and enjoy the status of commonly accepted truth.

Ideals of correctness, for example, ideas of accuracy, or ideas of appropriateness, are still powerful in English teaching – even though liberal models of English might feel embarrassed about enforcing them. Standard English remains the dominant and dominating model of the English language – as though all other variants, of writing and speaking, were aberrations or deviancies. These ideas might be inimical to the English teacher who wants to linguistically empower all her students, who wants to recognize the validity of the cultural diversity of the English languages in written and spoken form of all her students, and who wants to cultivate the unconstrained development of all her students' various language competences. But when it comes to examining students' performances in an official context and making formal assessments of language competence, ideas of correctness and appropriateness, the valorization of a certain mode of speaking and writing, cannot – in present conditions – be evaded. Liberal and progressive versions of English, though they may represent themselves as distinct from official definitions, have failed to address the politics of grading and assessment in English, just as they have largely failed to address the politics of language and textuality – preferring to allow certain assumptions about how these things work in the field of English in education to rest untroubled by theoretical analysis. There remains in liberal ideas and practices of English an adherence to the idea of the creative subject, for example: an idea belonging to an essentially conservative mode of thinking, a mode of thinking giving precedence to the individual and (necessarily) lacking a theory of the discursive, the social and the political. Belief in English or aspects of English as creativity must necessarily be ignorant of, or ignore, the sociolinguistic analysis of the positioning of the language of the subject within the institution of English.

The positions expressed in public documents representing institutional authority are eminently 'deconstructable'. Take for example this reference (from the GCSE assessment criteria for English for 1994) to the role of some pre-twentieth century works of literature 'whose influence in shaping and refining the English language and its literature is recognized'. It can be seen that a number of assumptions are at work in this statement. For instance, it is assumed that the works in question – though never specified – will be universally recognized. But that is not, of course, necessarily the case. What are those 'works'? Are they listed somewhere? Do all English teachers know what they are? It is unlikely, even if the general truth of the statement were granted, that all English teachers would agree on what those pre-twentieth century works would be. But the statement does not specify at all *who* would agree, or would be in a position to agree or to make judgements about the development and refinement of the English language. We assume that it does not refer to the general populace, or does it? How can the confident assertion be made that these things are agreed – whether universally or by the appropriate professional body or in some other way – without the implication that it refers to some simple and universal truth?

And yet if we examine the idea, can it be asserted that some pre-twentieth century 'works' have 'shaped' and 'refined' the English language and its literature? It's difficult to imagine what evidence could be cited to substantiate the claim. But even if some kind of ethnographic, historical, statistical, sociological research *were* to be undertaken to test the proposition, its verification or falsification would still depend on the acceptance of the implications of its key terms. The term 'the English language', for example, could be taken – utterly against the grain of any sociolinguistic description – to refer to something we all know and recognize as a unitary whole with a clearly defined identity. Alternatively, however, we could claim that there is no such thing as *the* English language, that it is simply an idea used to impose one version of the language in a position of power over other versions. We could claim that there are many different kinds of language spoken in English and we could also claim that their differences are closely related to cultural and social differences, that the English language is plural and divided. We could further claim that the development of the English language has been thoroughly diverse and uneven. On what basis, then, could it be claimed that the development of the English language, this changing plurality, has been a process of refinement? Is the English language more refined now, because of the works that have shaped and refined it? More refined now than it was when those works were produced? More refined now than the language used in the works themselves? Are the early works, then, less refined than the later ones – which would use an English language refined by the earlier ones? And what does this word 'refined' mean? Less gritty? Less crude? More pure (in what sense, though)? More abstract? More elegant? More expressive? More socially refined? What? The claim is clearly untenable – an established, officially sanctioned kind of nonsense.

It's evident that the assumptions contained in the statement quoted above are ideological. Asserted as self-evident truth, they take their force on the understanding that the ideas will receive 'universal' acknowledgement. They also take their force from the fact that they are stated from a position of institutional power *and* ideological power. The document the statement is taken from is produced by SEAC (Schools Examinations and Assessment Council), the body invested in the UK with the power of surveillance to supervise and control what kind of English is examined. Here, in this merely fragmentary but thoroughly representative instance, ideology and institutional power can be seen hand in hand, defining the material authority of the subject.

The GCSE criteria for English (1990) – for example – would actually tell an uninitiated observer very little about how English works in practice. It would tell very little about the different kinds of activities and approaches there are at work in the everyday business of English. It seems to take for granted that the variations will not be significant, that certain universals will be accepted by all and that everyone to whom the document is addressed will recognize what it means in terms of a practice of English teaching. This cannot be done simply by exerting institutional power, but depends on the understanding that the established discourse of English at a certain level will prevail, and that this discourse will be acceptable in all the many and various thousands of institutions it inhabits. It is clear that the document illustrates an important point about language and its relations to politics, ideology and institutions.

The example above illustrates a number of points about how discourses operate in relation to ideology and institutional politics. The writing of the document belongs to a particular type of discourse: say, the discourse of educational management and control. It makes assumptions and leaves enormous gaps because it knows that the assumptions will be recognized and the gaps filled in. In order to do that it must assume that there is an audience ready to make the appropriate and necessary responses to make sense of the document and to carry out its implications in the context of practice. It addresses a knowing subject. The knowing subject is tied, in this instance, to the institution of English teaching, and tied in turn to the institution of the school. It is part of that knowing subject's professional identity to recognize the terms of the discourse operated within the various institutional contexts it inhabits. And professional identity – impersonal and public – in our culture, at least, is linked closely to personal identity.

The practices of English, though, may – and evidently do – exceed the restricted definitions of the subject as stated, for example, in official documents defining GCSE assessment criteria or in syllabuses. The 'unofficial' practices may involve notions of English that contest the assumptions made by official documents and syllabuses, while they remain within the specific institutional contexts of English. To effectively – and thoroughly – contest the assumptions and practices of English would necessarily involve contesting its language and its ideological structure in a theoretically informed and coherent way. But it would also entail contesting the way in which the language of English positions and defines its various subjects – in order to maintain its present forms and effects. If we accept for the sake of argument the notion that there are many different forms of the English language, and if we entertain the idea that institutionalized English marking is largely determined by the criteria of a particular and dominant model, then we may go on to question the identities ascribed by grading procedures defining some of the subjects of the discourse as ranging from A to G on the basis of written samples of their languages.

A dual-certification English and English Literature syllabus makes reference to a number of key points that may be taken as representative of a line of thinking – involving a model, or a theory, of language and of textuality – installed in established practices of English. (Please note that these key points draw upon the now fully installed National Curriculum criteria). Among other things, references include:

candidate's ability to understand and convey information;

understand, order and present facts, ideas and opinions;

articulate experience and express what is felt and what is imagined;

recognize implicit meaning and attitudes;

show a sense of audience and an awareness of style in both formal and informal situations;

the detailed study of some texts and wider reading;

acquire a first hand knowledge of the content of literary texts;

understand literary texts, in ways which may range from a grasp of their superficial meaning to a deeper awareness of their themes and attitudes;

a sensitive and informed personal response to what is read;

opportunities must be provided for students to read for various purposes both literary texts (e.g. short stories, novels, auto-biographies, poetry, plays) and non-literary material (e.g. newspaper articles and advertisements) and respond in a variety of ways to what is read. These must include detailed study of literary texts in all three forms (drama, prose, poetry);

opportunities must be provided for candidates to develop a variety of styles of writing in what may be termed 'closed' situations (e.g. the writing of letters, reports and instructions) where the subject matter, form, audience and purpose are largely 'given' and in what may be termed 'open' situations (e.g. narrative writing and imaginative/personal response to a range of stimuli and experience) where such factors are largely determined by the writer. Response to reading may include the opportunity to explore themes, ideas and the ways in which writers achieve their effects.

(NEA 1990)

All of these snippets have the status of injunctions and determine the criteria by which students' work – the expression of their being within the arena of English – is to be judged. They are the requirements of the syllabus, of the publicly authorized version of the subject at a certain level. Many assumptions are made – about the difference between the 'literary' and the 'non-literary', for example: that language articulates experience; that 'literary texts' have 'content'; that there is such a thing, unproblematically, as 'informed personal response'; that there are 'three forms' of 'literary texts' that 'facts' are different from 'ideas'; that in 'literary texts' there is a difference between 'surface meanings' and 'themes and attitudes' which require 'deeper awareness'.

All of these assumptions rely on their acceptance being taken for granted, as if there was never the remotest possibility that any of them could be contentious or problematic. Their expression constitutes a particular model, or theory, of language and textuality. There is the assumption too that what is expressed throughout the document in question refers to central and essential aspects of language and textuality.

To theorize language and textuality means to examine the assumptions contained in dominant models, or theories, in the first place. It also means to propose alternative ways of looking at language and textuality. Theorizing in this sense doesn't mean the displacement of one theory by another, but entails putting theory into play explicitly in relation to the identity and construction of the subject. Asking questions about the terms the subject is set in and its institutional being, examining alternative models from the dominant, promoting consciousness about the practices and ideas of the subject, its particular frames of reference and its assumed difference from other subjects, its place in the whole curriculum and the meaning of how that place is construed: all of these are aspects of theorizing tending to promote a reflexive position, a position that may address the institutional identity and being of the subject. It seems to be clearly the case that to 'deconstruct' the restricted categories of established English can engender a whole range of new practices likely to engage students in more varied and more interrogative approaches to the field of 'literacy'.

For teachers of English, the theorizing of language and textuality – entailing a sustained questioning of the fundamental categories of the subject – is much more likely to render them powerful in the face of public and institutional forces that may appear at times to threaten their domain with intrusive edicts, pseudo-debates that falsely polarize subject terminology, and trivializing misrepresentations of attitudes and practices. A self-conscious and self-reflexive practice is always more powerful, being forearmed in the face of external attack. Liberal models at present have no theory of how English positions its various subjects, for example, within its various institutional contexts. Liberal models have no understanding of how English works as a kind of technology of the subject, producing, or at least reinforcing, certain dominant notions about individuals and individuality. Liberal models have therefore never made a fundamental issue out of grading procedures, procedures discriminating between different kinds of language use, different kinds of response under the guise of universal criteria of value. To introduce theory into this context, to question the fundamental assumptions of grading in English, is not necessarily going to make it immediately go away. But it is likely to provide the grounds for a reappraisal of how grading works, and is likely to 'de-naturalize' grading. Theory, in this context, might conceivably produce the grounds for change in institutional conditions.

THEORY AND THEORIES: SOME ISSUES

In what follows I've chosen to elaborate certain theories that have a bearing on language and textuality – theories, I believe, offering possibilities of re-orienting the subject, addressing its relations to political aspects of 'literacy', and of resolving issues that currently polarize differences about the nature and function of English in schools. These are theories, not *theory*; theory is everywhere, all the time, whether made explicit or embedded in attitudes, practices and assumptions.

I've chosen these particular theories because they represent a power of ideas capable of addressing the fundamental issues at stake in English teaching. They can be used to make necessary connections between language, textuality and social practices. They have no value, I believe, on their own, nor for their own sakes. They make problematic cherished assumptions and open the ground for new practices – and that *is* their value. They have the capacity to foreground questions about values. They stand against the values of grammar, detached literary criticism, standard English and correctness, as well as against the values of self-expression, of creative writing, of personal response. They are anti-common-sense, and may be used to expose the various ideological underpinnings of what gets taken for granted as significant. They enable the subjects of English – its teachers and its students – to come to grips with its relations with sociology, with history and with politics. For in the field of language and textuality, all these things, which have persistently been seen to be outside of the domain of English, in conservative and in liberal models of the subject, are always in play.

I've tried in all of this to avoid making reference to the proper names that are associated with some of the theories I've elaborated and attempted to demonstrate in use. I've done this not to claim these ideas as my own: for – as I've often felt obliged to tell students I've been teaching – these ideas are not mine, nor anyone else's, really; they circulate among many different people working for different purposes within different institutions. I don't believe it's necessary – in the context of English in schooling – to cite names to establish credentials for ideas. And I think it's generally agreed to be an irony of the way theory in higher education has operated that the so-called 'death of the author' has resulted in one pantheon of great writers being substituted by another.

A MODEL OF THEORY

The model of theory I've tried to describe in the following sections, might be diagrammatically illustrated as in Table 2.1

Discourses

Linguistic activity, linguistic life, can be divided into different types of discourse. A discourse might be characterized as being a specific kind of language, or 'language game' – a language form associated with a particular activity, a particular kind of knowledge, a particular group of people or a particular institution.

Table 2.1   Aspects of theory – language and textuality

discourses: a general theory of particular language practices and their institutional contexts – how they · organize statements, define texts, promote meanings, construct fields of knowledge and position subjects.
semiotics: a theory of the structure of signs and sign systems, and of the movement of meanings in specific cultural practices and contexts.
phenomenology: a theory of subject/object relations; about how we know what we know; a critical theory of identities, including ideas of *perspective, position, aspect, idea* and questioning the notion of the *object-in-itself.*
psychoanalysis: a theory of the relations between the individual subject and language, texts and discourses; a theory of identifications – proposing a subject divided by different orders of being: the *real*, the *symbolic* and the *imaginary.*

Deconstruction: a general theory of language and textuality, sceptical of identities, meaning-in-itself – and critical of ethnocentric positioning of subjects – where ethnicity may be considered to vary according to class, race, gender and other (cultural) differences.

A discourse will have its own terminology and its own rules of expression, including, in some cases, a special type of grammar, and will have rules about what kind of statements are appropriate, as well as rules about who may speak when and who may say what to whom and in what circumstances. In any discourse, there will be differences in the distribution of linguistic power. Within the general discourse of schooling, in a classroom, for example, students are permitted to say certain things, write certain things, and not others. Teachers generally have more flexibility in what they may say in this context, and have more power in determining the boundaries of the discourse and the limits of the discursive positions taken by different members of the group. Also, in different types of classroom – distinguished by different subject identities – in the formal discourses of learning, different ways of making statements, as well as different kinds of statement, will be deemed to be appropriate. The people involved – in this case teachers and students – don't necessarily make the rules, though they can, to a degree and within limits, alter them. The rules of the discourse are often unstated, though they may at critical points be made explicit, may even be contended. The discourse is dependent, for its proper maintenance, on the often concealed presence or exertion of power. The people involved in the discourse can be characterized as the 'subjects' of discourse – and they will take up particular positions in relation to its power.

Discourses have powerful determining force – and exert powerful influence in determining what kinds of linguistic exchanges take place. This applies to all kinds of language situations. The power of discourses exerts control over oral statements, over what gets written, how it gets written, and, equally, over what and how things get read and interpreted. All language is discourse and is variously bounded by discursive controls.

English in schooling as an examination subject is a discourse with considerable institutional power. Although the activities of examination English may appear to be quite liberally open, very strict constraints operate over how, for example, students' writing gets judged. These constraints are expressed most explicitly in assessment criteria, but are also expressed in the processes of assessment which are not inscribed in documents – the kinds of assumptions, comments and judgements that examining teachers make when examining. The criteria and the processes of assessment have considerable controlling power in determining how students are positioned in the examining process; a process having important effects in defining students' opportunities within the education system. The criteria and the ways they are applied are powerfully discriminatory – as markers of qualitative difference. Nevertheless, much of their power depends upon the willing acceptance of their authority by their subjects, in this case students and teachers of English. This is a crucial point about the idea of discourses – in the way it highlights how discourses produce, not just statements, grammars, forms of exchange, but also *positions* for their 'subjects'. These positions are always more or less hierarchically structured, though they tend to enjoy a kind of 'naturalized' status, being assumed to belong to the order of things, to the way things are.

Teaching students themselves about discourses might begin by an invitation to consider different types of discourse; their special vocabularies, grammars, their rules of exchange – and their likely ideological inflections. How different discourses operate can be quite straightforwardly demonstrated by identifying and analysing particular – and divergent – cases such as football, geography, business, playground, religion, romance and so on. Students may then be asked to consider the various contexts and institutions of the discourses they've identified – and also how they position their various subjects. This can be done by asking about the places or contexts, the groups of people, the kinds of exchanges, the organizations of the identified discourses.

Of course, discourses don't always fall into these rather neatly bounded categories, and may not have such easily definable institutional contexts. For example, the discourse of 'romance' might be understood as the discourse of being in love. As such it may refer to the kinds of things people say, think and write when they are in love. Or it may refer to romantic feelings as expressed in novels, in popular magazines, in songs, and so on. It may also be said that there are less easily placeable discourses, like male discourses about women, discourses of family life, discourses of pleasure, for example.

By considering these kinds of example, it may be pointed out that discourses are not necessarily uniform in all contexts. The discourse of football, for example, inhabits many different contexts – and may take on a different form in each context. Football played on the street may employ different terminology and different forms of expression from football that is presented on 'Match Of The Day'. It may also be pointed out that any discourse can be divided by different ideas about how to operate it and attitudes towards its ways of positioning its subjects. So the discourse of religion, of religious experience, may be defined as divided, contested and plural. This plurality could refer to divergent attitudes about the way a discourse positions its subjects, or could refer to fundamental aspects of its contents – as might be said to be the case with religion.

This last point leads to a consideration of the how discourses may be involved in struggles, and in changes, and of how the power of discourses may be contested. To change the way that English works by challenging its assumptions and practices, and by offering alternative ideas and practices, would be one example of contesting the established power of a particular discourse. The challenge, to be effective, would, of course, have to address not just the language of English – its established terminology and forms of expression – but its positioning of its various subjects, and would have to contest its institutional position and power, too.

With students, the challenge to the discourse of English – its ideological and institutional power – may be initiated by a consideration and analysis of discourses, introducing a theory of discourses and some of its terminology, in dialogue with what the students already know, probably inexplicitly. The particular line of development taken by this analysis may be very varied. Examining how a particular discourse works and attempting to formulate, with the students, alternative ideas and practices of the discourse can be productive in a general sense relating to the general topic of discourses. For instance, fairy tales may be taken as an example of a specific type of discourse, particularly related to issues of reading and writing. An examination of fairy tales – their general structures, the kinds of stereotypes they employ, the types of closure they work towards – may lead into ideas about transformation. Students may engage in proposing alternative forms; they may put forward a critique of fairy tales which involves producing new forms to contest the dominant forms of the discourse. Implications concerning contexts and institutions can also be explored in relation to the specific example of fairy tales. The kind of writing which may be produced, and which may be eligible for coursework examination, could include analytic writing, critique and story writing, and would, at least implicitly, by being contained within a single piece, challenge the categorization of different types of writing established in English syllabuses. This writing could be used in turn for the beginnings of an explicit critique of the fundamental categories and practices of the discourse of English.

Semiotics

Semiotics is the study of signs, and deals with the theory of signs in general, examining how signs work, what sign systems there are and how they work as systems, also examining the relationship between signs, sign systems and the social contexts they belong to. As a general theory, semiotics addresses all kinds of signs and sign systems – and so might range from road signs, to signs used in maps, to signs as they operate in TV adverts and signs in written and spoken language. Semiotics would tend to regard sign systems as operating according to common fundamental principles, or, at least, as being subject to certain fundamental questions and forms of analysis. So semiotics would tend to propose that all signs systems are a kind of language and that language is a sign system – and would also tend to see the world as saturated with signs, organized by sign systems actively constructing the world, rather than simply reflecting what's in it.

In dealing with language, semiotics has been particularly concerned with naming – examining how the process of naming in language operates to produce different identities for the different things named. The kind of analysis of naming undertaken by semiotics may be used as a simple and direct way of challenging common-sense assumptions about language and the way it works, as well as common-sense notions about the relationship between language and what it is supposed to represent. Semiotics can therefore offer an immediate departure from ideas about language which see the correspondence between words and things as simple and direct, also failing to acknowledge the ideological inflection of all language practices.

Teaching semiotics can be a simple matter of introducing a few terms with explanation and discussion, and then applying this theorizing to specific texts and the signs used by particular cultural practices. This kind of exercise could begin with familiar examples of signs – traffic lights perhaps – and then consider simple single words. The terms initially introduced would be the signifier, the signified and the referent – where the signifier would be the material component of the sign (in traffic lights the colours red, green, amber), the signified would be the idea or concept conveyed by the sign (in the case of traffic lights stop, go and the third more ambiguous, uncertain idea), and the referent would be what the sign refers to (the actions of stopping, going or whatever happens when the lights are on amber).

A number of important and fundamental issues may be drawn out from this particular description of the sign, using these particular terms. It's evident and easy to see or indicate that the relationship between the signifier and the signified is arbitrary. There is no necessary connection between the colour red and the idea of stopping, just as there is no necessary connection between the colour green and the idea of going. The sign system operates by establishing differences between signifiers. Anyone unfamiliar with the system would be unable to make sense of it, if confronted by the sign system alone – without the particular practices that go with it. The terms within the system are empty in themselves. They only carry meanings within a system of differences that is established and that operates according to social conventions. Once the social conventions of behaviour at traffic lights is known, then the meanings are evident. When the workings of the sign system become familiar and everyday, they may appear to be natural and inevitable: of course, red means stop and green means go (although the meaning of the term amber is likely to be taken to mean a number of different things – remain stationary, go, get ready to go).

The analysis of language as a sign system might begin with consideration of single words, words obviously operating according to the description implied in the signifier/signified/referent terminology. The word 'dog', for example, is a material signifier – a sound or written image. To define the signified conveyed by the signifier 'dog', though, is no easy matter. It might, for example, be defined as the concept 'dog', but this concept in itself is no more definitive than the signifier. Or the signified might be defined as Alsatian, dachshund, Pekinese and so on, but it is evident that these definitions are themselves other signifiers referring directly to no particular dog, and themselves requiring further elaboration in order to be defined. The referent of the word 'dog' would then be dispersed along an endless chain of signifiers and would be defined only as a dispersal of possibilities. For the word 'dog' to have any kind of meaning, then, it must refer to what is conventionally understood by the term in the social practice which names and distinguishes dogs – or, strictly speaking, ideas of dogs. It must also be placed within a specific language context in which the term – 'dog' – is distinguished from other terms in a 'chain' of meaning, but a chain that operates according to a principle of difference, above all.

This leads to another important idea generated by a semiotic analysis of the sign in language: meanings are always contained in syntax, that the meaning of a sign in language (the signified of a signifier) is contained in a movement, in a sequence in time; so that signifiers are set in a structured relationship of positioning – and part of their capacity to mean is determined by this contextual positioning. Signifiers convey meanings that are conventional and established in the cultural practices of language, as elements in a system of differences that defines different identities for different terms, like the difference between 'dog' and 'cat', and like the difference between 'Alsatian', 'dachshund' and 'Pekinese'. These words have established, conventional connotations; but they also bear meanings dependent on their position in a specific context. In the sentence, 'the Alsatian chased the dachshund down the road', the signifiers are assigned roles determined in the movement of the statement. These roles are not necessarily conveyed by the conventional, established connotations of the signifiers 'Alsatian' and 'dachshund', though they may, in this case, be associated with them. If the sentence were changed to read, 'the dachshund chased the Alsatian down the road', the roles would have been changed, the meaning of the terms would have been changed, though the established, conventional connotations of the signifiers would have remained the same. Although, of course, they do not always remain the same. The plurality of the meaning of the word 'dog' does not simply begin and end with the classifications of a certain kind of animal. The word 'dog' can convey quite other meanings, too, and the meaning of the word 'dog', whether in relation to a certain kind of animal or to other things, is subject to changes in time and in social context.

This in turn leads to a consideration of the difference between language as a system and the particular utterances or statements that the system as a whole gives rise to – another important distinction established by semiotics. The meanings of words are structural: they take up a position in a system of differences. And particular statements are ordered according to rules of grammar and syntax; words are set against each other in particular forms of ordering determined by the rules of language. The meanings of words are not simply present when the words are used; they are not explicitly defined in each statement they find themselves in. Nor are the rules of grammar and syntax which generate the patternings of statements all present in each particular usage of language. The whole of language, all the meanings it contains and the rules that govern its orderings, can never be present; language in this sense, as a totality, can only be apprehended from particular occasions of its use. This means in effect that any particular statement depends upon the items present and their orderings referring to a whole system which can never be made present. Meanings are always caught up, then, in an endless interplay of presence and absence. (This theme of presence and absence in relation to language and meaning is developed radically by deconstruction – and is also a theme with important implications for a psychoanalytic perspective on language and meaning.)

Neither the words themselves nor the rules are what they are by necessity – which is why different languages can have different words and different rules of grammar and syntax. Language is a system, a structure, a self-regulating form, not directly connected to anything beyond itself. According to the implications of a semiotic interpretation of language, language does not reflect or represent the identities of things in the world, but creates them. Language does not refer to 'reality' so much as construct it. And this construction always takes place within specific social contexts within specific cultural practices.

The issues that can be pursued with students from a consideration of these relatively simple examples could be summarized as follows:

The relationship between the signifier and the signified is arbitrary.

A language is a system of differences.

The signified is, in effect, a series of other signifiers.

Signifiers and signs are always substitutes or metaphors for the things they signify.

The meanings of signs are always established in particular contexts in particular cultural practices.

The world of words creates the world of things.

As well as considering some of these theoretical points – and as a development and exploration of them – students could also be invited to engage in active use of semiotic terms and analysis in relation to specific texts and specific cultural practices. An obvious and productive example to take would be to examine two powerful signifiers – 'man' and 'woman' – and to relate an analysis of these to some texts: for example, popular magazines, children's stories and TV adverts. This can be done simply, in the first instance, by asking students to write down signifiers relating to the signifier 'woman' and signifiers relating to the signifier 'man' – and this could take the simple form of a pair of lists drawn up side by side on a sheet of paper. The associations of the words on these lists could then be explored and questions asked about how each list differs in the sets of associations it constructs. Further questions could then be asked about how these signifiers relate to the identities of men and women, and whether the associations they produce are to do with anything essential or whether they are culturally generated. Moving on from there to examine how signs of gender operate in particular cultural practices could involve students identifying signs of 'woman' and signs of 'man' in children's fictions, in popular magazines of various kinds and in TV adverts and soap operas, for example. The point of all this would be to develop the theory of semiotics with students in relation to a particular aspect of the creation and recreation of meanings within sign systems, meanings embedded in cultural attitudes and cultural practices, rather than necessarily out there in 'the real world'.

Phenomenology

Phenomenology is concerned with the appearance and knowledge of things – in any kind of context. The main importance of phenomenology is deconstructive, in so far as it uses quite common-sense ideas in order to 'deconstruct' common-sense notions about how we know what we know, and about the identities of the things we know. Deconstruction in this sense doesn't simply mean taking apart, or demolishing, but implies review, revision, critique and re-ordering. Phenomenology has radical implications for considering how language can represent things, how objects and texts get read and interpreted and what they can mean. It provides a theory for understanding how everyday objects in everyday life are always given identity in relation to ideas about what they are – rather than being simply there in themselves.

The topic of phenomenology is very easy to teach to students, since it uses ready-to-hand terms. All the main issues at stake in phenomenology can be activated by using a few simple terms, a simple diagram and a number of questions or points. The terms are given below.

object (the thing itself),
subject (viewer/spectator),
perspective (point of view/position),
aspect,
idea.

As shown in Figure 2.1, the spectator, or subject, according to this

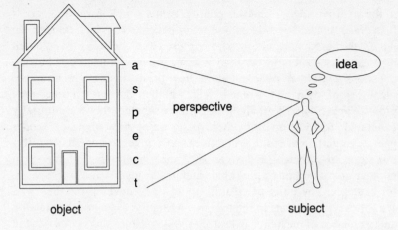

Figure 2.1 A simple diagram of phenomenology

model, stands in a particular position in relation to the object in view. In any 'viewing' situation, then, it is clear that the subject is positioned. This positioning determines the perspective that the subject will have on the object. The positioning of the subject will also be an element in determining what aspect of the object is revealed to the spectator or subject – for the object cannot reveal all its various aspects to the subject all at once. All aspects of the object cannot be perceived by the positioned subject, though they can be construed by the subject from the already existing knowledge – or assumptions – of the subject.

The subject recognizes what it sees, not in relation to the object in itself, because what the subject sees – how the subject identifies the object – will be determined by the idea of the object. This idea can be the subject's own idea derived from its perception or perceptions of the object, but this is unlikely to be the case very often, and gives no guarantee that the object is what the subject defines it as. The identity of the object is determined by the idea of the object logically preceding its perception by the subject and allowing its identity to be recognized by the subject. The object itself is never knowable by the subject, because the idea of the object determines what it is for the subject, and because all possible aspects of the object cannot be revealed simultaneously to the subject, and because the subject is always positioned in a way that determines what the subject's idea of the object is.

The subject is positioned culturally – in a number of ways. Ideas about what objects are must be culturally determined through language and sign systems that give objects identities. And just as there are no objects in themselves, there can be no subjects in themselves either. For every subject is also an object for other subjects, and every subject is an object for itself, its understanding of itself equally determined by ideas, perspectives, positioning and aspects.

With students, the topic of phenomenology – initiated by introducing the diagram and the terms, and developed through explanation and discussion – can be summarized by using the following questions, questions perhaps forming the basis for discussion or written work:

How is perspective determined? What different factors might be involved?
How do we know what objects are?
Can we know objects in themselves?
How do we discover aspects?
Are the object and the idea of the object identical? How can we know?
Phenomenologically can we ever know anything?
Can we ever know anything except aspects of ourselves?
Are the aspects of ourselves that we are aware of our entire selves?
Can there be an entire self?
Can we know all of a text (a textual object)?
What is all of a text?

Phenomenology offers a way of thinking through issues of the relations between subjects, ideas and the way that objects in the world are perceived. In granting importance to perspectives, aspects, ideas and the positioning of subjects an understanding of phenomenology may engender important shifts in the ways we understand language and texts. Phenomenology also has important implications for the ways we may understand our own subjectivity, our own cultural positioning and our own perception of ourselves and our identities.

Psychoanalysis

Descriptions of language activity in English – in so far as they belong to its dominant modes, or its more progressive modes – tend to emphasize language as self-expression. The language used by anyone is an expression of their essential self – a self that may grow and develop as it is nourished by engaging in developing activities with language or as it comes into contact with texts that open horizons and that allow the individual self to extend, to encounter other worlds, to experience other lives, other ways of seeing, and so on. This might be described as the positive aspect of a dominant model of language in general currency in English teaching. On the other hand, and less explicitly, there is the negative aspect, the implication that restricted language – such as a student gaining a grade F or someone who has been excluded from the enhancing activities of a progressive or developmental model of English might display – implies a restricted person, someone who is less fully alive, less fully competent, less aware. This would be a highly dubious notion in a number of ways, but would be consonant with a liberal model of language in education, proposing a sense of generalized, individual development. Much of the use of so-called 'creative writing' in English has been justified by the idea that certain forms of writing are liberating, in so far as they may unlock possibilities for the individual self concerned. Much teaching of literature has been justified on similar, 'personal growth' focused grounds. Countless examples of this kind of thinking could be cited.

There are fundamental problems, though, with this position. Firstly, the valorization of certain kinds or forms of writing above others is likely to indicate that other forms are being excluded or devalued. The grounds of inclusion are hardly ever likely to be very explicit – and are almost never likely to be open to challenge. The idea of language in the classroom as a form of self-expression denies the importance of the institutional context of writing. The emphasis on individual self-expression obscures how what might be termed sociological factors play a determining role in this writing scene. Secondly, the theory of writing in English as self-expression offers no adequately formulated ideas about the relations of the subject – the writing/reading/speaking individual – to language, and in failing to do so leaves unanswered some fundamental questions about language, the individual self and the relations of these to culture, cultural forms and institutional practices. This failure is not only a failure of omission, not a purely innocent oversight; it is also, and crucially, a distortion of a strictly ideological nature.

Psychoanalysis addresses the important issues of the effects on the subject of the acquisition of language and of the effects on the subject of being, not simply a language user, but a *subject* of language. What this might mean and how this particular theory of the relations between the individual – the subject – and language might operate can be introduced to a class by considering the division between the conscious and the unconscious. This can perhaps most easily be done by presenting a representation or model of the mind, which will give space to indicate the contents of the conscious and the contents of the unconscious, making clear the division between the two, as shown in Figure 2.2.

This may form the introduction to a number of questions. The introduction may be done with a whole class using a board to fill in the

Conscious (ego)

_____ 'Bar'

Unconscious (id)

Figure 2.2　A representation of the mind: division between the conscious and unconscious

details, or using the kind of representation shown above produced on a printed duplicated sheet, or both. The point is to invite students to consider what goes into the unconscious and what is in the conscious and to begin, thereby, to define the relations between the two. This process needn't be lengthy nor very complicated. For example, it may be decided that memories, dreams, fears, and so on will go into the unconscious, while knowledge, ideas, sense of self, awareness of the world, and so on might go into the conscious. These issues can be explored through discussion in a number of ways and following a number of different tracks of thought. A series of questions could accompany the filled in version of the above representation in order to prompt discussion, such as:

How do memories get remembered?
Are all memories always remembered?
What happens to everything you've forgotten?
Why are some important memories forgotten?
Do memories change?
How can you tell if your memories are 'true'?
Does the contents of the unconscious change?
What happens to dreams? Do they get remembered?
How are dreams constructed? What forms do they take? How are they experienced?
Do dreams have meanings? If so, how can you know what they mean? If not, what are they?
Where does language go? Vocabulary (think of all the words you know)? Rules (think of how you know how to put words together to make statements, and so on)?
How do you know what words or statements mean when you see or hear them?

How do you know what to say before you've said it – or even thought it out?

How do you know when to say things in specific situations (and when not to say things), and how do you know what specific things to say (and not to say)?

Can you ever think without using language?

Who decides what words mean? Who made the rules of language?

A host of issues can be made explicit following the implications of these questions through exploring and creating a workable theory based on a relatively simple (though perhaps the most fundamental) point – the difference between conscious and unconscious – from psychoanalytic theory.

It's evident, anyway, that language must go into the contents of the unconscious. It can easily be demonstrated that language cannot be adequately explained without some reference to the unconscious. Where is language when it's not in use? The unconscious component of language might be characterized, then, perhaps using the ideas below, or something similar, as pointers.

Language – words and meanings – cannot be present to consciousness all at once.

The meanings of words – even when in use – remain, except when consciously explained, unconscious.

The rules of language – how to put words together: syntax and grammar – are also largely unconscious.

Language in action is also largely unconscious: you don't necessarily rehearse each statement you make before you make it.

Simple exercises can be devised to demonstrate these points. Evidence for the existence of the unconscious can be found in the way that language works, as well as in other phenomena classically associated with the idea of the unconscious, such as dreams and memories which will have an important bearing on a development of ideas about the relations of the subject with language.

The question: 'What form do dreams take?' can lead into a general discussion about the signifying qualities of dreams, covering questions such as those given below.

What is striking about dreams and about the way that they work?

What different kinds of dreams are there?

Are dreams ever stories? Always stories?

Who writes – or composes – your dreams?

Do you always/ever understand your dreams?

What are dreams most likely to be about?
What do dreams mean? Are dreams ever meaningless? Are meaningless dreams experienced as meaningless? Who can decide – and how – what (your) dreams mean?

It's clear that dreams – if you accept that they are meaningful, or are experienced by the dreamer as meaningful – operate according to some kind of logic, ordering or rules. It's also clear that they utilize a kind of language in some way connected with the language of everyday, waking conscious experience. But it's also clear – from people's experiences of dreams – that they are often mystifying, difficult to understand, and that their meanings are elusive. In other words, dreams operate according to a different set or sets of rules, although they utilize the same signs and symbols. If these rules are not conscious then they are not dissimilar in that from the rules of conscious language use, and if the meanings of the signs and symbols deployed in dreams are not conscious, or under conscious control, then they must operate independently of the dreaming subject. The same kind of consideration, about rules and about the meanings of signs and symbols, applies equally to the speaking, writing and reading subject – the subject who does not consciously deploy the rules of language in every utterance, and the subject who cannot determine all the possible meanings of the signs and symbols inhabiting the subject's relations with language.

In dreams, the subject confronts most obviously an alien and often disconcerting discourse. Something is at work which is not under conscious control. The dreaming subject and the waking subject, then, may be said to be fundamentally and radically alienated. The subject is split; the conscious and the unconscious may speak to one another, but in ways neither will fully comprehend.

Memories, like dreams, can be characterized as symbolic representations, using signs and symbols in accordance with rules of organization. Memories, too, are a kind of language, and are most commonly recounted in verbal form. This also has implications for a theory of the relations between the subject and language. For it is clear that memories are a kind of mental writing or reconstruction: past experience becomes transmuted in memory into linguistic and symbolic form, and memories become a kind of cataloguing of past experience. Memories frequently take a narrative form which shapes their meanings, enclosing them within a specific form of discourse. The speaking, writing subject does not necessarily control these forms. Nor does the speaking subject control the meanings of its own memories, which may shift and change with time and may be 'rewritten' in the light of a changing, shifting identity. Memories, then, can be seen to form, for the subject, a mobile and dynamic 'intertext' – a way the subject may represent its past experience to its present identity in a more or less constant movement of replay and revision.

This is not just to say that memory is unreliable – though that in itself has important implications for the subject's relation to ideas connected with 'truth', for example. Conscious memories, and their meanings, are unstable, not fixed, and reveal that the subject's relation to memory, as a linguistic phenomenon, is complex – and is essentially a textual relationship. The contents of conscious memory may, to a degree, be under the subject's conscious control (though this is certainly not predominantly the case), but the forms of memory are not. The subject is subjected to these forms in its relation of its memories to itself.

It is also – and perhaps obviously – the case that memory is a selective procedure and that the selection of memories is not under the conscious control of the subject. Remembering particular events or experiences, their details, and specific contexts also involves, necessarily, the forgetting of other events or experiences. What kinds of things get forgotten? How do things forgotten sometimes get remembered? Are all memories lodged in the unconscious? If so, what does the unconscious do with them? Or are some, important, memories kept in the unconscious, and kept from the conscious? However this process of selection and censorship, of remembering and forgetting works, it is clear that it is not under the control of the subject. The story or the history of the subject's life – like other stories and other histories – is a story and history of gaps, exclusions and repressions.

Psychoanalysis proposes a critical importance for language in the construction of the individual subject. The subject is, according to this theory, actually constructed and positioned by language. The subject is always a divided subject, divided between conscious and unconscious. A large part of the knowledge and experience of the subject belongs to the unconscious. The conscious subject does not know itself; its identity is split, as illustrated by the strange quality of dreams, by the absence of control in remembering and forgetting, in the ways the operations of language work – and in the different ways the subject may identify itself – as separate from itself – as 'I' or 'me' or a proper name, all of which are signifiers, substitutions, metaphors taking up positions within the orderings of language in its systematic organization of differences.

. The subject in psychoanalytic theory is divided between conscious and unconscious, but according to some versions is also divided by different orders of experience or of 'being'. The orders are a) the imaginary, b) the symbolic and c) the real.

a) In the order of the imaginary the subject identifies itself with its mirror image as whole and complete, denying the fact that it is divided and subject to the incompleteness experienced as desire. In the imaginary the subject may also identify with others and see its own self reflected in them, thus confirming its own sense of its identity and, at the same time, temporarily borrowing the identity of the other. In imaginary identification, according to the theory, the subject may break down the difference between self and other and take pleasure in its release from subjection to a particular form of identity, from subjection to feelings of dividedness and separation. This can be demonstrated in relation to a spectator watching a film and identifying with an identity in the film. But there are complications involved in this, since the spectator might identify with different identities or positions the film uses. The film may invite the spectator to identify with a hero, but what happens if the spectator is a woman and the hero is a man? The imaginary identification involved might cut across the symbolic ordering of things determining more or less set identities according to gender.

b) The symbolic order is the order of things in the social world, established and maintained by the organization of identities in language and in sign systems. The symbolic order keeps things in place, grants identities and confers meanings. The subject is subjected to the symbolic order most significantly with the acquisition of language to which the subject must submit its individual will or desire. With the internalization of language the subject is divided into conscious and unconscious and is 'inhabited' by the symbolic order. There is no escape from the symbolic order as it overwrites the imaginary without doing away with it, suppressing its wayward tendencies.

c) The order of the real is, simply, what it would seem to be, but is also, rather mysteriously perhaps, never knowable or reachable by the subject, since the subject lives in the imaginary and the symbolic. The symbolic and the imaginary are like ever present filters through which the real is perceived, barring the subject from the real. It's not that the real isn't there; but the subject can never make direct contact with it. The difference between the real and the symbolic is perhaps most clearly illustrated in the subject's experience of another's death, where the other vanishes from the real but remains to inhabit the symbolic. The real is vague and disorganized, a totality without differences unorganized by the symbolic, impenetrable and totally alien from the imaginary.

The ideas suggested by the orders of the subject's experience of the world have implications for a theory of language and of textuality seeming far distant from ideas about language as enabling direct expression of the self, ideas often central to much thinking in general currency in English.

Deconstruction

Deconstruction is more of an attitude, an activity – or set of activities – addressing texts, writing and signs systems, initially in a sceptical manner; it's an orientation deploying a range of terms and concepts rather than a fixed, established position. Deconstruction draws upon and develops all of the strands of theory mentioned so far, but denies all fixed stances, either for its own positions and practices or for the positions and practices it addresses, preferring the mobile idea of things in play to the more static ideas of fixed structures and orders. And deconstruction may address any field of knowledge, any system of belief and any kind of writing – anything, in short, that may be described as textual, within which category it would claim all forms of language.

The procedures of deconstruction are generally based on a kind of radical semiotics. According to semiotics, the signifier (for example, a word in written or spoken form) and the signified (for example, the meaning of the word) are not attached by any necessary connection. The signifier, in effect, signifies – or brings into play – many other signifiers. Words may mean things, none of them contained in the words themselves without reference to other words – other chains of meaning. According to the logic of this position all meanings are always deferred: that is, they are not present in the statements that produce them, but are generated by a movement or 'play' – an interplay between the present word(s) and the absent, but invoked, 'meanings'. In this interplay of presence and absence, traces of meanings are mobilized in endless networks. Any resting point for meaning is always subject to movement and deferral. The idea of 'play' is a very important element in deconstruction's mode of critique. This means, though, that unless deconstruction is to be anything more than an academic textual game it must address *how* texts are given specific kinds of meanings. What forces are at work in producing and stabilizing meanings? For it might well be the case that, in some absolute and theoretical sense, meanings are always subject to movement and play. This doesn't mean, though, that statements and texts don't get given meanings that are fixed. It means that meanings, in so far as they are fixed, are located not in the statements or texts themselves, but in their specific, social, institutional contexts. Meanings are framed and determined by social, discursive, institutional contexts – and the codes and conventions they operate. ('Keeping it tight at the back', for example, might well mean any number of things, but within the context of football commentary, it will make a certain kind of determinate sense.)

According to the idea of the deferral of meaning in language, meanings can only achieve any stability within the contexts of specific practices, social forms and systems of ideas that stabilize them. These specific practices, forms and systems must always be located within history, or rather histories, and deconstruction – as a general mode of critique – addresses not just common-sense versions of language, textuality and meaning, but a whole set of concepts that have been operative in the history of western thought. Deconstruction, then, provides a way of examining ideology in its relation with, for example, reading and writing practices. It aims to expose the particular systems of thought at work in language practices, to indicate their relative and always provisional status. It aims to expose the rhetoric of texts as undermining any fixed centre, any determined meaning, any claim to be grounded in some kind of 'truth'. Clearly this must shift the question of meaning, value and significance from texts (or language practices) themselves; the logic of the deconstructive position would therefore locate any determinate meaning granted to texts within the contexts of their readings, within the established reading practices that grant them meaning, value, significance – and practice of deconstruction would also, therefore, need to address these institutionalized reading practices and their contexts. And, of course, these things don't get established by themselves. They are produced, develop, become powerful in particular historical circumstances. The implications of a deconstructive position would suggest that these histories of meaning might be addressed and analysed.

Deconstruction celebrates the semiotic principle of difference. Meanings in language, in texts, in systems of thought are produced by the interplay of differences, where positive terms, or identities, can only be established by being set, negatively, against what they are not. The tendency of all language and all texts is to establish systems of difference based on more-or-less paired sets of oppositions. Many of these 'binary oppositions' have general cultural currency and may act as nodal points holding together the slippery structures of meaning. The deployment of oppositions in texts will tend to have a 'normative' direction, with one of a pair of opposed terms being privileged over the other. In other cases, the interplay between paired terms may be more openly structured, though the pairings will still structure meaning. The pairings or oppositions – and the play of meanings they generate – are not necessarily under the conscious control of the particular language user that brings them into play. They already operate in what deconstruction might refer to as the 'general text' of language. The meaning of the interplay will be already partly determined by the possibilities of meaning granted to it in general cultural usage; again, this will always be located within a particular discursive framework. Examples of culturally loaded oppositions might be:

reason/madness	first world/third world
real/symbolic	representation/reality
fiction/reality	doing/thinking
material/immaterial	theory/practice
literature/popular culture	masculine/feminine
freedom/state control	nature/culture

One of the most important procedures of deconstruction is to examine these kinds of opposition in order to reveal that the paired terms cannot stand in a relationship of absolute difference to one another – in order to indicate that their difference is always a constructed one, maintained against the possible threat of their collapse, in order to sustain the symbolic ordering of things in language and within discursive formations. For these oppositions cannot, in any case, represent an absolute difference from one another. It can be shown, for example, that the difference between reality and representation is not really tenable, that reality is always produced in relation to forms of representation, is always represented, and is always subject to representation. Reality is always permeated by ideas, and is itself the product of an idea of itself – an idea that must be set against something other; unreality, fantasy, myth. The idea of a real reality, out there, uncomplicated by a subject's perception of it, must always remain an idea, given, for example, the specific position of any subject – what the subject 'sees' directly cannot be taken absolutely for reality. Reality is always caught up in subjectivity – and is always an idea produced in specific discursive contexts. That's not to say that everything is unreal, that the reality everyone experiences as reality is only a 'ghostly paradigm of things'. It means, rather, that there can be no free, direct, subjectless, extra-discursive access to the material reality of things.

Deconstruction doesn't have to deal solely with abstruse philosophical questions about reality, though these are, ideologically speaking, of great potential importance – in English, for example, where according to much conventional reading practice the idea of reality is used as a criterion of value. Deconstruction may equally address oppositions of more immediate political significance (though its academic practice has tended to neglect this potentiality). Take, for example, the difference between the third world and the first world, where it is often assumed that the two terms represent completely distinct realms of operation and of being. And yet we know that both worlds are very much inter-related and any attempt to represent them as different, as specific to themselves, is bound to be an effect of particular ideological positions.

The deconstruction of the 'masculine/feminine' opposition has been undertaken and articulated in recent times by feminism, with far-reaching effects on the way that these terms are understood in the sphere of the personal and in the sphere of the political, though again the popular feminist slogan, 'the personal is the political', signifies the deconstruction of that opposition, too. This particular piece of deconstructive work, undoing the assumptions contained in the man/woman opposition continues against the current of what might be called dominant ideology. This particular deconstructive move is perfectly easy to undertake – and to explain in these terms – with students, and may take the form of textual analysis and/or pieces of writing.

The idea of general writing and the idea of general textuality indicate ways that boundaries demarcating specific textual identities for forms of language can always be deconstructed. All textual productions and all statements in language always refer to other texts and other statements. This is a condition of their existence and of their meaning. It is not possible, for example, to make sense of a novel without already knowing how to read a novel, how novels operate, how they structure different identities and how they address a reading subject. A novel doesn't simply speak for itself – establish its own form of representation, its own terms of reference, its own characteristic features, its own structures and conditions of response – but must, always, refer to other novels, other forms of fiction – films, stories, soap operas – and other kinds of text, too. It always 'speaks' within a general network of writing or texts – or textuality. It's within a network of writing and meanings that a novel takes up its specific textual identity. It's always within such a network that its meaning is determined. Intertextual relations can be clearly demonstrated by examining, for example, the openings of novels; looking at how chains of meaning are brought into play with very little 'work' having to be done by the 'text itself'.

He rode into our town in the summer of '88...

(Schaefer 1957)

From this scant beginning a fairly detailed scenario may be quite fully elaborated – indicating innumerable details concerning the kind of hero, his physical attributes, the community he's about to enter, his past (or lack of it), his role in the drama about to unfold, the other main protagonists, the nature of the heroine (and his relationship with her), what he's riding, what he's carrying with him, the landscape, the time of day, the atmosphere and even the kind of closure we might expect from this text which is not yet a text, but the promise of a text that already deploys a host of intertextual references. A host of uncertainties and ambiguities is thus given definition by these intertextual references, though their meaning may radically alter depending on what genre is assumed for the text. And genre – where the text is placed within an ordering of categories – cannot be determined by the text itself. Of course, texts may confirm or disconfirm the expectations they generate, but they can never escape the intertextual network they are always already caught in. The same principle of dependency is equally the case for other kinds of text – news reports, science textbooks, fire drill notices.

Genre, then, is one of the discursive forces holding the text in some kind of order against its radical potential to deny identity and to disseminate itself into the order of general writing. Textual identities are always mobile and can only be held in place by conventions and established ordering within discursive frameworks. No text can establish its own identity; the boundaries of any text spill over – according to the principles of intertextuality and dissemination – and cannot be contained or controlled by the material covers of a book.

The idea of literature, for example, was an attempt to establish a fixed identity for a body of texts otherwise disjointed and disparate. The category of literature is impossible to maintain, though, because its limits cannot be set – and also because the values it has come to represent cannot, according to a deconstructive reading, be held to be inherent in the texts of literature. Literary values can only be a product of certain, limited, kinds of reading practices, and a limiting determination of textual identities dependent on the maintenance of the opposition literature/non-literature – a difference constantly breaking down. One way the special identity of literature has been, and to some extent remains, maintained is by the special significance attached to the idea of the author. The author has been used – in relation to literature – as a kind of guarantor of a unique quality seen as the expression of the author's special sensibility in textual form. The author is used as a point of origin – a point fixing the meaning, or potential meanings, of texts, determining also the *value* of particular texts in an order of relative greatness. Other texts, not written by an author in the sense of a canonical figure, may be deemed to display similar qualities, but these qualities will still be valued for their author-like properties, and still may be traced back to an originary source fixing their identity and their possible meanings. The author in this sense is no more than a set of assumptions holding together a limited category or type of text. To the identity of the author will attach certain notions, assumptions activating ready-made sets of meanings. The author, in this sense, is simply another element in the determining of genre. And always before the 'author', the individual language user, comes the technology of writing, the technology of syntax, of the ordering, spacing, punctuation, semantic relations and structuring which is the condition of the use of language. In this sense the very idea of 'use of' language is highly deconstructable. Language can be seen, alternatively, as 'the machine of writing', a ready-made and mobile structure which itself determines and uses.

Deconstruction is suspicious of any attempt to trace back meaning to any originary source. Any attempt to recover the meaning of a text by referring back to an original intention, for example, must be deluded. For where can this intention be expressed, if it's not realized by the text itself? Would the meaning and identity of *Hamlet* be secured if only we knew what Shakespeare intended? There is no way an intention can illuminate or verify a reading, or ways of reading, a text; for *Hamlet* partakes of the order of general textuality, the order of general writing, and is a complex intertext, enmeshed in an ordering, in a complex network of references, cross-references and identities it cannot now be extricated from. To attempt to recover a meaning for *Hamlet* depending on the assumption of a particular intention, or attempting to locate its meaning in reference to its relations with its contemporary texts or ideas would have to attempt to negate the way that *Hamlet* is located within a network of intertextual references that make its reading possible. The meaning of *Hamlet* can no more be grounded in the original moment of its production than it can be grounded by referring to its author's intention.

In deconstructive terms *Hamlet* is perhaps an obvious example of the principle of the 'intertext' deploying, in an ever active movement, the play of presence and absence. This theme can be easily demonstrated with students in relation to the importance of Hamlet's father in the text, a father whose presence is made significant by its absence, and who, when present, hovers in the ghostly realm of being/not being between the two. But it can be shown that similar consideration can be given to the figure of Hamlet, who appears and disappears throughout the text, who appears one moment in one guise, adopting the rhetoric of one form of identity, and another moment is different. Where, then, is Hamlet? And what is Hamlet when not 'present'? ('He' can never be fully present, of course, at any one moment because his being, such as it is, like any being, is structured by the movement of time in its constant deferral of the present caught up in the unceasing movement between past and future. What's more, his being can only be signified within a network of signs – dependent for their very operation on the interplay of presence and absence.) Hamlet dies at the end of the play. Is he, then, always already dead, even before the play begins, since the ending will determine the beginning and will also determine the intervening sequence according to the logic of textual movement, and since the ending of the text already exists before it is ever read from beginning to end?

In one very important, deconstructive, sense Hamlet is never there, anyway. Hamlet is an effect of language and, as such is signified by a series of signifiers acting as substitutes for the presence of Hamlet. In other words Hamlet is always a metaphor for something which isn't there but which is signified – or deferred by the presence of the metaphor. What applies to Hamlet in this sense may apply equally to anything in any text. Anything signified within a text must point to something, an idea or chain of associations, going beyond the limits of the text, outside the text. The inside of a text and the outside of a text is an opposition that cannot be strictly maintained.

This idea of the metaphor as substitution clearly has far-reaching implications in the way it breaks down the inside/outside opposition and undoes the possibility of clear limits to meanings generated by texts. Certainly an important aspect of deconstructive thinking about language is that the idea of metaphor – an idea in English previously specifying a limited kind of linguistic effect – is made into a general linguistic principle. All language is always metaphoric, substituting itself for what it is said to represent. Any kind of name is a metaphor standing in the place of what it names, and is a substitution for it – and gives it identity in a systematic ordering of named things, generally structured in series of oppositions. So too other kinds of language effects are also metaphoric in that they signify relationships between things in an equally substitutive manner.

This has important consequences for the status of all forms of discourse. Any claims any discourse may make to represent the real, or the truth, or the real truth, must be undercut by the recognition that discourses are always an ordering at one remove from what they may claim to be ordering. The logic of the metaphor in language is always at work whether the discourse in question is the discourse of football terraces, the discourse of scientific research, the discourse of family relationships or the discourse of news reporting. Truth and reality can only be expressed within these kinds of discursive regime, and can only deploy different kinds of rhetoric, intertextually infiltrated by other kinds of discourse, always subject to the logic of metaphor. The rhetoric of truth – of a discourse claiming truth for itself – would be seen by deconstruction as an expression of a will to power. Even the most scientific, 'objective' language is not immune from the sharp critique of deconstruction.

Finally, perhaps the most bizarre opposition that deconstruction has sought to undo is the opposition between speech and writing. Deconstruction would claim that all the features of writing can be equally ascribed to speech, but that speech has been privileged over writing in descriptions of language, descriptions particularly that have struggled to assert the victory of the individual over the 'machine of writing'. So, much writing about 'literature', for example, will speak of 'voice' – finding in this metaphor a guarantee for the presence of a person in the impersonal text of writing. Deconstruction, though, might suggest that texts – in terms of their material and ideological being – are far from personal.

POLITICS, IDEOLOGY, INSTITUTIONS

In what precedes this section I've attempted to illustrate certain theories – all of them having a bearing on language and texts or textuality. These theories all have a potentially interrogative inflection, in so far as they may be used to question established ideas, and may propose alternative ways of looking at powerfully dominant ideas. The ideas in this case belong to the field of English in education, but are not confined to that field, many of them enjoying general currency, or common-sense status. These ideas are concerned with reading, writing and speaking practices; they might be generally characterized as ideas about literacy; but it should also be emphasized that they are not 'merely ideas' that anyone is free to disagree with: they have been granted institutional power and operate within institutions that determine the identities of subjects.

The theory of discourses proposes an alternative way of looking at language in so far as it puts language into specific social and institutional contexts, examining how beliefs and attitudes are embedded in those contexts. On this model, language is an activity undertaken by various groups of people, and it is not simply an activity they do, but one which also organizes them – their ideas, beliefs, attitudes and values.

Semiotics indicates how sign systems operate according to a principle of difference, establishing distinctions between things and producing an order of things. Semiotics also indicates how signifiers are loaded with cultural meanings, and do not bear meanings on their own, outside of a cultural context, establishing a strict correlation between language and culture. Semiotic readings can reveal how signifiers – words, for example – create images and ideas that tend to be stereotypical. According to semiotics it's the world of words which 'creates' the world of things – an inversion of common-sense ideas about representation.

Psychoanalysis offers a theory of the subject – the reading writing and speaking subject – in relation to language and culture. In this model, the subject is not the author of meaning, but is ordered, constructed and positioned within and by language. The subject hovers between the imaginary and the symbolic orders, divided into conscious and unconscious systems, unable to make direct contact with the 'real'. A radical questioning of the idea of personal identity is entailed in this perspective.

Phenomenology theorizes the relations between the subject and the object, examining how perspectives, aspects and ideas position the subject's knowledge of the world. Phenomenology can be used as a model for reading – reading the 'world' as well as reading texts.

Deconstruction offers a very wide range of ideas about texts and language, ideas tending to 'deconstruct' the established identity of things linguistic and textual. Deconstruction is a critical, sceptical theory aiming to expose the grounds established thinking rests upon as problematic, contradictory and uncertain. Deconstruction generally proposes the analysis of rhetoric and sees rhetoric at work wherever there is a claim for meaning to be grounded in truth.

But if deconstruction claims that all meanings of all statements of all texts are always undecidable, what use can such a thoroughgoing scepticism be? If psychoanalysis proposes that the subject is used by language as much as being a user of language, what space is given for the subject to operate in? If phenomenology suggests that we can never know things in themselves, and that ideas and language always construct our knowledge of things, how can the subject – anyone – ever really know anything? If discourses determine what can be said and position subjects according to their own orderings, doesn't that leave the subject powerless in the face of impersonal forces that are far greater than the individual will? And if semiotics suggests that all meanings of all signifiers are predetermined culturally, how can the subject ever evade the replay of established stereotypes? All of these sets of ideas have a radically anti-humanist inflection; they rob the individual of the supremacy it enjoys in liberal humanist ideology; they 'decentre' identities, decentre the hallowed private individual, and put emphasis on social contexts and their structuring forces. Language is less an instrument than an external force – a force, though, inhabiting the individual in its most private spaces.

All these problems are important to the possibility of constructing a practice that aims to put the theories I've outlined into play in the field of English. They engender issues concerning the social contexts of language, meanings and textual practices. They therefore lead to a consideration of cultural contexts – which in turn must inescapably engage matters of ideology and politics. For theory to have any useful application, it is essential that it addresses how meanings are produced in specific social contexts, relating language uses and texts directly to the attitudes, beliefs, behaviours of general social life.

In effect this means that all language use is bound up with ideology – with views, attitudes and ideas making assumptions about the way the world is, about the identity of things, about the nature of people and of society. Ideology is not something belonging only to the external realm of the public arena; ideology – as language, forms of language, ideas, thought, attitudes, beliefs, practices, behaviours – is always also enmeshed in what might be called the politics of everyday life. In fact, it is never possible to clearly demarcate the difference between the intimate, the everyday, the personal and the external, the public, the impersonal. Ideology is embedded in the language we speak, in our ideas and in our most personal feelings. As subjects of discourse we are 'interpellated'; we make imaginary identifications with culturally constructed positions and identities. We are called upon, or 'hailed', and in responding we give assent to the positioning, the structuring being held out to us – within established institutional frameworks. This happens to teachers, for example, all day with great frequency – and is a feature of the political construction of the institution of the school.

Meanings and identities are produced by discourses – always within institutional frameworks. Language and textuality are always framed and produced and always have ideological inflection. The distinction between the political and the personal is untenable; the idea of a neutral position (even of a liberal neutrality) is not possible. There is nowhere to escape from ideology; it is impossible to stand outside of ideology in some 'objective' position. The value of theory is that it provides a means for understanding processes of meaning more fully. While this is partly a process of disillusionment, it is not absolutely so. Theory shatters the illusion of the individual's free creativity; but it makes more clear the kinds of choices that can be made, the kinds of positions that can be taken. This applies as much to the politics of daily social life as it does to reading and writing and speaking practices, which cannot, anyway, be separated from daily social life.

One political project consistently addressing the politics of meaning and identity in recent times is feminism. Feminism has utilized the theories outlined to analyse the public, cultural construction of feminine identity, has addressed all this to language and textuality and has undertaken deconstructive readings of institutional practices. This is clearly a political venture seeking to theorize meaning and identity to reveal its social construction. But feminism has also sought to go beyond the analytic, to provide an understanding of the mechanisms of social change and to effect changes – changes of an ideological nature – concerning how women are regarded, concerning assumptions about the social roles of women, and has contested these things to effect changes of an institutional nature, addressing, for example, the jobs that women do, women's organizations, discrimination, misogynistic behaviour and so on.

Feminism has addressed language and textuality to examine how existing, established reading, writing and speaking practices have defined meanings and identities in relation to women. The purpose of this theorizing has been manifold – but has included a thoroughgoing critique of patriarchal ideology as expressed in language and textuality and has also, positively, been able to propose different reading, writing and speaking practices constructing meanings and identities differently and having implications and consequences for the way things are – meanings and consequences that are ideological in effect and have a bearing on institutional practices within the arena of the politics of gender. An important implication of much work in feminism has been to question the way textuality itself has been seen as a privileged site in the construction of identities. Whether in relation to Literature, or to a broader notion of literature, or to the field of popular culture: feminism has sought, in effect, to break down these supposedly discrete categories, to break down the idea that they are especially the places where identities are formed, to break down the differences between them and other forms of social exchange. In effect the difference between text and non-text has been deconstructed by the way feminism has sought to address equally all forms of social practice, from a political perspective foregrounding language as ideology – a perspective identifying the political with language uses.

The example of feminism has potentially far-reaching implications for English and for English teaching. For while some aspects of feminism have been incorporated into the more liberal practices of the subject, they tend to remain within the sphere of the incorporated; that is to say, they become another way of looking at things along with all the others, rather than being centrally informative. This means that they remain, effectively, marginalized. The same consideration applies to the issues of race and of class. If issues of gender, race and class are simply additional, though, simply other or more things to take into account, then the liberal model must be, in the end, fundamentally untroubled by them, must remain essentially conservative and – it must be said – anti-democratic.

The theories I've outlined are not simply deconstructive in that they take things apart. They have the power of offering different models, of breaking down established definitions, and so of opening new spaces, ways of understanding formerly closed that can be used to change, to develop and extend, for example, current reading, writing and speaking practices in English in schools. New models of literacy, new and powerful ways of understanding literacy on many different levels become possible. The kinds of practices embodied in liberal and in established versions of English really use a very limited set of ideas; a deconstruction of these practices is the opposite of negative. It has the positive force of proposing multiple new practices: different fields of operation open up, different approaches become possible, new – and often surprising – combinations may come into being. Deconstruction unfixes, mobilizes, takes a dynamic view of discourses and cultural practices.

An application of the theories I've been proposing, an application maintaining an interest in ideology, politics and institutions, an application aware of the cultural implications of the issues, would, it's true, necessarily tend to deconstruct in the breaking down sense existing practices of English teaching, would tend to undermine the very identity of the subject. But existing practices have been largely founded, I'd contend, on very restrictive models of language, models blind to their own constructedness, blind to the political effects of their institutional situation, and blind to their implication in politically suspect systems of belief. Existing practices have been largely founded on a narrow definition of textuality, and have privileged certain kinds of textuality – certainly stories and poems, for example – over others. Existing practices have obviously then been founded on an inadequate notion of literacy.

To break down may also mean to liberate many other possibilities, to 'deconstruct' in order to allow a greater flexibility, or 'play', to diversify and expand in order to more fully and more explicitly incorporate a reading of language and textuality in relation to ideology, politics and institutions.

It may be argued that there's a danger in all I've suggested that teachers and students are to be robbed of their linguistic/textual innocence, that the pleasures people have clearly taken from reading novels, say, will be replaced by the solemn business of semiotic analysis, or the grimly analytical work of psychoanalytic deconstruction. This is not the case at all. This position would have to depend on the false assumption that textual pleasures are 'innocent' in the first place, that there is a clear distinction between pleasurable immersion and analytic reflection. It would also tend to associate textual pleasures with the privileging of the representational fictional text – a strange privilege when considering from where and how most people get most of their 'textual' pleasures.

Theory such as I've advocated here certainly has ways of addressing and analysing textual pleasures, of explaining the kinds of pleasure taken, for example, in the imaginary identifications people may make in relation to texts, and the pleasures to be had from various different kinds of closures of texts, of analysing the 'hermeneutic' pleasures generated by reading processes generally. The analysis of the pleasures, though, doesn't reduce them to any degree, any more than the analysis of football reduces the pleasure of watching or of playing football. It is also the case that there are pleasures associated with theory: that reflection itself can be experienced as pleasure. Analysing, theorizing textual pleasures does perhaps change them in so far as it may render them conscious – and in doing so is likely to make conscious choices more clearly available to reading, writing and speaking subjects. This is no reduction, no loss. It is, though, I would suggest, an opportunity largely denied by current practices.

3 On the subject of reading

THE ROLE OF READING IN THE SECONDARY SCHOOL

Although the *Bullock Report* (1975) claimed that no more than one school in ten made adequate provision for reading, the business of reading, one way or another, has been central to the practices and to the ideological structure of English since the subject began. The importance credited to reading is again given official statement by the 5–16 document on English containing the proposals of the Secretary of State for Education and Science: 'Good schools foster positive attitudes towards books and literature. . . . Literature helps secondary pupils to explore and express their own thoughts and feelings and moral and social values. . .' (*English 5–16*, 1989: 3.9, 3.11). Reading, here, is clearly equated with the idea of literature. In general, within the secondary context it's likely that notions of the value of reading will most often be connected to ideas about 'books and literature'. Ideas about what constitutes literacy are crucially significant in maintaining reading as an educational activity. In all officially commissioned reports on the teaching of English, the centrality of reading is unquestioned, even though the nature of the reading done, its particular texts and specific forms may not be very explicitly elaborated. Reading, apparently, is reading – everyone knows what it is, what it's for and why it should be done.

In secondary schools the place of reading in English takes many different forms. Some English departments will have established clearly formulated attitudes, policies and practices concerning reading. Others will be more partial, more haphazard and more cloudy in their apprehension and implementation of a policy for reading. The attitude of the school as a whole institution will have some bearing on what kind of reading community exists in the school. The kind of library the school has and the way it operates will be implicated. The whole school policy

– if it exists – may or may not accord with the policy of the English department. Whatever the situation – of a department, of a school, or within an individual English teacher's classroom – ideas about reading, what it is and what it is for will be a force within the institution, will influence practices and are quite likely to be deeply ingrained. The ideas in question may be more or less explicitly stated or may be wholly implicit, operating only at the level of practice. That reading is worth doing, though, is a truth (almost) universally acknowledged, though why it is worth doing – and often with whom it is worth doing – is likely to produce very varied, often divergent positions. *English 5–16* asserts one stereotypical view: 'Studying literature and encouraging others in that study is an enrichment for pupil and teacher alike.' (1989: 7.2) Traditionalists and progressives alike would mostly agree with this assertion. A theoretically motivated approach, though, might want to challenge it, beginning by asking questions about, for example, what is understood by 'studying', by 'literature' and by 'enrichment' on the grounds that all those terms represent ideas that can be and ought to be questioned and contested.

Among institutional variations of attitude and approach to reading, it is possible to identify dominant models and ideas largely, and necessarily loosely, based on the idea of studying literature as some kind of enrichment. These are expressed in what English teachers do in practice with classes, as well as in institutional structures, examination syllabuses, assessment procedures and official documents. The idea of literature, of there being certain texts or kinds of texts that are worth studying in themselves, is the basis for much of the teaching of literacy in secondary schools.

The focus of a challenge to accepted assumptions and commonly held notions about reading might centre on the following points:

1   the idea of literacy;
2   the idea of literature;
3   ideas about how reading works;
4   reading texts and ideology;
5   general reading – the contexts and organization of reading.

An approach to these issues would inform not only the teacher's perspective on reading, but would equally have practical implications for an approach to reading in the classroom and would determine the kinds of activities students engage in. The list above might well provide a title of elements in a course, to be approached explicitly with a wide-ranging textual focus. Literacy – in spite of its often taken-for-granted status in education and in public life generally – is a highly charged issue, loaded with social, cultural and political assumptions. The frequency of articles in the national popular press about English in schools, and very often about the identity of literature (as in the familiar 'Chuck Berry vs Chaucer' form – when traditionalists are set against 'progressive cranks') may act as an index of the importance of the idea of literature in debates about wider cultural issues. Judgements about literacy – sometimes represented as concerned with technical matters, like so-called 'reading-ages', for example – are ideologically generated. In schools and in English the ideological aspect of literacy is most often concealed. It could even be said that the business of English in schools is, partly, to conceal the ideological component of literacy. The very idea that there is something called literature, the idea that there are literary texts, the idea that reading is in itself enriching, for example, are all, of course, socially, ideologically produced ideas. They are therefore worth pursuing in an interrogative manner with students who are often and have been often immediately subjected to them. They are all part of the stuff of institutionally defined literacy.

Teaching 'literacy' could well involve some examination of the *idea* of literacy, rather than simply assuming that literacy is a comfortably established state that everyone recognizes instantly when they see it. It could also – and consequently – look at the idea of literature, rather than accepting it as a necessary given. Moving beyond literature – whatever that is – it might address ideas about the operations of reading in general. That would probably imply looking at ideas about texts and how they communicate, in turn requiring some kind of approach to reading practices and to ideology. Texts, though, inhabit and operate within contexts and within fields of organization. This, too, might be worth exploring.

LITERACY, LITERATURE AND THE LITERARY TEXT

It is an important assumption (made by the document *English 5–16* and preceding and subsequent reports) that literacy is closely connected with literature and the literary text. Literacy is thus associated with the authority of the book. Somewhere lurking in this ideological construct is the notion of a progression and development. This involves, in turn, an ordering, a hierarchy, a system of differentiation – as may testify reading ages, and reading schemes with their different levels. Children in primary schools are familiar with this view of literacy – as in many cases they still find themselves ploughing their way through Roger-Red-Hat, Billy-Blue-Hat, and so on (until, finally(?), and many years hence, they achieve the zenith of *Anna Karenina*?). The book itself can represent a symbolically important element in an educational rite of passage – as the goal to reach for above the lower level of the sentence maker. Literacy, graded and ordered, becomes an important focus of difference and distinction in educational contexts, and this is reflected outside educational institutions, too. The social, cultural, political significance of literacy and of the idea of Literature can be attested in many ways. The idea of being well-read, for instance, remains an important factor in social and educational identity – part of the small change of cultural currency.

Where does literacy begin and end, though? How can English teachers begin to tackle this enormous field of knowledge, of cultural, educational, general social practice? How can we begin to provide our students with more than merely received notions of things textual, of reading, of its discourses and its practices? This chapter attempts to propose an approach to some of the issues involved in teaching a more theorized, more conscious and self-conscious, more critical and questioning approach to literacy than has generally been traditional in the various practices of English in schools. What is proposed here is that the idea of literacy be examined – or deconstructed – in a non-systematic way. There is no need to start at one specific point and to move methodically through a series of precisely intervalled stages. No such starting point really exists. Work on writing, for example, might easily and equally be construed as work on reading – the clear distinction between the two activities being deconstructed by different ways of seeing them both. Illustrative texts, lessons, activities are designed to approach different aspects of literacy that are always inter-related and so don't need to follow a precisely ordered programme. In what context and on what occasion the question: 'What is literacy?' may be posed explicitly, will depend on factors such as the progress of the work, the kinds of questions or responses that arise, the readiness of the students. The intention, though, is that the question should neces-sarily come to the fore during the kind of work described.

AN INITIAL APPROACH TO LITERACY

With year ten and eleven students in secondary comprehensive schools, it's obvious that each student will arrive into any English class with a personal literacy history of their own. In many cases they will have been already graded and differentiated on a scale of literacy. They will also arrive with a set of culturally produced assumptions about literacy and the business of reading. A useful starting point might be to examine students' own assumptions, to create an issue, open a discourse, as it were, and to begin to attempt a fresh analysis of reading/literacy. A description of their own attitudes towards literacy and assumptions about it can be elicited quite easily by a number of questions. The material for the lesson is produced by the students themselves in the form of their responses. The following questions might be useful in this context:

> How is reading learned?
> What different kinds of reading are there?
> What is reading?
> What is reading for?
> What is a good reader?
> What kind of reading is done in schools?

Each of these questions could provide the starting point for several other questions. The question: 'How is reading learned?', for example, could be specifically focused to look at the contexts of learning to read, the kind of techniques used, the kind of reading material used, the way that learning to read positions and constructs reading subjects of particular identities, and so on – each of these points being laid open to question, with alternatives being considered. This initial exercise could be developed into a more elaborate exercise designed to put reading – and attitudes to reading – under interrogation. The questions above could obviously be used in many ways. Each question raises potentially contentious issues. Students could be invited to consider their own personal reading histories – and the implications of the questions of their own position in relation to literacy and its institutions. Students could be asked to develop their own – more detailed – set of questions to use with one another; reading questionnaires could be discussed and devised to provide a survey of the field.

An ethnographic study of attitudes and ideas on literacy, reading and literature might be developed, based on questions addressed to a wide cross-section of members of a reading community. Responses from different members of the community could be analysed, and identities could be defined, explored, challenged, in relation to the perspectives offered by the process of survey. A school is a good example of a reading community – obviously with radically differing identities ascribed to individuals within it according to how they stand on a scale of literacy, what their attitudes towards different kinds of reading are, how they represent themselves as readers, what their personal 'literacy inheritance' is, and so on. Using this approach, the specific ways literacy operates in a community within an institution, an institution clearly linked in with other powerful institutions, can be explored. The materials for such an enterprise may be devised by teacher and/or students and may, of course, vary in degrees of sophistication and detail. The end product might furnish materials for students to present in written, spoken or video form. It's critical, though, that the questions get raised, that they get seen as *possible* questions, possible approaches to the business of literacy. Further questions might be proposed following the initial inquiry; questions such as:

What different purposes are there for reading?
Are some kinds of reading more functional than others?
Do different groups of people do different kinds of functional reading?
Are some kinds of reading done purely for pleasure?
Do different groups of people read different things for pleasure?
Are some kinds of reading better than others?
What different contexts are different kinds of reading done in?
What different kinds of institutions might be associated with different kinds of reading?
What different kinds of reading are done in schools?

Whatever activities might follow, asking these questions addresses a different set of issues from the general approach to literacy in schools. Pursuing particular issues generated by these questions might begin to open a new agenda for reading practices, a new approach to the idea of literacy – and to institutional practices of literacy.

INTRODUCING THEORY: A PHENOMENOLOGY OF READING

A phenomenology of reading would simply seek to re-address the business of reading at the level of a general question as simple, but demanding, as: How do we make sense of what we read? This initial question can be broken down to a series of questions that – simple though they are – may enable a review of the whole business of the perception of reading 'matter', defining and making sense of reading 'objects' – and may also encourage a questioning of the everyday assumptions generally used to define reading processes.

The analysis of how reading works – sometimes referred to as 'reception theory' – would involve looking first at the nature and definition of the textual object, and second, at the nature of the reading process – or the field the object is placed in, defined and interpreted. Any attempt to address the reading process would need to take into account the nature of the reader and the reading audience, the nature of the reading context, as well as dealing with the conventional tendency to see reading as a simple interchange between a reader and a text.

According to the model of phenomenology outlined previously, texts are not perceivable, any more than anything else is, as objects in themselves. Their identity is always already determined by the particular social configuration; within it they take up a specific place; within it they are already granted a specific identity, already catalogued, as it were, within a system of distinctions organized into categories. Although this 'system' is not necessarily explicit, and isn't written down in detail anywhere, it is powerful in determining modes of reading and the production of meanings. The way established reading practices determine particular meanings is well illustrated by most of the practices associated with literature in education – where certain specific types of reading and certain specific types of meaning are called for, or demanded.

Texts don't stand on their own as bearers of their own self-defining meanings. Any text is always read from a particular point of view, by a subject (or subjects) positioned at a particular point. As the model of phenomenology makes clear, the object *in itself* is not perceivable by the 'spectator', and the object *in itself* – the 'true' text – is never more than an abstraction, an idea distinct from particularly positioned readings of aspects of the textual object. This can be made clear to students without much difficulty, by using the phenomenology model, and by simple exercises in differential readings – looking at different aspects of texts from different perspectives using different ideas – following through the implications of a group of students' own reading of a particular text.

It is very important, though, that the phenomenology of reading should not end in the (banal) reduction to pure individualism, a position likely to claim that reading, and all readings, are purely a matter of individual preferences or personal predilections. This is where the idea of reading practices is important, reading practices being those attitudes and habits that are institutionally rooted and that have established status of common-sense inevitability. The liberal model of reading asserts on the one hand that any kind of reading is possible – that a single text may contain a range of varied and even contradictory meanings. In not acknowledging that this position has a tendency to totally negate the idea of literature – since any text can mean so many things to different readers – the liberal model also fails to recognize how its own preferred modes of reading are structured and restricted according to established habits of thought. The range of readings on offer in established liberal reading practices is in fact a range within a very limited notion of what constitutes a reading.

Any attempt to construct a moderately inclusive and general theory of reading must go beyond presently dominant notions. A phenomenology of reading is required that can explain, on the one hand, variant readings and, on the other hand, how readings are embedded in particular social, institutional practices. Theory – of various kinds – can do just this: a sociology of reading is also necessary, though, to make sense of the relations between questions of textual identity, questions of meaning and their social contexts. Taking a wider view of reading than is offered by the limited model of the reader and the text, literacy may be addressed in the social context of the school. The school, in turn, can be seen within its general social and cultural context. It's possible, then, to conceive of a teaching of literacy dealing with general notions about literacy, explicitly placing textually specific meanings in their wider cultural context.

Practical examples of classroom work that follow are offered as an attempt to construct a phenomenology of reading that engages students in the process of consciously developing theory in relation to textually focused activities.

THE TEXTS OF LITERATURE

Textual analysis has been the adopted, favoured form of literary encounter in most practices of English and certainly tends to be the way that literary study is presently organized. The single text is read and studied, then perhaps compared with another similar or contrasting text – though usually a text of like form and identity. The form of the approach generally ensures that it is the unique characteristics of this particular text that are being addressed, and that the text is a bearer of certain meanings, though all of this tends to be very hazily formulated. Generally, the text is represented as an object of positive value, worth studying in itself.

The idea of literature is crucial in maintaining the idea of a text being valuable in itself. It's rather curious, though, that English Literature in schools in many cases has been based on texts that could only be described as being rather dubious examples of English Literature. The familiar texts of English in schools, texts the subject English Literature has been based on, are not, according to any formalized or traditional view, official texts of English Literature. They must, however, curiously and paradoxically, bear the status of *literature*, otherwise they could not be claimed to be worthy of study in themselves. Even though it may be conceded that the focal texts are inferior – to the established texts of canonical English Literature – the assumption remains that there *are* texts of intrinsic merit, even though exactly what they are cannot be determined. In the business of literature, much must be left to personal preference – so long, of course, that it's personal preference for the right kind of text. This confusion – between freedom and very strict constraint – is at the core of English Literature as practised within schooling and remains at the core of the idea of English in general.

Lord of the Flies; *Kes*; *Of Mice and Men*; *An Inspector Calls*; *Animal Farm*, *Across the Barricades*, *Talking in Whispers* and many of the other texts that have figured in secondary English have never existed officially and unequivocally within the borders of English Literature. These texts have been brought together by no recognized procedure at all. No-one has ever attempted to justify the existence of this secondary canon. There is no common agreement on what texts exactly are to be included in it or where its limits might be drawn. No-one has ever determined why these texts are peculiarly suited to the study of English at this level. Why they are there remains a mystery; their unofficial status remains unjustified. They represent the practice of a subject that is – in a philosophical sense – ungrounded. Recognition of this significant gap in the construction of the subject argues strongly in favour of a complete redefinition of the textual field considered worthy of attention.

THE GROUNDS OF READING

The modes of study of literature in English have also been formulated on indefinite and questionable principles. The idea of personal response, for instance, is a highly dubious notion – effectively limiting the scope and constituency of the subject. Personal response is formulated on a very restricted notion of textuality. Allied to personal response are dominating concepts like 'character', for example, and other categories of response and analysis that have governed reading practices in English. Although these ideas have alienated the majority of the subjects of English, this has not deterred their continuation, and has, perhaps, been the reason for it.

In the following sections of this chapter is an approach to texts and textuality attempting to reformulate the field of enquiry, according to different sense of textual identity, addressing a broader textual field, taking different approaches to texts, attempting to change the grounds for the study of texts, to begin to deploy a different vocabulary, a different set of terms and ideas to engage with a wider field of textuality.

TEXTS AND TEXTUAL ISSUES

One of the things that theory does with the content of English in its established and conventional forms is to suggest different ways of looking at things that are ensconced as the everyday material of the discourse. This will necessarily tend to imply a different kind of vocabulary, so that while conventional practices with texts may refer to character, a theorized view might refer to an identity or a symbolic function – in this case stripping the notion of any direct connection with reality, with the idea of character in fiction as being in any way continuous with character in the real world. The constructed nature of fictional identities is thus suggested while, at the same time, the process of granting identity in language forms, contexts, genres and discourses may be seen as related to the granting of identities in general and real social exchanges. The idea, then, is not simply to deconstruct ideas about fictional texts. There would only be a limited purpose in examining, for example, fairy tales for their structural features and forms unless the implications reached beyond the limit they themselves represented. In this sense, theory foregrounding the cultural and political dimensions of things linguistic and textual, does not simply deconstruct the particular terminology of established ideas to displace them with another set of terms tackling the same entities. The general effect is to alter the grounds of study, to direct attention beyond the limits of the immediate textual focus, to see how local textual effects, details and functions are configured within and correspond to the large and general effects that infuse all things linguistic, that are central to the way we experience and interpret the world.

A practice of language and textual analysis that goes beyond established terminology has, at least, the virtue of offering choices, of indicating that there *are* different ways of looking at things. Established practices tend to remain – in spite of their protestations of freedom, allowing free individual responses – within the same repetitively restricted frame of reference. It's a frame of reference representing itself as the natural terminology of response – but it is, of course, very much a constructed terminology of a particular kind of practice. These differences in terminology – between routine notions of response and theory – may be represented as a series of alternatives in the following rough tabulation. The sense in which the two sides of the table represent strictly direct opposites is, of course, loose – partly because the terms borrowed from theory don't address the same identities signified by the conventional terms. Ideas about the very standard stuff of textual analysis are often represented as being natural common sense. These ideas about things as apparently simple as time, place and character are eminently questionable, though. They are also prohibitive of other ways of looking at texts, other ways that can be much more varied and revealing, that might develop and extend thinking without restricting and suppressing the features of texts that might be described as textual and constructed. Table 3.1 offers an initial view of some possible options.

Table 3.1 Conventional and alternative ideas about texts, and textual analysis

Conventional/established ideas	*Alternative ideas/views*
status and identity	intertextuality and institutional ordering
independence, uniqueness	genres, discourses
characters	symbolic code – elements and identities
setting	interplay of presence and absence
places	
objects	
story	syntactic/narrative structure – opening/closure
development	hermeneutic code
time –	
of the text	cultural code/reading practices
meaning or meanings	phenomenology and reading practices
response, empathy, identification, enjoyment	interpellation, symbolic order; addressing and positioning the subject of discourse, pleasures
truth to life, realism	regimes of truth

To move from considering objects and identities in texts to truth and regimes of truth covers a great deal of thinking. The range of issues, from the relatively fine points of textual analysis to the larger questions about meaning and truth, might seem daunting and unwieldy, yet is no more inclusive than established practices that deal with these things, but that don't make them explicit or subject to a questioning process. Although examining something like the hermeneutic code in fairy tales, for instance, might seem at odds with addressing regimes of truth in texts and discourses, these things are interlinked. Thinking about the genre of fairy tales can lead to considerations about genre in general and to a sense of how textual identities are organized by regimes of discourse. Discursive regimes are always configured in some relation to the idea of 'truth' or 'reality'.

Established practices of English have locked the possibilities of thinking about texts into certain entrenched modes. Theory can offer the opportunity for more mobile and more probing ways of looking at texts – addressing at the same time issues that would conventionally be passed over. How texts engage attention, for example, can be re-examined in ways that go beyond present explanations. Phenomenology begins to theorize the position of the subject or audience in relation to the text. Models that reach beyond the limits of the naive idea of individual response or textual meaning may be constructed and developed. Textual pleasures, for example, are assumed simply to be a property of reading, a matter between the text and its reader. Theory, though, might encourage teachers and students to reconsider *how* textual pleasures are activated, what kinds of pleasures there might be, how these relate to genres – how texts may address subjects in discourse, how they may engage identifications, how they may address the 'symbolic order' and the subject's position within it.

The scope of the differences outlined above may reflect a number of demanding issues and may represent a kind of working model for a project of teaching that seeks to reconfigure what passes for textual, linguistic study and practice in schools – what's generally undertaken in the name of English. Each item listed above might constitute the material for a substantial project.

A general approach to textual analysis, taking one text initially and trying out a number of angles, might, however, be useful. The study of individual texts can be quite simply – initially, at least – 'theorized' by applying a formula for textual analysis, a formula recognizing the text's configuration within a larger textual arena. One such formula is given below.

Textual identity: the status of the text; genre and the text.
The context: where, when, social setting.
The time of the text.
The symbolic structure: important roles, objects, places.
The narrative structure: from – through – to.
Questions and gaps in the text.
The ideology of the text.

A literary text, a text from popular fiction, a TV soap opera, a detective film, a wildlife programme, a documentary – all these different kinds of texts might be addressed using this outline.

The question of textual identity is certainly not a question very much probed by established, routine practices of reading and literature in English. This first point invites consideration of the text in the textual field and the text in relation to the institution – so challenging the idea that the text has a meaning and function independently of those things. The second point asks about the context of the text – where is it set and when, but also invites consideration of how the text represents social relations. A question such as: 'What differences does the text seem to construct in relation to different identities?, for example, would be a generalized way of addressing this point. A more specific way of beginning to address the issue would be to ask: 'How does this text represent, for example, the relations and differences between men and women?'

The issue around the time of the text touches upon crucial matters of interpretation and identity. The time of *Macbeth*, for example, made explicit as an issue, includes examining how a time sequence might be represented textually and what assumptions are commonly made about time sequencing in texts; it may also touch upon the question of the time of the writing of the text and the assumptions that this may carry with it. The time of the writing of the text, of course, is not identical with the time of the content of the text – the time of its setting. How might these time differences be addressed? The critical time of the text, though, might, theoretically, be construed as the time of the reading of the text, shifting the sense of its moment of production from some imagined originary point in time, to the present time of its production or reproduction – the present time being the time that determines the kinds of meanings that are given to it.

The idea of 'opening' – allied to the idea of 'closure' – might be used to initiate a discussion of when and how texts begin and end. This is not necessarily just a matter of examining specific beginnings and endings, how they operate, how they might address and position a reading subject, but might go further and engage with issues about textual forms and identities and the kinds of expectations, constructions of meaning and limits on meanings those things might involve. Students can be invited to consider these issues in relation to specific examples, but they might also be invited to think about general features of opening and closure in an explicitly theoretical way. Specific openings of texts might easily be linked, for example, with the idea of genre – looking at how openings of texts confirm, merge or affront genre expectations. Endings can be looked at in similar ways, and might be used to explore notions of where the limits to the meaning of the text might be set. When Shane rides off into the glowing west from whence he came, the conflicts at work in the earlier phases of the text have been resolved. Not everything, though, will necessarily have been resolved, and some problems that the text presents will have been left unaddressed, not dealt with by the closure. In the case of *Shane*, the relationship between Shane and the boy's mother is to an extent an unresolved issue. Its implications would be difficult for the genre of the classic western to pursue. Asking a question like: 'What kind of questions might this ending leave you with?', would be one way of inviting consideration of how meanings generated can spill over the apparent limits of any text, and might in turn be used to ask about how meanings of texts might be held in place by things outside of texts.

Conventional reading practices have no way really of linking signifying processes with the general cultural meanings they engage, produce and reproduce. In addressing the idea of 'character', though, utilizing a different kind of terminology can provide a perspective that examines more clearly and fully how verbal entities are construed in reading processes as character identities and given specific symbolic functions and roles within a text. In this way, specific practices of reading and writing may be highlighted – and examined for the assumptions they make about language and textuality. Textual elements are demystified from their established formulations. Identifying and looking at different textual elements enables textual construction to be seen. Looking at the materials of the construction make it possible to see the kinds of orderings that hold texts together. This necessarily means looking at cultural practices and identifying cultural meanings. These practices and meanings may then be addressed from different perspectives, different attitudes towards them being made possible.

The idea of narrative structure highlights the sense of the text as an ordered entity, in which the ordering is not inevitable, but is a feature of an active process of construction. The ordering may follow certain definite patterns that can be identified in practice by looking at different assemblages of textual elements, the kinds of ordering differing according to different genres.

All narrative texts in their movement from one thing to another pose questions that may be answered in the continuing progress of the narrative and all leave some questions unanswered. Different reading practices will produce different sets of questions to ask of texts and will construe the questions texts raise differently. For example, one reading of *Great Expectations* might propose the question: 'Does Pip marry Estella at the end?' Another way of reading the text would put a different question, say: 'Why is Estella restored to the text, albeit briefly, in the final moment, and what kind of closure does the text therefore seem to be seeking to effect?'

The ideology of the text is to do with how the text seems to represent the world and how it seems to configure different identities. Obviously this is a large and critical issue. It relates to all the other kinds of features of texts that might be addressed using theory. But it is important to identify ideology at work in texts, to represent the case that texts offer particular views of the world rather than standing in some direct relation to it. Addressing ideology it's important to raise the question of whether the ideological content of the text – its meaning – is a property of the text itself or whether it is produced by modes of reading. This can be examined by looking at one text and seeing how different readings – making different meanings for it – may be produced.

Questions and gaps are features of all texts and may be just as revealing of how they work in terms of genre and ideology. Gaps are necessary for texts to function at all – but it is in their gaps that texts may be said to reveal their ideological constitution most. Gaps and silences indicate the places where meanings that are generally current and dominant will tend to fill in. 'He rode into our valley in the summer of '89 . . .' sets a number of stereotypes into action, gaps initiating questions like: 'What does "he" signify'. 'What was "he" riding?' and so on, which are quickly and noiselessly filled in by ready-to-hand meanings. Of course other meanings are perfectly possible and perfectly plausible, but they don't push themselves forward with the same instant alacrity.

Textual issues could be represented by the following questions that students can apply to a number of different types of text:

Identity
What kind of people read this text?
Where? Within what institutions?
What would they do with it?
What kind of text is it?
What social activity or activities is it associated with?
What other kinds of texts is it distinguished from?

Context
What places are represented in the text?
What interiors are there? What exteriors?
What public places are there?
What era is the text set in?

What tense is the text represented in?
What social relations are evident in the text?
What differences are there in status, in identity and in role?

Time
What era is the text written in?
What era is the text being read in?
How does the era of the text's reading represent the era of its setting?
What movements in time does the text signify?
What movements in time do readers have to assume?

Symbolic structure
What identities, or 'agents' are there in the text?
What are their different roles and functions?
What objects are there in the text?
What symbolic meanings can be given to these objects?
What places are represented?
What is the symbolic meaning of these places?

Narrative structure
From what situation does the narrative begin?
What changes are there?
What instigates each of these changes?
What direction is the text moving in at its moments of change?
Are there any changes in direction?
What kind of ending does the text have?
How does the ending organize the movement of the text?

Questions and gaps in the text
What questions does the text leave open?
What possible answers are there to these questions?
What answers are most likely to be given?
What assumptions are these answers based on?
Are there any unanswerable questions?
What gaps are there in the text – in terms of explanations, details/
descriptions, actions, location and time?
How are these gaps likely to be filled in?
Are there gaps that cannot be filled in?

Textual ideology
What ideas about the way people behave does the text seem to promote?
Does the text represent people differently according to – race, class
and/or gender?
How does the text organize its different identities?

What ideas and attitudes about the world does the text seem to promote?
What ideas and attitudes about the world does the text assume?
How does the text seem to address the reader or audience?
What assumptions does it make about the reader or audience?

The issue of genre may be approached by considering fairy tales as an example, examining two or three texts. The procedure can be relatively simple, involving constructing a structure box; identifying elements and the ways they tend to get organized. One way of concentrating focus to begin with might involve considering the idea of genre in relation to the symbolic structuring of gendered identities, for example, looking at the kinds of roles assigned to male and female characters; looking also at the different ways that texts address male and female identities; and looking at the pleasures these texts seem to yield – in relation to the issues of gender they activate. This example of genre might then be put alongside other genres to see what the differences and similarities are according to the identified points of interest. Example 3.1 shows a structure box and follow-up activities which could be presented to students.

The structure box offers the opportunity to look at general features of the genre, or discourse, of fairy tales. Inside the structure box may go all the elements that might make up fairy stories – elements such as identities, places, events, time and so on. The box can easily be filled in by the students and its contents discussed. The other activities may develop ideas in practice, playing upon the idea of the difference between conventional and less conventional forms and the structuring of elements. The elements of the genre may be identified and explored. The extent that those elements themselves produce certain kinds of meanings can be examined by looking at the possibilities that the genre may offer for redefined meanings. In this way, meaning – the creation and the reading of meaning – may be understood as at least partly a property of genres, and certainly not as something that a text may make for itself, by itself. The example of fairy tales, organized in this way, might also be useful for asking questions about texts and the idea of reality. To what extent might fairy tales be thought to stand in some kind of relation to the way things are outside of fairy tales? Given that fairy tales are understood to belong to the realm of fantasy, a number of ways of looking at them might be considered and discussed: for example, the kind of treatment of fairy tales by psychoanalysts who read unconscious symbolism into them might be considered, their relations with ideas about gender might also be looked at, as might their connections with other narrative forms.

Example 3.1   Examining the structure of the discourse of fairy tales

---

Structure Box

including, for example:

identities
events
beginnings
endings
time
places
objects

Is the reader inside or outside the structure box?
What about the author?

Activities

- Write your own fairy tale using a conventional structure and contents.
- Write a fairy story that changes or challenges the conventional structure and contents.
- Read *Rapunzel* and *The Company Of Wolves*: and discuss in the light of what you have found out about the structure of the discourse of fairy tales.

An important aspect of this work – an eminently deconstructive issue – is to examine the idea of what is inside and what is outside the text, so prompting questions about the very identity of the text. The things that are in the text must also refer to things that are outside the text. The idea we may have of the text being something inclusive with clear boundaries cannot then be maintained. All things in the text being also outside of it – even if only as ideas, stereotypes, general categories or common reference points of language – the text cannot then remain stable within itself, but must always hover between its inside and outside. This hovering might be expressed as what the text is. The elements of the text must have meanings that are independent – or outside – of the text, and the configuring of those elements must also correspond to forms of organization that are not unique to the text – these are conditions of the text being recognizable as the kind of text it is, and are also conditions of its being able to mean something.

Then may come the question of the reader – whether the reader is inside the structure of the text or whether the reader stands clearly outside. What about the author?

The question of genre may be further pursued in a more definitely comparative way by going beyond the limits of one genre to look more explicitly at genres of different kinds – examining the issue in a more generalized sense, though still being able to refer to specific instances.

A sentence maker is, in fact, a kind of writing machine and one that usefully provides a way of looking at textual elements and genre. One way children in primary schools are taught to write and to read (both at the same time) is by using a sentence maker. The sentence maker is a mechanism for writing – and makes use of children's already acquired ability to read. It consists of strips of paper pasted to card that has slots for cards with words written on them to be placed in. Children are given words that they can read and are then asked to put them into some kind of order on their sentence maker. An example is shown in Figure 3.1.

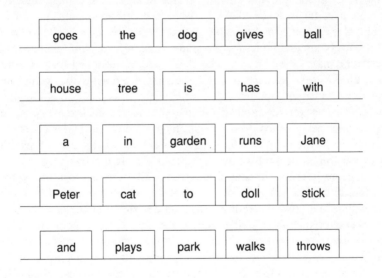

| goes | the | dog | gives | ball |

| house | tree | is | has | with |

| a | in | garden | runs | Jane |

| Peter | cat | to | doll | stick |

| and | plays | park | walks | throws |

Figure 3.1 A sentence maker
Note: The cards may represent several instances of the same word.

The sentence maker is like a rudimentary language consisting of prepositions, verbs and nouns. The child makes up sentences by selecting the elements and putting them into an order, as the following examples may illustrate:

Jane goes to the park with Peter.
Peter has the ball.
The cat runs to the park with the dog.
The dog has the stick in the park with Jane and the cat.
The tree is in the house

The words are elements of meaning that have to be recognized by the child. But to use the sentence maker the child also has to know how to put the words into a meaningful order or sequence – according to the rules of syntax. The child needs to know, among other things, the conventions of language that enable the elements to be put together into sequence – the roles and functions that the elements have. While this knowledge may not be conscious – active knowledge about language rarely is – it is absolutely necessary.

This is both a writing and reading machine. In fact, the distinction here between writing and reading may be shown to be unclear – and thus the childish example may illustrate some important 'grammatological' points like, for instance, the way that genre determines meaning. The point of the sentence maker in the context I'm proposing is that it provides a relatively simple model for the study of genre and syntax in texts. A sentence maker may be imagined that could be designed for use with any kind of text and would simply consist of elements that would be available to be put into order. So, for example, it is possible to imagine a sentence maker for football commentary or for nuclear physics. In each case the sentence maker would have its own particular elements and in each case the user would need to have knowledge about how the elements might be put together in order to operate it effectively.

A genre sentence maker might have different sets of cards for different textual genres – to illustrate how genres may determine meanings and how different genres may determine how elements may be characteristically combined into sequences. Students could work on producing sets of cards that had on them the characteristic elements of different genres, and could then put the elements into play using a sentence maker to place them and move them around as necessary. In doing this they might explore the 'rules' of syntax as they work at the level of genres – determining how narratives get shaped, what identities have what functions, what genres have what kinds of closures; they might look at any of these things in a broad and general way or in a detailed way – depending on the number of elements required to make up a set. The point of this exercise would be to illustrate how genres operate, how the elements and their ordering may be made conscious, and how genres may be 'interfered with', manipulated and altered. The last point may be part of learning how certain genres may deal with certain kinds of cultural stereotypes – familiar images and forms of representation that might be playfully but consciously challenged. Example 3.2 shows how this type of exercise could be presented.

Example 3.2   The sentence maker or forms of fiction

Construct sentence makers including necessary and possible component parts for each of these various types of fiction. The components might consist of identities, places, time, events, objects, beginnings, endings and ideas.

- a detective story/novel
- a romantic love story/novel
- a boys' adventure story/novel
- a nineteenth century story/novel about growing up
- a horror story/novel
- a story/novel about World War II
- an anti-war story novel
- and so on

The sentence maker can consist of a number of cards with single elements written on each. These cards can then be dealt, at random, and then configured into a characteristic ordering of the genre in question. The structure of fictions can then be looked at across a wide field and can be understood from different perspectives: initially from the point of view of their constituent elements; and from the point of view of their forms – the narrative forms that shape and organize the elements. What may also be considered is the different ways these genres tend to configure identities, the different ways they may be read – different kinds of attitudes towards them, different statuses different groups may accord to them. Some kind of speculation might take place about these differences and what produces and maintains them.

It would be important, though, to move beyond the limited realm of fiction for work on genre to have general significance. The extension of the textual field may link, in the first place, cinema narratives with the genres of fiction. But other – equally important though perhaps less likely – connections may be made between genres of fiction and other kinds of writing and representation, such as news items, adverts on TV, newspaper reports and magazine articles on topical issues. A great deal of work could be done examining TV news genres and how these get organized into news programmes; analysing the different kinds of reports there are, what their characteristic elements are, how they get presented, what ideas they generate and what general forms they take.

The connections between genre and ideology and how these things might position readers or audiences can be developed in relation to a specific example, in this illustrative case, by examining the newspaper report below, going on to answer the questions raised in Example 3.3

Treading the Path of Tears
Jan, a sturdy little police collie, tore into the earth of the haunted moorland wilderness. Dank mud caked her black and white fur as she dug relentlessly into the ground, her finely tuned nose seeking to lay the ghosts of Wildcat Quarry. For handler Sergeant Neville Sharp, of West Yorkshire police, it was a horror revisited. He gritted his teeth and held back his fury and tears as his seven year old dog scratched furiously into ground that holds secrets and terrors. Two decades ago he was a young copper assigned to help dig up the mutilated victims of the deranged madness of Myra Hindley and Ian Brady. He had watched as the bodies were exhumed and taken away. 'I was just a lad at the time,' he said yesterday. 'I was so sad, very sad, when I saw those little bodies. I'm a 43 year old now with two daughters of my own. But I shall never forget what I saw on that awful day.'
Sergeant Sharp is one of the eight-strong sniffer dog team who will be minutely inspecting every blade of grass, every mound of earth and every rock on this desolate moorland called Saddleworth. It is a disturbingly grim place, hovering above the Dove Stone reservoir. Little of this bleak landscape has changed since the stomach churning discoveries that first shook the nation all those years ago.
  In the quiet village of Greenfield, just two miles away down a winding muddied road, the people are bracing themselves with grim lips to relive the horrors. The village pub, The Clarence, is the place where Brady and Hindley calmly and callously played dominoes after their frequent trips to the moors.
  It gives you a feeling of chilling eeriness to stand on Hollin Brow knoll where the abused and tortured body of Lesley Ann Downey had been found. Or to walk across the charmingly named Isle of Skye road and stare at the earth where the mutilated remains of little John Kilbride were discovered.

(*Daily Mirror*, 21 November 1986)

The question about what kind of writing is involved here might provoke some consideration of genre; and this might usefully be directed towards considering the difference between fiction and non-fiction,

Example 3.3 'Treading the path of tears': ideology and interpellation
– addressing the subject

What kind of writing is this?

What is the function of / what is represented by:

- Jan, the police collie?
- Sergeant Neville Sharp?
- the pub?
- the village of Greenfield?
- Neville Sharpe's daughters?
- the Dove Stone reservoir?
- Saddleworth Moor?
- the ghosts of Wildcat Quarry?
- Myra Hindley and Ian Brady?

How is the reader expected to respond to each of these various things?
How is the reader positioned by each of them?

How is the reader interpellated and positioned by the story?

---

examining whether, in this case, a strict difference between the two
categories can be maintained. The positioning of the reader by the
textual deployment of ready-to-hand stereotypes is clearly evident in
this example. Each of the things identified – textual objects, places,
identities – carries specific symbolic meaning and orients the reader in
certain ways of seeing, thinking and feeling. The police collie associated with Sergeant Neville Sharp clearly represents a kind of natural
good. The landscape – Saddleworth Moor, Wildcat Quarry, Hollin
Brow Knoll – are associated with a natural eeriness that complements
the representation of unfathomable evil in the 'story'.

This type of exercise can be usefully compared with generic features
of fairy tales and might be done as complementary to it. It's possible to
use this example to highlight the way established reading practices
invite you to give 'character' a certain kind of reading to produce the
appropriate and inescapable responses. How could you not reject the
horror of the Moors murders? Equally, how could you not feel the
essential goodness of Neville Sharpe – representative, quintessential
policeman, father and kindly dog-handler – a decent man bewildered by
senseless, horrific evil. The text promotes the idea of normality –
symbolized also by the village with its pub – violated by the outrages of
the murderers, and positions the reader to accept these stereotypical
identities and meanings as essential, natural and inevitable. The text,

though, does not do this on its own; the reading practices, the positioning of the reader, the intertextual echoes and references, the stereotypes deployed work together to produce the effect.

The theme of genre, the positioning of the reader or audience, and ideology might be pursued in relation to gaps and intertextual references using Example 3.4, which takes the text of *Shane* (Schaefer 1957) as its key text.

Examples 3.4 Shane: gaps and ideology in the reading of texts

---

Extract

He rode into our valley in the summer of '89

. . . he was weaving quick and confident. It was incredible, but they could not hurt him. . .

He was the man who rode into our little valley out of the heart of the great glowing west and when his work was done rode back whence he had come . . .

From reading the extract above:
• define the possible heroine
• describe important aspects of the setting
• produce a cast-list – with defining characteristics
• outline significant stages in the plot
• describe the hero
• identify important objects
• identify important ideas

and, finally, consider how it is possible to answer all these questions.

Most of the essential components of the narrative and its developments are somehow contained in these brief lines. The responses from students presented with the following questions are likely to be fairly developed, fairly precise and 'accurate'; but the critical question, in relation to the kinds of responses that may be produced, is concerned with where this knowledge comes from and how – unconsciously and apparently automatically – it gets transferred to the few clues that are offered by the textual material. It seems that a whole range of details, a whole body of knowledge may be triggered into play by a few textual clues. This seems to be something that is a feature of how meanings are generated by signs. Visual and linguistic signs may operate in quite similar ways, and the text above – the radically pared down version of *Shane* – could be compared with images from Clint Eastwood films, images that generate very similar sets of stereotypical responses and ideas. It could also be compared with and set alongside a range of other texts that would seem to activate very similar stereotypical images and ideas; and the business of where meaning comes from and of the relations between meaning, texts, and culturally produced sets of meaning may then be – in a preliminary way, at least – explored. Adverts of various types, for example, might provide ample material for comparison and development. Popular music, popular forms of fiction of certain types, and many cultural products would be relevant. At issue, explicitly and immediately, could be the question of masculine identity and its various different representations in culturally powerful media forms.

The main questions asked of the *Shane* extracts could be broken down into a host of questions, such as those below:

Who was he?
What kind of past did he have?
Was he married?
How old was he?
Where did he come from?
What was his ethnic identity?
What kind of clothes was he wearing?
(What colour clothes was he wearing?)
Who is 'speaking'?
What is the gender of the speaker?
How old 'was' the speaker 'then'?
How old 'is' the speaker 'now'?
What is the ethnic identity of the speaker?
What is going on in the valley?
Where is the valley?
Who are 'they'?
What gender are 'they'?
How many of them were there?
Did they want to hurt him?
How long did it take to do his work?
What was the work that was done?

There are many more questions like those above. How can it be possible to answer these questions? It obviously is possible. That it is possible – actually necessary for there to be a story – indicates how reading literary texts depends on the operation of assumptions and familiarity with genres. This puts a decisive emphasis on the role of the reader, but it is important not to assume that the reader has a free choice in answering these questions. The answers are strictly limited by dominant cultural ideas, and these dominant ideas – or ideological conditions – are written into established reading practices. It is evident, from the exercise above, that the text is dependent for its meaning and its functioning on meanings outside of itself, meanings it brings into play via reading practices. These theoretical points – antithetical to common-sense accounts of reading – can be made available to students using the above exercise.

The business of addressing the wider textual field is necessarily complemented by the placing of texts within a field. This implies consideration of how texts are given differently defined identities. In turn, this implies a system regulating and determining the identities and statuses of texts, though the system may not be explicitly formulated. Students may be directed to look at aspects of texts apart from what is conventionally designated as content. Signs of the identity of the text within a system of differing textual identities may be examined. Questions may be asked about how these identities are maintained, and whether they operate with equal force within different contexts.

While looking at the 'packaging' of books may now have become a fairly standard kind of activity, it would be a significant development to go beyond the examination of individual texts looked at in their disparities and to begin to build a sense of texts being placed within a larger – mobile but structured – textual field. It would be important for the exercise outlined in Example 3.5, for instance, to consider other kinds of texts as well as those conventionally addressed by routine English.

Similar analysis could be applied to other texts – TV programmes, sporting events and their representations in various media, material objects and their representations in adverts, for example. All these 'texts' could be looked at in terms of the way that their identity is readable from various features granting them status, placing them within a specific arena or textual field.

An important aspect of this work is that it addresses the idea of the textual field in general and the idea of different texts and media producing different textual fields. In relation to the idea of the textual field, students can produce readings of novels alongside readings of other texts of a very different order. Once the textual field is opened and addressed, the idea of reading practices – practices like those in English, for example, that favour only certain kinds of texts – can be set alongside and seen against others. A network of texts and fields can be produced. Students may be engaged on a project to begin to tabulate

Example 3.5 Fictional Identities

Choose 3 novels and examine each for clues as to its identity such as:

- the front cover
- the back cover
- first paragraph
- names in the text
- kind of language used
- kind of print
- point of view of narration
- references to objects
- places
- any indicators of cultural context

Write about how, in each case, the identified features work to give the text an identity.

---

different fields and texts. A model might be produced that begins to figure how different texts could be positioned – a kind of intertextual network – illustrating how various texts and kinds of texts are differentiated and connected. Examining the textual field in this way, it can be shown that textual identities are configured in certain ways by particular reading practices; reading practices that, in turn, can be shown to belong to particular cultural practices and to particular kinds of institutions and institutional practices. Emphasis is given, then, to an idea of reading practices moving well beyond the scope of English and its idiosyncratic predilection for fictions of a particular and limited kind.

This project, although beginning with looking at the identities of different kinds of fiction texts by reading certain 'external' signs, intends to a) place texts within fields and within a larger field, and b) demonstrate that texts, their meanings and the reading practices that give them meaning are variously and differently situated and defined. So questions about meaning – and how it operates within particular cultural formations – may be pursued, looking for example at how meanings produced by ways of reading Shakespeare might be compared with meanings produced by readings of Levi jeans or *Rambo*, or Black and Decker power tools. Different discourses, it can be shown, employ interconnecting ideas, using similar and different signs to produce related meanings, meanings, though, that retain some consistency of identity in their cultural contexts – and that are not intrinsic to special texts.

It might be useful for students on courses currently titled 'English Literature' to consider examples of what is signified and understood by the designation. The following approach to *Great Expectations* offers a way of reinscribing the text – or elements of it – into other forms, providing a positively deconstructive approach to its identity and status as English Literature. More information could be provided about the outline of the narrative. Students could be asked to fill in gaps and construct the outline of a 'drama' using a list of some structural functions, such as those given in Example 3.6 below.

Example 3.6   Great Expectations: some structural functions and extracts

---

Structural Functions

- an orphan boy, brought up in a country forge who has a wealthy benefactor
- an escaped convict, later captured and deported to Australia, who returns in secret a wealthy man much later
- a powerful London lawyer
- a bizarre and very wealthy old woman jilted when young
- a beautiful but cold young woman, 'adopted' by the old woman
- the forge where the orphan boy is brought up
- the eccentric old woman's ramshackle house
- the lawyer's office
- the orphan boy's London lodgings
- Newgate prison
- a file
- a large inheritance
- moving from home in the country to London
- falling in love
- an unexpected return
- an arrest and a trial
- a fire
- a final meeting

Extracts

My father's family name being Pirrip, and my Christian name Philip, my infant tongue could make of both names nothing longer or more explicit than Pip. So, I called myself Pip, and came to be called Pip . . .

I took it upon myself to impress Biddy (and through Biddy, Joe) with the grave obligation I considered my friends under, to know nothing and say nothing about the maker of my fortune. It would all come out in good time, I observed, and in the meanwhile nothing was to be said, save that I had come into great expectations from a mysterious patron. Biddy nodded her head thoughtfully at the fire as she took up her work again, and said she would be very particular; and Joe, still detaining his knees, said 'Ay, Ay, I'll be ekervally partickler, Pip,' and they congratulated me again, and went on to express so much wonder at the notion of my being a gentleman, that I didn't half like it. . .

I took her hand in mine and we went out of the ruined place; and, as the morning mists had risen long ago when I first left the forge, so, the evening mists were rising now, and in all the broad expanse of tranquil light they showed to me, I saw no shadow of another parting from her.

More information about *Great Expectations* might be provided, including, for example, an account of the narrative and how it configures the structural functions. Students might be asked to consider, in relation to the limited material they've been given, what themes might be in play. They might also be invited to consider what kind of narrative structure is involved, what kind of narrative position is taken and how this may place the position of the reader. They might also be asked to take into account the identity of *Great Expectations* within the order of English Literature, considering how this might determine the kind of reading it would be given and the kinds of meanings that could be made of it, as well as considering the kind of audience this would tend to imply. All these issues could be dealt with by discussion or by providing further material – perhaps by providing sets of questions dealing with each.

Practical work, though, could be organized around the idea of transposition – raising the question of what happens to the identity of *Great Expectations*, and to its 'meaning', if it gets transposed into other forms. Students could be invited to transpose the narrative features of *Great Expectations* they've been given into the following types of text: an American soap opera, a UK soap opera, an Australian soap opera or a Hollywood detective film, and might devise storyboards and produce dialogue for each different type based on a few chosen scenes. They might also be invited, for example, to produce scripted 'trailers' for each kind of text, considering what kind of audience, and what kind of audience interests, they want to address. Other kinds of transposition could also be considered, for example: women's magazine stories, TV adverts; conversations held by different groups of people in different contexts could also be considered.

According to this kind of procedure, the identity of the text, its structural properties, its themes and its meanings can be seen to belong to a particular context – the context of English Literature – in the first place; but all those things can be transposed into many different contexts, shifting the text's identity, shifting its meanings, too, so that the idea of special properties and special meanings belonging to specific texts in any kind of essential way may be effectively, practically deconstructed. In the process many important points about the placing of texts within different arenas in the textual field may be raised.

Understanding ideas like textual fields and discourses producing meanings is not very closely allied to the practices associated with the idea of personal response – not in its routine forms, anyway. Structures of meaning generate structures of response too, and institutions, like the institution of English, for example, also legitimate, organize and control appropriate and proper responses. This is, no doubt, one of the time-honoured functions of English. In spite of the theological aura of the mystical that sometimes attends references to it, there is nothing mysterious or subterranean about the business of personal response and (there's nothing much *personal* about it, either). English quite clearly *demands* certain kinds of responses to certain kinds of writing – and what English syllabuses mean by personal response is really quite strictly restrained. Unconstrained personal response is likely, in certain circumstances, to get you into trouble, or at least to exclude you from entry into the charmed circle of legitimate attainment. However, exercises may be constructed to examine the business of reading and response, and theory can be produced that analyses forms of response in a quite direct manner. The suggestion in Example 3.7 inverts the text–response formula, in that is *begins* by looking at likely responses.

The business of personal response, though, may be more complex than this outline of structural features suggests. A different approach to personal response – one that addressed ideas like interpellation and identification in a theoretical manner – would be required to reach beyond the apparent limits of the idea as it is predominantly conceived by the official versions of English and by its dominant practices. Questions might be asked about how English demands these kinds of response, how other kinds of response are excluded, what the consequences might be of refusing certain forms of response, and so on.

This kind of analysis of specific genres of poetry and their habitual forms of expression may well be linked in with other kinds of work on genre – genres of fiction, for example. The sections defined by the points above enable students to analyse how features, and responses,

Example 3.7 Poems and personal response

Write a list of appropriate responses to each of the following types of poem:

- a poem about a scene in nature or a natural object
- a war poem
- a poem on time and death
- a poem of forsaken love
- a poem of the urban environment

- Write a list of metaphors/similes for each of these types of poem.
- Write a list of metonyms for each of these types of poem.
- Write a list of words signifying objects for each of these types of poem.
- Write a list of words signifying moods for each of these types of poem.
- Write a list of rhetorical features appropriate to each of these types of poem.

How, then, are personal responses to all of these things organized by these different types of text?

---

are produced by the deployment of genres – and how, in turn, the genres will tend to delimit the kinds of expression that are possible. This kind of work could easily be analysed along with the kind of treatment of poetry that demands personal response – when personal response may be a good deal less intimate and individual than imagined. Another direction that this work might take would be to transpose the signifying elements and responses onto different forms, so that exactly the same kinds of responses and features that are attributed to poetry as a special category can be attributed to other – and often contrasting – forms of expression. It might be demonstrated that a John Donne poem can elicit similar responses to a TV car advert. That kind of exercise could be undertaken in a general project, one of the effects of which would be to deconstruct the identity of poetry, to demystify its special status and to demonstrate that, as a special category assumed to be worthy of attention in and for itself, it is not really plausible. While the kind of work outlined above could be simply used to identify structural properties of certain kinds of poetry, it would be more critical and more adventurous not to leave it at that, but to pursue questions about the institutional identity and value of poetry.

The identity of poetry in general may be subjected usefully and positively to deconstructive critique. Another aspect of this kind of project might involve some comparative analysis of texts belonging in a thoroughly established sense to official English Literature. The texts in question hold their place according to the notion of English Literature that still remains institutionally dominant. The specific texts of English Literature are in it because they are believed to be of value in themselves. They represent fine expression, sensitive feeling, cogent thought and other admirable qualities. Exposure to these texts gives access to these special qualities – at least, that has been the theory of English Literature and the justification for its continued existence.

What happens, though, if we analyse the apparent values of English Literature as expressed in some of its representative texts? What happens if we set these texts alongside texts that are generally deemed by the institution of English Literature to be inferior, to belong, in themselves, to inferior modes of representation with inferior forms of expression; texts that are deemed, by implication, at least, to be more crude, less subtle and to be of less sensitive emotional quality; texts that are deemed to be decidedly inferior, if not altogether absent, in quality of thought? What happens if these different texts of divergent and, in some senses at least, opposing identities, are examined in relation to one specific topic that seems relevant to their apparent content?

The contrast elaborated in Example 3.8 invites comparison between various texts differentiated according to their modes, their identities and their relative statuses. Within the field of English, Marvell must occupy a position distinct from Madonna, and that distinction must be based on the notion of superiority of some kind – otherwise the idea of English Literature as valuable and worthy in itself must collapse. But if we compare these texts from the point of view of how they represent women, how they address women and how they seem to position male and female readers, it's difficult to see how the texts of English Literature – according to conventional reading practices, anyway – can escape the charge of an intransigent sexism. Here – in relation to all these texts – important questions about texts, their identities and their meanings can be pursued. Taking a specific perspective, the difference between textual identities – construed as a difference in quality – collapses. What are the implications of this deconstructive effect?

'Fiction and reality' represents a complex network of issues that might take analysis and classroom activity in many different directions. The largeness and complexity of the topic though need not –

Example 3.8   Madonna and English Literature

Texts:

English Literature
   To His Coy Mistress
   The Flea
   Goe Lovely Rose

Madonna
   Like A Prayer
   Cherish
   Express Yourself

Answer the following questions in relation to these texts:

- What different kinds of language do these texts use?
- What different identities are likely to be given to these texts?
- What different kinds of status are likely to be given to these texts?
- In what different contexts might these texts be given different identities and statuses?
- What words or other signs are used in these texts about women?
- What images of women are there in these texts?
- What assumptions or ideas about women do they seem to portray?
- What attitudes towards women are expressed in these texts?
- How do these texts position the reader?
- How might different readings of these texts be made by men and by women?
- What are the implications of this comparison – between English Literature and Madonna – for the identity of English Literature in education?
- And Madonna?

---

and should not – prevent its being tackled. The classic way that literature in English has of dealing with the issue is to equate certain texts with certain kinds of representation of the real – thus suppressing the problematics of representation, evading the business of textual constructions and the force of the 'imaginary'. No text can escape from the medium of its representation; texts cannot reach directly into reality and demonstrate it. Texts are deemed to be real or realistic on the basis of decisions that determine them as real or realistic. Habitual ways of reading – of watching TV, for example – are often highly conscious, in their everyday terminology, of the constructedness of texts. Texts, though, are not constructed by processes that are unique to themselves.

They make sense through reference to recognizable signs, signs that get deployed in other texts. In all these senses the representation of reality – or rather the assumption of reality – is something affirmed by particular perspectives on reality. Reality itself – in some pure and direct sense – is no more directly representable than it is directly perceptible.

'Drama and the representation of reality' is a topic that might usefully address issues of representation while also addressing what might be called the idea of the autonomous drama text. Some attempt at this admittedly unwieldy project could begin with a single text that enjoys the status of a 'drama text', such as *Romeo and Juliet*. The initial complication in this case is the fact that the drama text in question is also a relatively popular film – popular in English in schools, anyway. The following points or a selection of them could be addressed as a generalized way of looking at *Romeo and Juliet* – as drama text and film – before beginning to approach the issue of what drama is and how it might or might not stand in relation to the representation of reality:

- the context – setting: in terms of time, place and social order; the interplay between order and disorder in the text;
- the style of the text: language, mode of presentation, points of view;
- the direction of the narrative – as tragedy;
- the symbolic ordering of the texts – significant figures and objects, their roles and functions;
- stereotypes deployed in the text: other texts, and kinds of texts, they connect with;
- textual ideology: ideas and issues promoted by the text and how they are represented;
- the status of the text and its institutional identity: the position the text takes up in the textual field; its identity in relation to other texts similar and different;
- alternative views of the text: other ways of interpreting it, or other ways of perceiving it – from the established;
- the context of reception, the context of reading – how this might affect the kind of meanings that get made of it and responses to it;
- the different forms of the text: reading text, film and play, and how these differences might determine meanings and responses.

This more inclusive approach to a single text can be useful in so far as it tends to offer multiple ways of looking at the text, offering different perspectives on meaning and identity that suggest strongly that the text is not some simple unity held together by itself, defining its place in the order of things textual, or giving itself specific and limited meanings. The effect of all this is to problematize, though perhaps indirectly, the idea of the presentation of 'reality' and, by implication, at least, to suggest that reality itself, in relation to texts, is always something constructed and represented. If the meaning of the text is uncertain, ambiguous, shifting according to different factors, and if the identity of the text is granted to it, temporarily, by social convention, then the notion of some kind of direct communication of the real or of truth, is not really sustainable.

The identity of the literary text – as a discrete category, with special meanings and subtleties of its own – can be neatly deconstructed along with the idea of textual place, time and context. In Example 3.9, the idea of a special context for a literary text is deconstructed by placing it alongside a contemporary text – of very different status – and finding a number of similarities.

Example 3.9   Why Summerbay and Verona are the same

Look at the way each text – *Romeo and Juliet* and 'Home and Away' – represents and organizes a sense of place.

What features of place are shown and what are their different functions?

Look at how the following things are represented by each text and compare them:

- clothes
- young love
- generation differences
- the family
- masculinity
- femininity

Exercises can also be devised that effectively deconstruct the integrity of textual meaning and textual identities by examining how different meanings might be construed for the same text. Looking also at how the same meanings or differences in meaning might also be construed for texts of widely differing identities, the idea of special qualities belonging intrinsically to specific categories of text is also deconstructed, as shown in Example 3.10. Unusual connections might be made, and a whole class might work together to create unusual combinations.

Example 3.10   Contradictory readings: common-sense and alternative approaches

---

Take a text – perhaps a 'standard' text from English Literature, *Macbeth*, say – and decide on three important themes, ideas or topics 'in' it. Do the same with another kind of text – for example a soap opera such as 'Eastenders'.

In *Macbeth* for instance you may choose the family, gender difference and personal identity. For each of these find three sections of the text and explain how a) a common-sense reading, and b) an alternative reading might use these sections of text.

Consider the implications this exercise might have for textual identity and status.

From the starting point shown in Example 3.10, work could be done on an oral presentation or a piece of writing showing a) how texts can be subject to contradictory reading, and b) how *Macbeth* might produce the same kind of contradictory readings as 'Eastenders'.

While it might be useful, and interesting to examine single texts as examples of types or genres or specific textual identities, it might also be useful to do some work that directly addresses categories of texts. The suggestions in Example 3.11 about dealing with the idea of drama might well be transposed to refer to stories or poems.

Most of the examples of work that might be done with classes so far has had a specifically textual focus, and the texts in question, while not necessarily belonging to the established order of English have, none-theless, been recognizable as texts. It would be important to emphasize, though, that all language is textual – is structured by form, genre, context and identity. It would be important, too, to bring the general textuality of language into play in teaching that addressed reading – or writing or oracy, the clear distinction between these categories being open to deconstruction along the lines suggested by the work addressing textuality. It would certainly be a move towards liberation from specific textual categories to examine a range of texts incorporating things that would be unlikely, under the present regime, to be considered texts.

A RANGE OF TEXTS

In English lessons reading has traditionally, but questionably, tended to focus on the single text. The reading of the single text, depends on certain notions of meaning and value. It effectively limits the scope of

Example 3.11 Deconstructing drama

We can look at the idea of drama in relation to different forms and the representation of reality, considering such aspects as:

* staging
* roles
* audiences
* performance
* construction

Consider the ways these ideas can be applied to:

* an Australian soap opera
* an Indiana Jones film
* a news broadcast
* a sporting event

Looking at drama, narrative and the organization of identities and meanings, consider the way these different kinds of drama 'stage' and represent:

class	the family
gender	race
gender orientation	individual identity

---

ideas and activities, in an ideological sense as well as in a practical sense. Comparative textual work – where it does occur – still tends to put together texts of similar identity and status, when more productive effects might be achieved by looking at texts of disparate kinds and by looking at cultural phenomena that are not usually defined as texts. This might be construed as a deliberate move away from the idea that 'reading' itself is identical with literature, or with what *English 5–16* refers to (rather indeterminately) as 'the literary text'.

The idea of drama, 'the drama text' is a case in point. At GCSE, or 'Keystage Four' – even on 100% coursework courses – there has been the requirement that drama be one of the categories of literature statutorily studied to meet the demands of the literature syllabus. The integrity and distinctness of the drama text, since it is never specified nor elaborated, is assumed. A different approach to the idea of drama, to the idea of the drama text, though – interested in definitions and identities – might explore a far wider field of materials than the routine notion of drama allows for, might put together combinations of different cultural products and phenomena. The point is not simply to produce unusual combinations, but to give explicit recognition to the idea that there is a textual 'field', and within that field texts are positioned, given certain kinds of identities, and that the meanings of texts belongs to the general kinds of cultural meaning given to signs that move within the general field. Deconstructing the established identity of texts in this sense doesn't mean that you simply deny differences. It means that you examine where differences come from, how they get established and what assumptions go with them. It also means that you make explicit *systems* of meaning that go beyond the limits of one single text or one single category of texts.

Putting together disparate texts is perfectly feasible within the 'real' limits of English in schools. In order to look at drama in the first place students might be asked to consider what is understood by that term. What different kinds of drama are there? Theatre, TV plays, films, soap operas, are common forms of drama that are readily recognizable. But what, then, does *drama* mean? Is it necessarily related to acting, to roles being put into play, with dialogue, with action, and so on? If so, then other activities may surely be construed as drama. What about sporting events? Or 'real life' dramas? What about items in a news broadcast? And what, then, might be the essential difference between drama and fiction in novel form? Is there an *essential* difference between drama and items in a TV news broadcast, or between drama and certain kinds of item in newspapers that may include features ascribed to drama? Comics, of many kinds, may well be regarded as drama. Looked at in this way the idea of drama – and therefore, surely, of the drama text – seem to spill over the conventional limits.

There's no reason why the film *Witness* – to begin with one example among innumerable possibilities – should not be studied as drama text. Although, it might be argued that it doesn't come within the scope of the subject, not only is it as 'good' a text as any to study, it is as 'literary' a text as any, and as much a drama as any 'scripted' drama text – as much scripted, too, though with a different kind of script perhaps. Any doubts about these matters are produced by the illusory identity of literature. Doubts about the authenticity of *Witness* as drama text – practically, in terms of what the letter of the syllabus might demand – can be dispelled by rendering parts of the dialogue into written form. With a script – so the conventional wisdom goes – it becomes a drama text, never suspecting that as a film it already has a written form, that film is just a different kind of writing. Indeed, watching film requires as much interpretative work as anything else. It is not – as is sometimes assumed – a 'passive' activity. As much 'reading' is required to make sense of *Witness* as to make sense of any other text.

In relation to *Witness,* an aspect of the text identified as 'literary' could be construed as the staging of 'traditional' American values associated with the conventional virtues of the cowboy film. These values and ideas can be identified as intertextually related to *Shane,* a literary text, as well as referring to countless cowboy films. Toughness, determination and independence in relation to masculine identity can be seen as factors in these different texts of different identity. Literary values can be seen as related to ideas that operate in cultural forms unlikely to be identified as literary. These values and ideas, though, are not exclusive to the cowboy novel or film. They can be perceived at work in any number of texts of so-called popular culture: Levi Jeans adverts, for example. They can also be seen to be at work in the more remote and revered texts of English literature. It is quite possible to construe aspects of the character and the role and the structural and symbolic functions of the Prince in *Hamlet* as perfectly in accord with certain kinds of qualities attributed to the cowboy hero. 'In what ways is the hero of *Hamlet* the same as the hero of *Witness?'* is a question that students might be invited to consider. There's no reason why this question of the idea of the hero should not be applied to *Twinkle,* the girl's magazine, or to any number of news items, sporting events or to a whole range of contexts and 'texts'. This kind of movement between texts is possible because texts must constantly refer beyond themselves, to other texts, to general cultural signs and meanings, in order to be able to make sense. The idea, then, of some special category of meaning, the 'literary', or 'drama', for example, can't really be maintained.

Special categories of texts demand that the texts in those categories have special properties. But the notion that texts contain the meanings they operate is one that's worth exploring. How can sense be made of the difference between what's inside a text and what's not? The interface between outside and inside of texts – and the implications this has for the activation of cultural meanings – may easily be approached by students, perhaps using the pointers outlined in Example 3.12.

Example 3.12   Inside and outside the text

Make a list of features in the text – objects, identities, places, words, images, ideas.

Underline all the features inside the text that might be considered also to be outside the text.

Give meanings to all the features that you have underlined – inside and outside the text.

This exercise can be extended to look at different texts, like *Hamlet*, *Witness* and news items where there might be features in common. The implications are clearly deconstructive for the idea of the integrity of the text. It can be seen that meanings move in and between texts, that they are not securely lodged within single texts.

Meanings change, are shifted and extended in relation to general cultural shifts. The meanings that inform the way that we make sense of texts are – theoretically, at least – the same in relation to *Hamlet* as they are in relation to *Twinkle* or the 'Nine o'clock News'. The meanings that are actually made of these things may be different and may depend on the position of the 'spectator', and the way the 'spectator' regards the identity of the text.

Deconstructing the idea of the integrity of the text by looking at what's inside and what's outside the text – and how this distinction cannot be maintained – might also be developed in relation to textual gaps showing how any apparent continuity of the narrative is illusory. Gaps in a text indicate, clearly, what's been left out. But, then, everything that isn't in the text has been left out. Some gaps in(?) the text, though, are more glaring than others, more present, as it were, by their absence. Any text depends for its effects on gaps – where questions that might be asked are not, and where the spectator must fill spaces by making assumptions. These assumptions clearly must come from outside the text, they must belong to a set of established assumptions that come into operation when reading texts. These might be referred to as reading practices. In the case of *Witness*, for example, many gaps might be identified. How did Rachel's husband die? When and how did John Book learn carpentry? It hardly seems significant that we don't know the colour of John Book's grandmother's eyes. We assume, though, that Rachel's didn't murder her husband, because that would be incompatible with her textual identity and textual function. We can assume almost anything we like about how or where John Book learned carpentry, if we want to, because the text doesn't invite such questions (though we mustn't assume that he learnt carpentry in jail where he was serving time for fraud under a false identity): it is simply necessary for the progress of the narrative and the symbolic ordering at work that John Book have carpentry skills. So, he has them. But it becomes increasingly evident, as the pursuit of questions relating to gaps goes on that the text 'in-itself' doesn't ask or suppress these questions; it's the reading practices that determine what the text is, how it functions, what meanings it bears. The 'events' of the text can be taken to show how the narrative structure is carefully and formally organized, yet may also illustrate how the reading process must assume and produce connections to make a meaningful sequence. Once the operations of assumptions are foregrounded, the whole of the integrity of the text can be seen to depend upon them, upon assumptions that are not in the text at all but must be always outside of it. Gaps and intertextuality may be used as initiating points for an explicitly philo-sophical enquiry into reading practices, into the production of textual meanings, or in other words – and to put it in the elevated language of formal literary theory – into a general grammatology.

Witness offers a clear example of the dependence of reading and interpretation on an intertextuality going in many different directions. Themes of order, difference and identity might be attributed to *Hamlet,* just as they might be attributed to *Witness;* but the same themes might equally well be attributed to any number of texts, including Levi jeans adverts, *Twinkle* magazine, or many features on TV news programmes. The idea of intertextuality does away with the idea that meanings are generated by anything strictly intrinsic to the text-in-itself. It's only by making reference to other, already established (textual) meanings – moments and codes – that the film can make sense. Traditional reading practices with their customary notions of the unique literary text engaging personal responses are unlikely to withstand the idea of intertextuality and the chains of meanings and connections it might mobilize. Focusing on intertextuality suggests a process operating always beyond – and against – the idea of the free-standing, self-contained text. Discounting intertextuality not only has a limiting effect on the procedures of textual analysis; it tends also to limit questions of meanings and values to the personal.

The meanings that texts deploy, the meanings that oscillate between inside and outside the text, are configured textually by the production of a context, though this too is produced in relation to ideas about contexts and textual settings. This issue also might be explored with students. It's often useful to examine the way a text's opening addresses the spectator, to examine the kinds of meanings it refers to by way of establishing a context. The opening sequence of *Witness*, for example, could be examined *as* an opening sequence, to look at how, meto-nymically, metaphorically, it evokes a period, an atmosphere, a com-munity, a set of expectations, how the music works, how we are being prepared for the fact that a story is about to unfold, and a context is being established. Further intertextual questions, addressing aspects of the identity of the text might be considered: What is dramatic about all this? What kind or kinds of drama does *Witness* enact? Quite disparate texts might be examined in the same kind of way.

By examining the relations between what is inside the text and what is outside, the idea of the integrity of the text is deconstructed. Listing, say, twenty important things inside the text, is a way of beginning. How many of these things are outside the text? Where, then, does their meaning come from? Where then is the meaning of the text? Inside or outside? And so on. Any text may be used to develop this kind of approach. The main point being that texts are not objects in themselves, but the occasions for reading practices to be played out. And reading practices put values into play.

Meanings – or rather readings of meanings – are related to the issue of genre. Genres might be conceived of as reading forms that carry with them established sets of assumptions. With *Witness*, questions might be asked about how the film establishes its genre identity, when there may be shifts in genre identity, what kind of effects shifts in genre identity might produce. An exercise in transposition might invite consideration of what would happen if *Witness* were read in the same way that *Hamlet* is read, or *Twinkle* or news items or Levi jeans adverts. Transpositions of this kind could be used to examine the different kinds of status that are accorded to texts. Suggesting that similar kinds of culturally established meanings operate in texts of widely differing status might have positively deconstructive effects.

As any of the above points indicates, the text in question is not the exclusive focus of attention; it is more of a 'pretext' for examining ideas about and features of textuality in a more generalized sense, for building up a new vocabulary for dealing with texts, and for providing a means for the critical examination of textual productions, and textual identities – and in the end for the institutions that maintain and purvey these things. An outline for work taking *Witness* as an initial focus might also be applied to quite different things.

In Example 3.13 specific features are examined in relation to 'textual ideology' – the meanings drawn from a general cultural arena, activated and organized by the text in question. Clearly this must involve looking at how features of the text refer to ideas beyond themselves – as metaphors loaded with meanings – and must also take into consideration genre as an organizing principle of meanings.

Looking at how particular identities are signified will indicate the components of a symbolic order of meaning. In the case of *Witness*, examples could be: McPhee as the callous, slightly dandified, villain, representative of an essentially corrupt world; Samuel, the Amish boy as innocent witness, vulnerable outsider, representing a world of simple, pacifistic, values, admirable but inadequate in the hard world of Philadelphia; John Book, tough, independent hero, essentially

Example 3.13   Textual and intertextual analysis

Read *Witness, Hamlet,* Levi jeans adverts, *Twinkle* and newspaper and
TV news items, and discuss and list:

- events
- objects
- identities and roles
- important images/stills

What do the above mean *inside* and *outside* the text? You may also wish
to consider:

- context: landscape and community/interiors: interiors and exteriors
- oppositions
- intertextual references
- gaps in the text – assumptions
- signs of genre
- status of the text

---

good, embattled with the forces of evil.

Objects in texts, like identities, can be seen to carry symbolically
loaded meanings, meanings that are organized by the context of the text.
In the case of *Witness,* Rachel's bonnet might be identified as an
example, signifying Rachel's attachment to the Amish community, and
so the film emphasises the moment of its removal as she gives herself
sexually to John Book (having, of course, already fallen in love with
him), who represents other attractions, different values. John Book's
gun signifies the difference between his world and the world of the
Amish and his Amish clothes signify his temporary belonging to that
community.

Particular moments will contain a cluster of symbolically loaded
effects. So, the moment of the murder in the station toilet can be shown
to establish the Amish boy, Samuel, as witness; it can be shown to
establish Philadelphia as the dangerous context of the 'real world'
where men must be more than usually tough. The moment of the barn-
raising establishes the positive, if limited, values of the Amish world,
values which are to be preserved and protected by the American way of
life, values John Book can admire with wry superiority from the
vantage point of someone who has their kind of skills himself (he's a
carpenter, of all things), but who moves more easily in a wider world.
The points made here could be raised with students by means of a series
of carefully directed questions.

Significant events, objects, moments: all can thus be perceived as different but completely interdependent aspects of a signifying system which operates according to already established codes and is inescapably ideological. Ideology here, though, does not necessarily indicate a fixed system. Although meanings deployed may depend on reference to stereotypes, and genre may control how meanings are organized, readings of these things may be shown to be mobile. A politics of reading – aware of symbolic orderings and variant readings – may begin to emerge, as the focus of this kind of enquiry moves beyond the confines of the single text. Objects, identities, moments and genres in TV adverts – Levi jeans, for instance – might be examined for their symbolic meanings. Objects, identities, moments and genres in news items might be looked at in a similar way. The way that meanings are activated and organized can then be explicitly addressed. Being explicit, alternatives can also be considered. Different ways of watching and reading can be considered allowing different contexts of watching and reading to be brought into play.

The section asking for an account of community is useful in raising ideas about the representation of culture, values and ideology. The textual construction of the idea of community – associated with the representation of place and of social relations – clearly engages matters of value and ideology. Views representing how the world is are features of the way texts position and engage audiences in relation to a context. Texts on this view construct *ideas* of how the world is rather than representing it as it really is. This applies as much to dramas like news items and documentaries as it does to *Witness*, *Hamlet*, TV adverts or *Twinkle*. Established reading practices have only partial resources for addressing the idea of the textual construction of reality, and they still preserve certain kinds of texts from any critical account of textual ideology and status.

In relation to the idea of drama, a body of work that looked at disparate texts and construed them as drama – or narrative, for example – might seriously re-address the idea of the representation of reality. Looking at texts in the way suggested above insists on the construction of 'reality', and, along with a phenomenology of the reading of texts, makes the whole idea of reality problematic, emphasising as it does the provisional nature of textual identities, meanings and interpretations while offering at the same time the idea of alternative reading modes.

Textual issues cannot be separated from issues concerning values and ethics. The reading of texts may depend on interpreting codes and on recognizing intertextual references. But codes and their meanings are not produced by texts, they don't reside with any stability within texts, nor do they exist independently of texts. They are themselves a kind of textual language, a language that may be interpreted differently, that is subject to ambiguities and to alternative forms of expression, just like any other language. A criticalview of text might ask – in relation to the matter of values – what values does the text seem to represent? What other ideas in relation to values might be brought to bear upon a reading of this text? What different cultural positions – with different values – might this text be read from? So questions of values may be fore-grounded by certain approaches to texts.

REDEFINING THE TEXTUAL FIELD

The idea of intertextuality is very simply demonstrable in this case. Students will have no difficulty in explaining the idea to themselves – nor in illustrating it. Any part of the film, visual moment, important event, or important object, anything going towards making up its signifying structure can only mean whatever it means because it refers, beyond itself, to the same or a similar thing in another text. All texts are connected with other texts, and could not be read if they were not so connected. The connectedness is not casual, either – not a haphazard kind of random cross-referencing. It is more in the nature of a dependency. In our own culture, for example, the reading of narrative (as narrative) fiction is determined, phenomenologically speaking, by the idea of narrative fiction preceding any reading of it. This, not usually explicit, idea will be influenced by the reading of films as much as by the reading of narrative fiction in book form. Narratives or stories are not, in the ways they function, strictly different from form to form. Films, novels, Shakespeare plays, TV adverts are all caught up in the play of intertextuality. And so we may return with a quizzical glance to the formulations of *English 5–16*: about 'positive attitudes towards books and literature' (Are they possibly different from one another? What is literature? What is a 'positive attitude'?); about 'the three main literary genres', and all the other many and varied references to literature and its importance. We may now question the ideas and processes that seek to keep the study of 'literature' as a discrete, but essentially unformulated category, separate from media studies and separate from a wider conception of textual studies. It is, of course, necessary to maintain the category of literature in order to maintain present definitions of literacy, present orderings and hierarchies of literacy. These definitions of difference are outmoded in terms of the real cultural experiences of our students, just as they are philosophically untenable and ideologically loaded. Is *Witness* a literary text? It operates according to the same principles and codes, and has fundamental qualities in common with any so-called literary text. This issue – and its ramifications – is worth pursuing with students, and will be partially developed in what follows.

A usefully provocative way of indicating the importance of inter-textuality and of deconstructing the privileged status of literature is contained in work that puts texts of disparate identity together ('Why *Twinkle* and *The Tempest* are the same'). This kind of deconstructive thinking can be pushed further, so that, for instance, titles like 'Why *Macbeth* is the same as a Black and Decker TV advert' might appear, or 'Why *Coriolanus* is the same as a Bosch power drill'. Phenomeno-logically speaking, material objects are also texts and take part in the general intertextual interchange, and because they are very obviously – and very significantly in cultural terms – ideologically loaded. The kind of reading that goes on constantly of material objects and of texts in everyday life doesn't count towards a literacy rating. Even though the same kinds of processes may be involved in the reading of these things, they do no enter into the charmed circle of literature. Reading material objects as texts, alongside the familiarly privileged texts of study, though, may be just a starting point. It is possible to extend the textual field to address all sorts of activities that are textually bound: examining conversations of various kinds, examin-ing social procedures like applying for a job from a textual and discursive viewpoint, or examining the kinds of texts that operate in the context of the family, the workplace and other arenas of textuality and discourses.

A RANGE OF ACTIVITIES AND APPROACHES

Most of the work done with reading, literature and texts generally in English takes as its focus particular texts, as does much of the kind of work outlined above. An attempt to introduce a theoretical per-spective on a practice addressing texts and textuality in a much wider field of operation, would need to look beyond the specificities of particular texts and address reading in more general terms. An example of an initial approach to general reading is offered by the survey in Figure 3.2.

Students might use the above model to develop their own ques-tionnaires. They could then begin a kind of ethnographic study, could define groups, collate responses and organize their findings. Findings

What people read

What ideas people have about reading

Attitudes towards/ideas about fiction

What kinds of fiction readers read

Why fiction readers read fiction/why readers read particular kinds of fiction

Diffreent kinds of bookshops: what gets sold, how much

Booksellers' ideas about reading

Publishers' ideas about reading

Publishers' marketing strategies

Figure 3.2   Reading survey: fiction

about fiction could then be measured against findings about other kinds of reading that people do. Some kind of account of reading fiction could then be configured within a more general field of reading, and the idea of reading here could be extended to include a wider range of 'reading' such as reading different kinds of 'cultural products' and 'events'.

TEXTUAL PLEASURES

Analysing texts is no more obstructive of textual pleasures than analysing or discussing football. The idea that there is a simple and innocent enjoyment of texts – an enjoyment that analysis is likely to distort – is highly doubtful.

In relation to textual pleasures students might look at a range of issues including:

identification and interpellation;
the effects of reading genre;
the reading context – where, when, with whom, in what conditions.

The issue of the relations between textuality and subjectivity is a complex one that has been highly theorized in recent times, especially by academic theorists of the cinema. In the context of English in schools, though, it is certainly possible to construct theories of textual pleasures that are accessible and that still deal with issues not generally approached by conventional practices of the subject. Questions on identification, for example, might go into many different aspects of the issue, without being dauntingly difficult. Questions about how identifications work, what kinds of pleasures they may yield, what different kinds of identifications are involved in any one single text might be profitably and easily pursued. 'How does the process of identification engage with gender differences?' is a question that might be asked of any text, involving looking at different kinds of responses, different ways subjects may be interpellated or addressed by a text, and might involve considerations of acceptance and resistance of offered positions and identifications. Studying genre has obvious implications for an analysis of textual pleasures, and here research that has been done into audience responses to certain kinds of texts from popular culture might be considered, and similar kinds of analysis – of a local and limited scope, perhaps – could be undertaken by students. Although these projects would necessarily be limited in terms of the ethnographic field they address, they might nevertheless furnish sufficient material for theoretical work to be done on different modes of reception.

Examining textuality and pleasure in a more open field than English habitually has been used to dealing with is very likely to surmount the common difficulty found with students who are deemed to be either non-readers or apathetic readers. Most students – just like most people – are actually constant readers. Most students have considerable experience of textual pleasures, though these pleasures aren't always associated with the texts, nor the pleasures, allowed by the narrow definitions of English.

CONCLUDING

This section has attempted to suggest some ways of opening up the study of reading in English lessons. It has been proposed that the idea of literacy itself be explicitly raised and questioned. It has been proposed that current definitions of literacy be examined. The *idea* of reading – what it is, what it's for, how it works – has also been suggested as a useful line of enquiry, beginning with the students' own personal and collective experiences. Some illustrative examples of reading have been offered, too, with the intention of suggesting ways of approaching reading within a theoretical framework, and thus going beyond – and often against – the established practices of English. There is no kind of necessary ordering in any of this. These are certainly not the only kinds of activities that might be used to achieve similar effects.

Almost everything described so far has been conceived as a whole-class activity, though none of it need be; any of the topics or texts proposed could be done with small groups or with individual students. I would also suggest, though, that the English department, or the English teacher, as part of an approach to the study of literacy and reading, should reconsider the form of the so-called 'private' reading lessons. If students should, once a week or so, be able to spend time in class reading, for pleasure, something of their own choice, what sort of limits are to be set on the kind of text permitted? It can be useful, for all sorts of reasons, to get students to bring a reading text along to every English lesson, to regard it, that is, as an indispensable piece of equipment. It can also be useful to keep a record of the students' reading, a kind of handy diary or account book, recording their reading experiences. The encouragement of private, individual reading has become a fairly standard practice. If the identity of reading is changed, though, by an extension of the field of reading and, the notion of literacy itself, then many different kinds of text must be considered as points of reference in any account of reading experience.

A record of individual reading experiences constructed from a wide variety of different texts can be referred to usefully during any analytical work on reading that may be going on. It also constitutes a text or a body of texts that the teacher – and the institution of English as it stands – is not in a position to dominate and control. Such a policy for reading, promoting it by giving it time and status, but avoiding the simple – and in many cases alienating – valorizing of the book, can have positive effects. It can work against the narrow definitions of literacy that – scandalously – define many of the populations in secondary comprehensives (quite absurdly, of course) as uninterested, unmotivated non-readers. It can also promote freshly positive attitudes to a freshly defined field of reading.

4 Grammatology for beginners

PROBING WRITING

If students – or 'subjects' – of English are habitually invited, in the name of English, to write stories, essays and other things; if writing is of central educational significance and also of general cultural significance, then it must be worth trying to theorize this phenomenon, in spite of the daunting scale of the task. The practices of writing in English invite many questions. Any serious attempt to review, question, or to reassess the content and values of the subject would need to look again at writing in a number of ways. Such a venture would need to examine the practices of writing in English and the ideas about writing purveyed by English.

Writing is, as obviously as reading, an *essential* component of English, a taken-for-granted, fundamental category and practice. This is so much the case that in the general run of things writing in English tends not to be theorized or justified at the level of practice at all. The only kind of theory you get at this level is likely to be one-dimensional, or to be simply aligned with criteria of assessment and judgement, or it might unambiguously promote the virtues of writing as self-expression. This kind of uncritical, implicit theory takes the form of saying something prescriptive like: 'This is good writing; this is what you've got to do to get a good grade'; or in a more liberal manner: 'This is the kind of good writing that will enable you to express yourself more fully, and will enable you to explore yourself and the world you live in'. Why this particular form or that particular style of writing is considered good is unlikely to be the focus of many, if any, lessons. Alternative views of the subject of writing are unlikely to be proposed. How a practice of writing that valorizes notions such as self-expression, for example, becomes ascendant is equally unlikely to be explored.

A deconstructive attitude, an approach that did attempt to rethink – with the students involved in the process – the practices and ideas of writing in and beyond the confines of the established conventions of English, could be instigated as an important part of a redefinition of the subject. The implications of this kind of interrogative approach would be to effect a radical expansion of the field of writing, making what gets addressed in relation to writing in English much more diverse, more wide-ranging and more philosophically probing than at present. This extension of the scope of the subject's encounters with writing could mean much more than just examining different kinds of writing; it could also work to redefine the idea of what writing is. To address the field of writing in a much more extensive and more interrogative sense – making explicit ideas about writing – does seem to be more educationally adventurous, more intellectually creditable than rehearsing the standard practices simply because they are there, in the uncritical acceptance of precedence or in accordance with principles that have been found to be inadequate, or compromised as partial.

There are a number of ways in which ideas about writing in English – and in education generally – might be theorized and restructured by doing some theoretical analysis. There are several possible, practical starting points for theory to begin to address the field of writing. To engage in the practical theorizing of writing simply means approaching the ordinary, everyday, established activities and ideas of writing in English from a quizzical angle. It means reviewing assumptions, and 'making strange' the often deep-seated assumptions that present themselves as common-sense truth. One of these deeply rooted assumptions, about writing is that reading and writing are distinct and clearly separable things that operate according to quite different procedures. To put this differently, to challenge its status as truth might be to claim something to the effect that the subject of reading is equally the subject of writing, is the subject of language and textuality in a thoroughly general sense. This implies attention to the general cultural production and dissemination of meanings, as well as examining contexts of exchange and the effects these things might have on subjects of language. Writing might be looked at as a specific type of language, having a particular correlation with 'general' language, and might also be looked at as representing general features of language.

Obviously, this is a large kind of project. The initial probings offered here only suggest a partial way towards deconstructing the habitual forms of thinking about writing – and only partially suggest ways of deconstructing the assumed differences between writing and reading, writing and speech, writing and other media. Plenty of other practical examples of writing-related activities could follow from the ideas proposed. Any ideas suggested here could, for example, be used by students to produce ethnographically based work to gauge people's experiences of and ideas about writing.

THEORY: ASPECTS OF WRITING

A framework for an initial expedition into the theory of writing might organize the practices of writing, the categories of writing, ideas and attitudes about writing using the following points:

1 The public/established categories of writing.
2 The individual subject and writing.
3 Institutions and writing.
4 General writing (or 'grammatology' – to give it one of its names from 'high theory').

These four categories of enquiry could be used as an initial conceptual framework, itself open tò question as the project develops. Ideas concerning the four areas suggested here could be developed in the light of specific work on particular issues with particular texts.

The following questions indicate the directions of enquiry. It might be useful to broach all these questions with students at some point. They may be applied to any piece of writing. A similar set of questions can be devised by discussion with students, or by students working together.

1 *The categories of writing*

What kind of writing is this?
What other kinds of writing is it 'related to' ?
What kind of people might be expected to read this?
What kind of activity is it linked with?

2 *The individual subject and writing*

Who wrote this? What position is being assumed for the writer of this?
Who is being addressed? What position is assumed for the reader of this?
What – if anything – can you tell about the writer, or about the condition of its production?
What assumptions are being made about the reader?

3 *Institutions and Writing*

Where would you expect to find people reading this?
Would the meaning of this change somewhere else? if so how?
What special, specific terms are used?
Into what kind of groups would the people reading this be organized?

4 *General Writing*

What key words are there? What key contrasts are there?
What conventional ideas about the world are presented?
What alternative ways might there be of reading this?
What would happen if it changed into another form: a film, a video, a tape?
What might examining all these questions tell us about writing and meaning?

These questions differ quite markedly from the standard set of questions applied to texts in the established categories of English. They address a completely different field from the standard questions about meaning and effects of texts. In the context of classroom practice, they could equally well be applied to written texts placed in front of students, to texts that were about to be written or to texts in the process of being written. They could equally well be applied to texts that were simply under consideration, whether they had been written or not, whether they actually were about to be written or not. They are generalizing. In other words, they address the field of writing in an open sense that does not make distinctions at all times between writing and reading, between what *is* a text and what is the structure – or form – of a text, between language, text and writing. These questions represent potentially deconstructive issues that can be pursued to varying degrees. The main point, though, is that writing is being differently conceived. Different kinds of writing can be examined in different ways – from specific perspectives that move away from the restricted notion of the individual writer. There are plenty of other potentially deconstructive perspectives with other kinds of questions – those posed by sociolinguistics, for example – that might be put into play to do similar or complementary work.

1   The categories of writing

Obviously there are many different kinds of writing. Any specific instance of writing can be looked at in terms of the category it belongs to. All writing, though, belongs to more than one category and could be placed in different categories according to different ways of organizing writing or looking at writing. A story, for example, might be a children's fairy tale. A newspaper article might also be a story, though in a different sense. One thing, for example, that might be involved in putting writing into categories is thinking about what kind of people would be interested in this kind of writing, what kind of people would read it or write it. Another aspect of its identity might involve considering what kind of social activity or activities it would be associated with. The identity of any piece of writing may change according to its context. Writing identities can be mobile and varied, but they can also be fixed by contexts, like the context of English in secondary schooling. All these different considerations might be involved in thinking about categories of writing.

2   The individual subject and writing

Writing involves the individual subject in many ways. Some writing, or kinds of writing, seems to have more individual quality to it: a letter to a relative would be different from a set of instructions on how to use a power drill. All writing can be said to be written *from* a particular position. Equally, all writing can be said to address someone or some people in another position or other positions. The writing in question will make certain assumptions about the reader, depending on the kind of writing involved. Writing will address the reader or readers in certain ways, ways that will vary, depending on both the writing and the reading context. It will assume that the reader belongs to a group or category of people. The individual addressed by writing is generally conceived of as belonging to a group or type, except in certain specific circumstances. The point can be made that writing positions subjects and may have a positive, determining effect on subjects' identities; writing may actively group subjects. In certain specific contexts writing organizes differences between subjects – in a general sense this might be related to gender, in a more specific sense it might be related to education, to examination English – where writing is often subject to control and judgement.

3   Institutions and writing

Writing takes place within many different and varied institutions, but is always written and read in some kind of institutional context. Even when you may least suspect it, writing is organized within the context of some kind of institution. It may be the institution of the school, the family, or football. *This* writing is framed by the context (among others) of the school – a specific type of institution with all sorts of ideas and behaviours of its own. The institutions of writing *organize* writing, writers and readers. Writing may use specific terms that identify it as being attached to a particular institution. Writing in one institutional context might not make much sense – or might make a completely different kind of sense – in another.

4   General writing

One way of looking at writing is to see it as being structured around certain key words. These words can tell you a lot about the kind of writing you're dealing with. Writing also tends to be structured around key contrasts – opposites that are set against one another. In all of this, writing always refers, one way or another, to ideas about the world. Writing is about ideas and is ideological. Some of the ideas activated by writing will be conventional – readily recognized and understood or stereotypical. Some ideas produced by writing, on the other hand, might be strange or might challenge stereotypes. It is generally difficult to say whether ideas are contained *in* writing or whether they are more produced by readers, reading, or reading practices. The idea of general writing tends to break down the strict differences between reading and writing – finding common processes at work in both – and tends to propose that any kind of sign production is a kind of writing, that it operates in the same way as writing. Writing practices get structured in certain forms, or genres; knowing genres means knowing what kinds of meanings are conventionally available for specific kinds of texts.

Discussion and analysis of some general principles about writing could well begin by applying the questions – with or without the explanatory guide-lines – to different, disparate examples of writing.

STORY WRITING

Story writing – tied to a loosely conceived notion of creativity – remains a more or less central activity in the commonplace practice of English in schools. An interrogative approach to story writing might be conducted by looking at particular aspects of stories and what happens when they actually get written – using the classroom as a site of analysis and production, making explicit the necessary connection between these two processes. This kind of work with stories – giving emphasis to structural and ideological features – is not the same as 'imaginative response', a practice tending to deny consciously theoretical aspirations. It does, though, suggest that reading stories cannot be an activity totally distinct from writing stories; writing being a kind of reading of forms, procedures, processes.

An important aspect of a project to review the practice of story writing would also involve reviewing the *idea* of story writing, not just in a generalized and abstract sense, but by reviewing its institutional functions and the kinds of assumptions – of an educational and social nature – that inform the practice, explicitly or implicitly. This might involve students being invited to ask questions about the predominance of story writing in schools – and might lead into a general consideration of narrative and its significance in general discourse. This, in turn, would be likely to involve deconstructing the idea of the story in its present sense in English, giving attention to the many different kinds of stories that circulate in many different cultural forms and cultural products. In this context it might also be possible and useful to examine some other ways of reading and defining texts other than as narrative, including deconstructing the idea of stories as belonging to some special realm of experience or knowledge.

Using a particular perspective, a simple beginning might be devised to engender reflective possibilities. Taking the general topic of stories and gender, as an example, looking particularly at representations of feminine identity might be profitable in itself. A more or less self-contained set of activities relating to gender could also be used to formulate an approach to writing and stories, to begin to investigate some of its processes, its structures, its effects. Practical analyses can be given theoretical inflection and can be used to address general theoretical issues.

The following approach to stories and gender activates a simply formulated question with far-reaching implications: What is involved in the apparently simple, innocent activity of writing a story? This question may provide an approach to some of most far-reaching issues of cultural theory. Students may be invited to examine quite critical theoretical issues of writing by being invited to write their own simple story – deploying stereotypical representations of gender differences. What they have written themselves may be set against other instances of writing, other texts that deploy stereotypical gender images. A few disparate examples may serve:

Elle magazine;
a few children's stories;
soap operas;
TV ads.

Students can examine these in relation to:

images of women / men and boys / girls;
ideas expressed about women / men and boys / girls.

The stereotypical images of gender found in these may then be compared with those in the other examples from students' own pieces of writing. Students can produce simple lists indicating their findings for each of the above. These lists, drawn from different media, may be used to indicate how cultural meanings circulate through different sign systems, and how the kinds of meanings available in writing are already determined by these systems. This kind of approach can be used to indicate interconnections between different kinds of writing; and can be used to ask questions about where generally available meanings and sets of meanings come from, and how they are held together. Questions also about the individual writing subject's relations with these systems or sets of meaning may be considered. The implications of all this is to work against the simple idea of the creative individual, with its mystical overtones, and to address – potentially with a great deal of specificity – the available meanings and position of the writing subject in relation to them.

The points of focus shown in Example 4.1 can be identified for students to consider and apply to different texts.

Example 4.1   Stories and gender

Examine the following in relation to various stories, and other texts, thinking particularly about how they seem to represent gender identity and gender difference:

- nouns/identities: meanings and cultural encoding
- sentence structures: syntax, orders and relationships
- identities, their roles, their functions: symbolic identity and structural functions
- actions, verbs and the way they position identities
- adjectives/descriptions: oppositions and values
- cultural references – to culturally specific objects or ideas

Write down examples of each of these. Compare your findings with the findings of others.

Effectively this activity involves identifying and examining the various components of texts and the way that they get organized in stories. Pointers might be given and questions asked about how these elements appear in other forms of representation, about what they signify. Connections can then be clearly made between writing stories and generally available meanings.

Activities that could follow discussion of the findings include the following:

- writing about how identities, relationships, structural functions and values operate in different types of story – and how these also relate to the same things as they are produced in other cultural products;
- writing stories deploying identities, relationships, structural functions and values as they have been found in investigations;
- writing stories that challenge by changing identities, relationships, structural functions and values that have been identified;
- producing writing adopting different forms, proposing or presenting alternatives to story forms, actively deconstructing narrative and intermingling images and ideas in other forms.

Writing doesn't have to be the mode of presentation for any of this. Students could equally produce oral presentations, audio or video tapes.

Among the issues raised by this approach to the business of writing is the assumed difference between the idea of writing as creativity and the idea of writing as producing meaning according to its ready established structures of form and meaning. In deconstructive terms, this point is expressed in a number of ways which invert the conventional wisdom of writing, for examples, the idea of the subject who writes as the subject *of* writing. What it is possible to write is largely determined by the predominant forms of writing, by predominant images and ideas. The writing subject can only reconfigure these already existing identities. One of the functions of the exercise can be to emphasize simply the issue of *values* in writing and where they come from. In this exercise, in responding to these questions, the idea of writing as a kind of neutral tool is called into doubt – to the extent that it's no longer tenable – and an alternative model has to be found or made. Words used by the writer, their meanings, the ideas and values they convey are not determined by the writing subject – just as the way they are put together is not and cannot be. The writer, in the case of the story, is under obligation to deploy already existing meanings, orderings and structures. Students may consider these determining factors; they may also consider how meanings may be constructed in relation to cultural powerful or dominant forces, and may consider alternatives to these. The case of gender offers an obvious instance of a cultural field – frequently configured by powerful systems of meaning – that can be approached from different perspectives, where different meanings can consciously be constructed.

Here the relations between ideology and writing may be explored in a directly interrogative manner. The following questions may be applied to the stories read and written in this work:

1 What ideas about the world seem to be present(ed) in this writing?
2 What different ways might there be of looking at this writing?

There are two main, and critically interlinking strands to this topic in relation to an alternative, deconstructive approach to writing. One concerns how writing engages with ideology through language and structural forms; and the other concerns how stories might get received differently, effectively how the meaning of writing might be differently construed by readings. To emphasize the idea of the reception of stories – how they get read, what kinds of meanings are given to them, what kind of identity they are granted – consideration can be given to the specific and immediate context of writing, that is to the institutional location and functions of writing done within the arena of the institutions of English and state education. Such writing is done in a self-reflexive mode, conscious of its own situation and the limitations that this imposes on it. This kind of approach positively enables a number of moves beyond the reaches of conventional approaches to story writing.

THE IDENTITY OF WRITING

One aspect of an attempt to extend the narrow attitudes to writing of English involves raising questions not normally broached. The big question: 'What *is* writing?' represents an attempt to open up fresh perspectives on writing, to explore some of the issues in relation to writing that a renewed sense of enquiry might demand. The impetus of the demand can be seen partly in terms of the state of the subject – a state that has been broadly described as 'in crisis', but might also invite less neutral terms to describe its uncertain condition.

In previous times, it might have been possible to secure a practice of writing on notions that are now really untenable. English Literature once could signify a kind of excellence to which writing could aspire. This idea may have been completely illusory, but it held a kind of symbolic value that could hold the idea of the subject together. Education in English was partly about emulating these models of excellence, appreciating writing of particular subtlety, perhaps, or metaphoric power, in order that some of the effects might rub off. The cultural narrowness of this idea hardly needs emphasizing now.

Simplified notions of language – largely stripped of its social dimension – have also played a part in holding together the identity of the subject. If teachers didn't, as authorized purveyors of English, believe in Literature, or didn't believe the students in their charge were capable of appreciating its subtlety or metaphoric power, then at least there was the English Language to fall back on. Everyone knew good English when they saw it, and even those poor unfortunates who were not blessed with it could recognize it when they heard or read it. If you didn't know exactly how it worked in all its parts, then you could always check it in Fowler. Writing was the appropriate way for the painstaking promotion of good English. Good English – it was believed, and still is by a fairly large body of eccentrics – embodied the values of 'our' civilization. Sociolinguistics and virtually all modern theories of language insist on the social and cultural specificity of cultural forms, making the very idea of *an* English language impossible, throwing into radical doubt all notions of intrinsically 'good English', though essentially that is exactly the idea embodied in assessment criteria. The means for judging and discriminating between different levels of attainment in this monologic model of language is, characteristically, writing. In this sense, at least, all 'subjects' of the education system are subjects of writing. And the model of good writing remains anachronistically tied to notions of standard form, notions that carry with them residual echoes of cultural domination.

More liberal and 'avant-garde' models of English over the past forty years or so have advocated writing in English as the means for self-expression. In a position sometimes different from and sometimes colluding with the 'good English' model, the liberal progressive version of writing in English believed that the personal growth of the individual could be developed by the practice of writing. More or less freely (though this problem was never really explored, never identified as problematic) expressing themselves, the subjects of English could explore their own inner being and the world around them through writing. The good intentions of this model are challenged by the social functions and dimension of writing, for one thing. For another, the whole idea of writing as self-expression runs fundamentally counter to most established theoretical positions that have seriously looked at the way language works in social contexts.

What is sketchily offered here proposes new ways of looking at writing as part of teaching its practice. Analysis and practice are not seen as different activities. What follows, initially, is an attempt to broach the question: 'What is writing?' afresh. This large and general question can be organized to direct an exploration of what writing is in the philosophical sense, how it can be defined and understood, what features can be ascribed to it and what useful ways of understanding its identity and general cultural significance can be constructed. This line of enquiry operates rather abstractly, quizzically asking what writing is. Beginning, perhaps, from simple ideas about writing as a technology of communication, issues can be tackled and ideas broached that previous models of English would have left untouched. More practical, but with philosophical implications, too, is the project to undertake an analysis of what different kinds of writing there are. The idea is to survey the field of writing – partly to establish that there is a differentiated field of writing – to examine the idea that writing takes different forms, occurs in different contexts, serves different uses in various institutions, looking at different social functions of writing, deconstructing the notion of universal categories or types.

TAXONOMY

One way to approach the theory of the extensive field of writing is simply to begin to produce a categorized list which aims to identify what different kinds of writing there are. The functions of this, and of the various lines of questioning that may follow, would be manifold. It is, fundamentally, a theoretic move engendering different potential lines of enquiry, all relevant to any attempt to address the field of literacy – to any exploration of language and textuality, as may be seen in Example 4.2.

Writing will have been organized into main groups, main categories and sub-categories. Where these different identities come from and how they are held together will also have been examined. Through discussion, different ways of defining categories of writing will be considered. In a sense, it is not necessarily of great importance how exhaustive this account of the different identities of writing and their institutional locations is. The idea is to produce a taxonomy – and not to pretend to simply reflect how things are. The taxonomy is a theoretic device, a model for understanding, and in that sense is a 'creative' production, like all such models. Part of the point of the process is to recognize that forms of knowledge and ways of organizing identities are subject to processes of production, and that the ensuing productions will be done from particular points of view and with particular purposes in mind – whether these operate consciously or not. These general considerations could be raised with a class that has been engaged in the activity and could be addressed in the form of a general consideration of the final point above.

It is evident that once a taxonomy of writing is produced, writing can be seen to take many different forms, having different structures, rules

Example 4.2   Taxonomy of writing

How to make your own writing taxonomy: a whole class or group activity

Make a rough list of different kinds of writing that you can think of: for example, letters, fictions; put the different kinds of writing you've identified into groups.

For each grouped item on your list – which we will call for the moment a main category – make another list comprised of different types.

Compare your main categories with other peoples; combine to make shared lists of main categories and subcategories.

When you have gathered – say – six main categories and a fair number of examples for each category there are a number of things to do:

1 Identify how different categories will be organized – where and among whom will these kinds of writing take place?
2 Try to say what kind of people in what kind of situations – and give examples of these – might be engaged in these kinds of writing; what might be the relations between readers and writing, what might be the differences?
3 Try to say also for what purposes they may be engaged in them.
4 Try to identify some of the main terms, or forms of language, that may be used in some of the categories of writing defined.
5 Try to identify the various different positions that people may take up in relation to your examples of different kinds of writing.
6 Consider how all of this work has changed the identity of writing – as it is understood by common sense.

---

governing its different uses; and, of course, different kinds of writing will be seen to have quite different contexts. This constitutes already a different approach to writing from any generally conceived by dominant practices of English. To have discussed these possibilities and formulated them in one way or another with a class of students constitutes a move away from the casual acceptance of the established categories and notions of writing that characterizes English. It provides a conceptual basis for further developments – in terms of both analytic and productive work – to take place.

A scheme of work complementary to the taxonomy of writing might begin by looking at different examples of contexts of writing, in the manner of a survey undertaken to categorize and distinguish different types of writing from a different perspective. The specific location of writing within different contexts – geographic, institutional, cultural – might then be addressed. Questions might be asked about how specific contexts of writing could determine the nature of the writing produced.

Pursuing the idea of a taxonomy by engaging with different questions, significant theory – abstract and specific – has been brought into play. The following conclusions may be examined and illustrated by students with specific examples.

1 Different forms of writing have different structures;
2 and appear in different contexts;
3 according to different forces of production and different processes of reception;
4 and are given different identities and meanings by different groups of people.

This introductory, theoretical approach to writing can be developed quite easily in relation to particular cases. The conclusions offered above might be applied to a number of different examples of writing. Particular examples of categories of writing could be addressed more fully and extensively. Further questions could be raised about how different identities are given to different forms, about where categories of writing come from and how they are maintained, why some forms of writing enjoy a higher status than others, and so on. All of this work could conceivably address writing and the subject English as a move towards deconstructing the presumptions of its established identity.

INTERROGATING WRITING

Another, different, approach towards theory addresses the question: 'What is writing?' in a more abstract manner, trying to explore the identity of writing, to investigate the properties of writing that make it what it is, to probe the attributes that distinguish it from and also connect it to other things. A philosophical analysis – opening general questions – would aim to reach beyond the limits of a common-sense or institutionally established understanding of these things. From a common-sense point of view this kind of questioning seems perhaps comically pointless. Everyone, surely, knows what writing is, and anyway, the most important thing is to learn how to do it well. Why waste time wondering about the meaning of meaning? Why worry over abstruse – and in the end probably unanswerable questions – of the impossible magnitude of, 'What is writing?' In response to these hypothetical objections, that nevertheless answer to the current state of things generally in English, it might be worth rejoining with a challenge to the assumed state of prevailing knowledge. Knowledge about language has not seriously been much incorporated into the general curriculum. It has now, curiously, become a requirement in English. Knowledge and theory, though, go hand in hand. You can't have knowledge without a context of beliefs and assumptions. The move engendering the question, 'What is writing?' is an invitation to look again at existing assumptions and to reformulate or at least to re-examine first principles. Why not engage students in this process? Why not attempt to provide the means and the context for them to engage themselves in this kind of fundamental interrogation? Surely asking those large, even cumbersome, questions must be the grounding for any kind of *critical* practice?

There are problems, though, in taking on a question as stupefyingly unwieldy as: 'What is writing?' (in any context, let alone with students). In the first place, it's hardly ever the kind of question we ask in the context of an educational 'philosophy' which tends to eschew abstract theoretical questions in favour of practical activity. Teacher culture and professional identity have to a large extent preferred a more crisply business-like, more bluffly practical approach to learning. Perhaps assured that its mission is essentially utilitarian – to deal in settled certainties or to be continually practically productive (according to the workshop model) – teaching culture has tended to rely on fundamental categories and favourite established forms, ranging from the certainties of formal grammar to the well-established comforts of story writing.

Considered in the abstract, the question: 'What is writing?' does seem difficult to get hold of. Writing is something we are so familiar with that it seems hard to find a perspective from which to view it effectively. It seems equally difficult to think of a possible starting point. Some forms of theory (associated with the general trends of post-structuralism) can most powerfully help to analyse fundamental aspects of this topic. Deconstruction begins, really, with a revaluation of ideas about writing. It proposes a new kind of field of study or science of writing – grammatology – but you don't, actually, have to be fully conversant with the ideas of Jacques Derrida to pursue some of the questions and ideas that might lead to a serious reconsideration of what writing is, questions and ideas that might produce ways of looking at and understanding writing; they are questions and ideas necessarily different from ideas about writing that have gone unchallenged for so long.

It's perfectly possible for students to begin to deconstruct dominant, common-sense notions about writing. Another thing students will be doing by answering the questions below is deconstructing the notion that abstract theoretical analysis is beyond their scope of achievement.

1 What are the characteristic features of writing?
2 What distinguishes writing from, for example, speech?
3 What kinds of *relations* are involved in writing
4 What kind of identities are engaged in it?
5 How does writing work? What kind of technology is it?

From this kind of open-ended beginning, it is possible to touch upon important ideas in relation to writing and how it works. The act of raising these questions opens a field of study with many possible developments. As shown in Example 4.3, a series of points for students to consider might help to approach the topic in a thoroughly exploratory manner, addressing specific aspects of the larger questions.

Example 4.3   The identity of writing

Consider and comment on the following points

1 Characteristic Features
  Writing is recorded words.
  Writing is technological.
  Writing can be read, can be understood by someone else.
  Writing is a way of organizing ideas.
  Writing uses rules.
  Writing uses recognized symbols.
  Writing deploys established meanings.

2 Writing and Speech
  Writing is different from speech because writing can be recorded.
  Writing is more permanent than speech.
  Writing is more technological than speech.
  Writing is less personal than speech.

3 Writing Relations
  Someone always writes to someone else.
  Someone sends a message to another person.
  It is always important to know who the writer is.
  You always know what the writer wanted to say.
  You always know what the message is.
  You can tell about the writer's personality from the writing.
  All readers read things differently.
  All readers read writing the same.

Some further general questions might follow from the exercise outlined above. These questions are intended to follow through and generalize from the deconstructive import of the points that have already been raised.

Is writing then fundamentally different from speech?
Is speaking a kind of writing?
Is maths a kind of writing?
Are maps a kind of writing?
Are pictures a kind of writing?
Are films a kind of writing?

Rethinking writing in this way might engender related questions more directly aimed at a reconsideration of the functions of writing in the school, and might invite students to consider their own situations, as students within a systematic organization of writing identities. All the points and questions are designed to offer opportunities for students to re-examine what writing is – to consider ideas that make connections between different forms of expression, that question how they work and how they have generally come to be understood. If students are prepared to entertain the idea that speech, for example, operates in ways very similar to writing or that pictures might be thought of as a kind of writing, having some of the features of writing, or that the meanings of writing are structured within particular contexts and by particular modes of reading and understanding, then both the field and the understanding of writing have been significantly expanded,

AN INTRODUCTION TO GRAMMATOLOGY

The points for discussion in Example 4.4 offer fairly explicit theoretical perspectives on the identity of writing – what it is, what it does and how it works – at a general level. They are formulated for open consideration, and might be put to work by referring to particular examples. They could also easily be broken down into smaller units and presented as a list of points to be ticked or crossed. Students could be asked to produce writing on all of this or to produce diagrams with notes, for example, indicating ideas and connections.

WRITING AS TECHNOLOGY

Whatever else it is, writing is a kind of technology. It might be worth considering the technological character of writing in two senses:

1 as a technology of inscription and duplication: as a means of encoding language in a recordable form, using specific material

Example 4.4 What is writing? Some ideas for consideration

Consider the following ideas and give examples of how they might work

Writing is:

- a system of signs: like signs used in a set of traffic lights, or in a film or in a picture. What signs does writing deploy? How do these signs work?
- an order of words: a way of putting signs together in a special *order*; change the order and what happens? How do particular forms of writing put things in order?
- a system of *substitutions*. Do words stand in place of the *things* they represent or of the *ideas* of the things they represent; language is always metaphorical – it means something different from itself, always refers to something other than itself. Think how words and statements are kinds of substitutions or metaphors: give examples and explain them.
- a way of putting ideas in *order*: words refer to ideas (not things? ideas of things? what they are and how they are?) and writing puts ideas into order.
- something to do with exchanging a *message* or a *meaning*? Do all kinds of writing work like this? Are all meanings and messages in writing clear? What decides what the message is? Does this change with different types of writing?
- always done by a writer. A writer is always situated in a certain position, with a certain kind of identity. Can there ever be a writing not situated by the identity of a writer?
- capable of being recorded, *repeatable*; writing can still mean something when the writer is not there. What happens to the ideas of the writer when the writer is not there?
- a system of *rules* and *conventions*: how do you think these are established? Who controls them? Are there *laws* for writing? How might the laws be enforced?
- depends for its ability to communicate on *recognition*. What different things have to be recognized – by a reader of writing – for the writing to be understood?
- something that *describes* the world, the way the world is; OR does writing *construct* our ideas of how the world is? What might be the difference?
- something that depends on *presence* and *absence* – at the same time.

The words are present, but the meanings – ideas or thoughts or things – are not; they are absent.

- is something that is done in different *contexts*, for different *purposes*, using different signs and orderings. Think of examples. Can there ever be a writing for *all* purposes and contexts?
- a *social practice*, done for specific social purposes: think of examples and consider their different social purposes. Can writing ever not be social?
- an *organization of identity* – of different identities: of the things being written about, and of the writer and the reader(s)
- something that can have conscious meanings but might also have *unconscious meanings* – meanings that are not present in the words themselves, but that come into play, whether in the writing or the reading. What might this idea tell us about meaning?
- something that is organized into different *genres*: news articles, poems, letters, fire drill notices, computer printer manuals, graffiti, autobiographies, shopping lists, and so on. What happens if you fail to recognize the right genre?

---

processes to inscribe its elements so that they may be repeated endlessly beyond the moment of their inscription;
2 as a technology of forms of thought, feelings and ideas, an aspect of the general technology of language, a technology not simply outside the subject and used by the subject, but inhabiting the subject, bearing and conveying general cultural meanings.

Writing may then be examined as a kind of technology in terms of the material structures of writing processes, allowing for inscription, repetition, recognition, but also in terms of what might be called a technology of *forms*. Only within the structures of established forms or systems can writing be done or be read. In this sense, writing can be seen as a technology of 'iterable' statements, guided by preset rules. In relation to this understanding of writing as a system, writing can be seen as a technology of meaning and values involving the manipulation of forms within various social contexts – specifically, institutions. The formal and structural sense that writing is a technology cannot be distinguished clearly from the consideration that writing is also a technology of thought and feeling – giving shape and form to readily established ways of thinking and feeling about things. The tendency of these considerations is to work against the notion that writing could ever be a kind of 'free' expression or a way for the individual to his or her unique and deeply inner being.

Students may be asked to examine these theoretical points explicitly and for themselves – points running counter to the practice of writing which regards it simply as self-expression or neutral tool. The idea of mastering this technology is then implicated in the idea of a technical know-how, but is more than just technical, and is something advocates of liberal English have hardly been able to confront. The idea of writing as a technology in the larger sense emphasises the importance of the material forms of expression as being the structures and forms of thought, rather than proposing some ghostly, unseen, shadow of thought that can't ever be known, assumed to hover spirit-like somewhere 'behind' the material forms of thought – or writing.

Looking at writing as a technology in this way would seek to develop awareness of how writing systems operate in different contexts – but also at different levels; and like any kind of technology, writing positions identities in relation to its social operations. This is clearly visible in the school context, where different levels of the technology of writing are used to differentiate between different identities of students, most crudely and blatantly in the grading system and in the criteria of assessment. Technology in this sense is very obviously implicated in institutional operations.

The following questions may initiate thinking on this topic and may lead to the practical examination of different kinds of writing.

What different technologies of writing can you identify?
How do they work?
Is speaking – like writing – a kind of technology?
What different *forms* of writing are there?
How do they work?
Do different types of writing 'ask' you to read them in different ways?
How does this happen?
In what kind of social situations does writing take place?
Do the social situations of writing determine the kind of writing that takes place?
Do they determine the form of the writing?
Do they determine what can be said and what can't be said?
What other technologies of communication can you think of?
How do they work?
Do different technologies of communication involve different kinds of thinking?
What people have most control of the technology of writing?
In what different ways might people have control of technologies of writing?

In what ways might control of different kinds of technology of writing be related to having *power*?

One example of how the technology of forms of writing operates might be furnished by considering fairy tales. A simulation of the technology of this form can be produced by constructing a kind of writing machine. This would simply consist of a set of cards having different components of fairy stories – events, identities, places, objects, beginnings, endings – written on them. The cards can be shuffled and a hand randomly dealt. The random arrangement of elements can then be organized into sequence, a way of demonstrating how genres structure the meanings of elements in writing, as shown in Example 4.5

Example 4.5   Fairy stories and genre

Introduce and explain the idea of genre

Explain the idea of the genre of fairy stories.

Explain the idea of a 'sentence maker' in relation to the elements of a genre of text.

Explain

a) structural functions (elements)
b) syntax (ordering)

and give 2/3 examples of structural functions and syntax at work (using the work you did with cards).

- Illustrate this in relation to *Red Riding Hood* and show how various structural functions carry with them symbolic meanings.
- Illustrate the same points in relation to two other kinds of text – for example, a TV advert and a story in a newspaper.

Conclusion, explaining how you've used the following ideas:

  genre
  structural functions
  syntax
  the idea of a writing machine

and consider the implications all this has for meanings of texts

---

A particular culturally common image in different forms might be examined to compare the operations of different technologies of representation, as can be seen in Example 4.6.

Example 4.6 Comparing technologies of representation

Text:

1 'La Figlia Che Piange'
2 The Nescafe TV advert using the song 'I Can See Clearly Now'
3 The Gucci magazine advert using the image of a girl on a motorbike

Consider:

- the three different kinds of technology of representation involved
- the images deployed by each in each particular case
- how these images produce or correspond to ideas
- how these images relate to other images in other examples of the same technology of representation
- how these images relate to each of the other examples
- how these images relate to images and ideas
- how each of these texts position and address the subject
- how each of these texts represents femininity

Students may be also asked to consider the phenomenology of perception or 'reading' as it is implicated in these different technologies of representation. This would mean examining what aspects of the 'object' may be viewed by the reader, what possible perspectives there are, what kinds of ideas of the object might be available, and it would also invite consideration of the position of the viewer or reader. All these factors may be brought into play in an examination of how the different technologies – the written text, the TV advert and the picture – work in their representation of a similar object or idea.

The kind of thinking involved in relation to the topic of the technology of writing engages, among other things, the topic of the subject in language – the subject in its relations to the technology of language. The subject – the individual – in this kind of thinking is very much perceived as the subject *of* language, shaped *by* writing at least as much as shaping it. Any shaping that is done must be done in reference to culturally available images, producing culturally organized meanings in forms that are culturally established technologies of representation.

The topic of grammatology – essentially a general interrogation of writing – might be approached by taking specific texts and considering what particular questions might be asked of them. The following is a suggested checklist.

Who is writing?
To whom are they writing?
What are they writing about?
What are they writing for?
When are they writing?
What are the main ideas?
What are the key terms?
What kind of language is used?
Are there any special terms used?
What kind of form is used?
What kind of time, place, social context, institution are invoked by a reading of the writing?

The specific issue of the cultural identity of writing might be approached by considering the following points, in relation to particular examples:

beliefs	behaviour	work
language	relationships	knowledge
social activities	dress	gender
objects	ideas	identities

Students might be invited to construct their own terminology drawn from the various topics they've looked at using material as presented in Example 4.7. They may be asked to consider terms from established theory and to transpose these into their own frames of reference. They may be invited to put these terms to use in relation to a number of

Example 4.7   A terminology of enquiry

---

terminology – dominant terms
discourses
special terms – specific elements of vocabulary
forms/structures – and what differences there might be
gaps and assumptions
status
form(s) of inscription/material production
rhetoric – including consideration of positions of address (what positions of address are being adopted?)
oppositions – contrasts and how identities of things are organized
institutional context
ideas about the world
symbolic order
genre(s)

---

different kinds of writing. They may also be in a position to examine this terminology with the standard terminology of response – that of common-sense or conventional English.

Students may also be invited to try putting these terms to use to inform analysis or preparation of their own pieces of writing. Their general function is part of a project to provide ideas for the more explicit awareness of writing, what it is and how it works.

EXAMPLES OF WRITING: AUTOBIOGRAPHY , GRAFFITI AND SHOPPING LISTS

Autobiography exemplifies a number of characteristic beliefs about the nature of writing. It is a thoroughly characteristic, cherished activity of English and represents beliefs about the individual and writing. In English in schools it epitomizes writing as individual self-expression, drawing together notions about the self, about identity, about narrative and about writing. An approach to autobiography from a radically different perspective could begin by opposing the ideas it's founded on; asserting the idea of writing as an impersonal symbolic ordering and, suggesting alternatively that the self is in fact erased rather than expressed in writing, that narrative form, usually used to structure autobiography, is a kind of strait-jacket preventing certain important aspects and ideas of the self from being expressed, and that the general cultural form of autobiography positions and defines the self in a limiting kind of way – in relation to important cultural notions of identity and personal history.

A way of approaching this topic with students might be to begin by considering the relations between autobiography and other kinds of writing it would normally be distinguished from. Putting together the examples of graffiti, shopping lists and autobiography may clearly illustrate issues and problems that can arise from a probing of writing and its familiar categories. It may, deconstructively, also lead to different possibilities of writing being brought to view, as well as raising questions of a theoretical kind. Deconstruction in this sense means analysing differences and identities, trying to examine estab-lished categories in order to see how – according to what procedures and what forces – they are maintained. In one sense this can simply be a kind of game; interesting enough, though, perhaps, undertaken for no further purpose. It can also, in this case, lead to consideration being given more directly to issues like the social contexts of writing, ideas about writing and the self, and might usefully make explicit points about what could be called the sociolinguistics of writing. It can certainly emphasise certain critical points about ideas that dominate writing in schools – where writing is a very significant component in constructing different identities for its subjects or students.

The apparently clear differences between shopping lists, graffiti and autobiography may, in the first place, illustrate simply how the form and function of writing varies according to its context and the (social) conventions that operate within that context. It may also illustrate how the technology of writing influences how we read its relative authority and significance. If the form of the autobiography is defined as being determined at least partly by the 'I' of the 'addresser', and partly by the narrative form, then the characteristic feature of a shopping list could be simply that it lists items. The characteristic features of graffiti would probably be more difficult to define, since graffiti may take many forms and may operate many different genres. To investigate these variously different identities might be usefully illustrative. For example, it is easy to illustrate that it might be possible for a piece of graffiti, written, say, on a toilet wall, to have an autobiographical form (indeed, some may aspire to do so). We might well ask, and not really decisively be able to answer, whether this graffiti is not, then, autobiography, or *an* autobiography? Does this piece of graffiti appear in the form of an identifiable genre? Is autobiography a clearly definable genre? Does the problem raised by these questions mean, in turn, that we can have and recognize autobiographical writing (an autobiographical fragment, say) which is not *an* autobiography? Does it also imply that we may not be able to tell the difference between autobiographical writing and autobiography – in the sense of the *true* story of someone's life? And doesn't the very idea of truth in this context run into trouble, in the sense that it might be difficult for an autobiography to claim *any* kind of objective truth? What might be the implications of this point, though, for other forms of writing claiming some kind of hold on truth?

To go further, what would or could determine exactly when an autobiography became, fully and unquestionably, an autobiography? Would it be appropriate, or even possible, to use the word 'exactly' in this context? And, to go further in this deconstruction of writing and its identities, isn't an autobiography, in the full sense, always doomed to be (in any form we can imagine for it?) nothing more than a series of autobiographical fragments, linked together according to the already established, thoroughly impersonal rules of narrative composition? The only coherence and unity the fullest autobiography could then claim would be textual. In that sense it would be a constructed coherence, imposed by an external pattern, a symbolic ordering, an instance of a particular kind of cultural technology, imposing its identity over the identity of the writing and reading subject.

It is also possible, in a deconstructive kind of inversion, to pursue this questioning in another kind of way. A shopping list may seem to be purely and simply what it is, without complication. Part of its being a shopping list in this uncomplicated way would be to do with its being used in the way a shopping list is used, although, of course, there are many different kinds of use for shopping lists. A shopping list, though, may take on a quite different kind of significance if it is introduced into an autobiography. A context may be produced in this case in which the shopping list, all or merely a part of it, perhaps a single item, would take on a new and different kind of significance, well beyond and totally different from the significance it had, or may have had, in a shopping expedition it may have been intended for. Here we come upon further complications, leading to further questions opening upon further lines of enquiry into the terrain of writing.

Within the autobiography, the significance of the shopping list may take on a new and different dimension or direction; but, it might well be asked, is it ever possible, with clarity and confidence, to know what the meaning of a shopping list *is*, without, that is, knowing all about the kind of living context it appears within? A shopping list found on the ground outside a supermarket may have no more meaning than a wayward piece of indecipherable graffiti. Such a shopping list would forever hold the secret of its own life story, its origins, its function and – in the end – its meaning, unless we could recover detailed knowledge of its history. Was it discarded as useless, or as over-optimistic, perhaps, on the way into the supermarket? Was it exhaustive, or were other items to be added as the trolley was wheeled around? Or did it have some other kind of role within a scenario that must forever remain mysterious? Was it, for example, a dummy or decoy shopping list, used as a pretext in a complicated network of relationships. And so on.

Analysis of the list's contents may or may not reveal important points about its 'author', although it would be impossible to say with any conviction what the status of these points would be, according to the logic of the questioning procedure outlined above. And here, the deconstructive idea of *undecidability* in relation to texts and textual meanings has been illustrated and may be brought explicitly into play. Texts and meanings, writing and meanings, writing and interpretation, writing and production of meanings: from these examples may be opened up a whole complex of critical issues, issues modern post-structuralist theory, in its own very limited context, has sought to propound. The shopping list on its own, then, may yield a very productive line of enquiry touching upon fundamental questions about the nature of writing. Being fundamental, though, does not mean that they are simple or simple minded. Similarly, because they may be complex and demanding, doesn't mean that they are therefore beyond the reach of any students. If, as is clearly the case, students can understand how a shopping list may be read as a fragment of an autobiography, if they can also understand how a shopping list may be read as no more than a piece of haphazard graffiti, significant points relating to the idea of writing in general and to the categorization of writing can have been introduced. The students in question may demonstrate their understanding of these points in a number of ways – and these ways may be explicitly theoretical or illustratively practical. To play around with these identities – in this case 'shopping lists', 'graffiti' and 'autobiography' – is both actively theoretical and practically productive.

Students may further be invited to consider how, for example, an autobiography may consist of graffiti, gathered together in a certain kind of order, or of shopping lists, perhaps dated and illustrated with jottings, ticks, crossings off, marginalia and so on. They may be invited to consider how an autobiography may consist of a gathering together of different kinds of writing – graffiti, shopping lists and other – to produce a kind of document file which may, or may not, be an autobiography. Questions about the identity of different kinds of writing can be posed, questions throwing the idea of a natural order of writing categories into serious doubt. Links between quite disparate forms of writing – like, for example graffiti, and shopping lists – can then be forged in new ways when the context changes, in this case into autobiography. This kind of linking can be productive of a lot of thinking – of a lot of writing even – which is positively deconstructive. A useful task might be to compose an autobiography figuring both graffiti and shopping lists as significant features. The composition would not necessarily have to be complete; it might only be an outline, and that outline in turn might be used as the occasion for a commentary on the different kinds of identity of different kinds of writing, enfolded, as it were, in one piece of writing. Questions about meaning and about modes of reading are involved here, also. The meaning of any of the elements – the shopping list, the graffiti – clearly changes when enclosed in a new context. The items on the shopping list, for example, might take on a new significance, being granted special meaning or meanings in relation to connections made with other items in the text. Is this because they *have* a new significance, or because the different kind of reading they are now being given in this new context constructs their meaning differently?

Putting different texts together, or putting together different textual identities or ideas of text, and asking some questions of all of them, and of the relations and differences between them, can have the effect of penetrating the aura of common-sense and established ideas that surround writing with their penumbra of obviousness. Clearly, doing this on its own doesn't produce a revaluation of attitudes to and ideas about writing and meaning. It is necessary to find some way of discussing the possible effects of putting textual identities into play.

What follows here briefly proposes one way the pursuit of the topic of autobiography might proceed; hoping to show how this topic may be a) taken far beyond its usual forms, b) usefully illustrative of fundamental issues, and c) demonstrative of the extremely limiting forms of much commonly accepted and celebrated practice of English teaching at this level.

The topic of autobiography can be used, then, to address a number of significant issues in the field of writing. Some of these issues may be specific to the topic of autobiography, but they all touch upon important aspects of writing in general. A theoretically alert approach to the topic of autobiography with students could follow many different lines, pursuing several issues, or could be more focused, concentrated and selective. Some of the issues raised might be concerned with writing and identity, writing and being, writing and memory, writing and the construction of the self – all issues emerging from some consideration of the relations between the individual writer and the system of writing. While these may appear to belong to the more sophisticated matter of deconstructive thinking, they can be dealt with in ways that are accessible. Of equal importance, they can be approached in a way that highlights issues of general relevance to any kind of subject claiming language and textuality as its proper business.

Autobiography may reach out into a great number of topics. In conventional, or liberal, English the possibilities of expansion for the topic are seldom really explored. The conventional, well established and most common approach to the topic is simply to invite students to write their own autobiography – an invitation that belongs to the best traditions of liberal, progressive English, where students are encouraged to express themselves fully in their own language(s). Autobiography, in some quite obvious ways, might be seen to be central to this kind of English project. The invitation might well be accompanied by an outline, giving guide-lines to students, providing a structure for their autobiography. Settling for an uncritical narrative approach, *questions* about autobiography and narrative, narrative and (in this case personal) history, narrative and subject positions, and, for example, narrative and the idea of truth are not generally explored.

The structure of the conventional autobiography in English is fixed and perfectly predictable in its adoption of a direct, chronological narrative form. This, it's suggested, *is* autobiography – and all the problematics of the topic are thereby denied. The question, for example, of how an autobiography can be in any meaningful sense 'auto' – if its form and structure are already clearly established – cannot be raised in the context of this model for the topic, nor, indeed, for this model of the subject, English. From background, through early memories, to hopes and fears for the future – this progress is presented simply as *the* shape of a life's experience, rather than the shape of a particular form of writing. The idea of there being a problematic relationship between the two – the life and the writing – is never entertained. The idea of that relationship being worth examining, that it might produce interesting ideas and might engage with significant topics in the field of textuality, language, identity and meanings in general social life cannot even be considered. It seems worthwhile to examine approaches that engender a great many more possibilities for different kinds of writing, approaches that students may adopt to produce work required by the subject, or to engage with ways of thinking that are not encompassed by currently dominant practices of English. There is no necessary ordering for any of this work; it is all intended to promote thinking about issues in relation to autobiography with an open and mobile structure. Initial discussion of the topic might be conducted perhaps in relation to some specific questions, or to some specific text or texts, such as the film, *Stand By Me*, the novel, *Great Expectations*, and/or an instance of standard autobiographical writing, or *Bonnie, Frieda and Annie*. The board notes in Example 4.8 represent the kinds of consideration that may be given to the film, *Stand By Me* in relation to an interrogative approach to autobiography.

Example 4.8   Autobiography: board notes for *Stand By Me*

Title

Solidarity	nostalgia – memory
togetherness	recollection
male bonding	sentimentality
love song	censorship

death – Chris

film narrative = body search
Teddy dices with death
Gordy's brother

Gordy = man in car at beginning = narrator + main character

Gordy = man at word-processor – writer of story (+ Stephen King – writer of horror fictions)

Death of Chris Chambers at end *and* at beginning – does the beginning determine the end, or the end the beginning?

(What is the significance of the deer?)

film = flashback
   also includes flashbacks
   + memories
   + dreams
   + memories of dreams

film = autobiographical text (of whom, though?)
not an autobiography?
fragment? fictional reconstruction?
partial text – exclusions, editing, censorship,
repressions, demands of narrative sequencing
significance of male dominance – no women

identity, status of text?

The following points might be identified by way of focusing a deconstruction of the idea of autobiography:

> In what sense can 'my' 'autobiography' be mine, if it belongs to the order of writing?
> What and where am I anyway? If my identity and being are written in the first place in/by the order of writing, what remains of me in the writing?
> The subject of autobiography is split by the grammar of identity, the shifting signification of subject positions – I, me; I, you; I, she; I, he; I, we; I, they.
> My so-called autobiography is structured by the discourse of identity as narrative. This structure is a structure of gaps, absences and repressions.
> The excess of my being over the order of writing cannot be expressed within the order of writing.

A range of approaches to the topic of autobiography is offered in the formal outlines of Examples 4.9 to 4.13, indicating how theory might be put to use in relation to this general theme.

Example 4.9   Autobiography, shopping lists and graffiti: textual identities and meanings

List different statements that might be found in an autobiography –
characteristic statements? What different categories could these statements be put into?

List different types of graffiti – and consider the different types of
statements that graffiti might make. What different categories of
statement might there be in graffiti?

Draw up a couple of examples of shopping lists? What different types
of shopping list might there be and consider what kind of statements
shopping lists might make – and about what?

Write an outline of an autobiography – including statements, topics and
information. Write a commentary to explain the meaning of the
different things in the outline.

Construct an autobiography made up from different examples of
graffiti. Write a commentary to explain the significance of the different
elements contained in this autobiography.

Construct an autobiography made up from different examples of
shopping lists. Write a commentary to explain the significance of the
different information that might be conveyed by this autobiography.

Consider these different outlines and commentaries using the following
perspectives on writing:

• writing and construction – the ordering and production of meanings
• discourses, terminology and rhetoric
• writing and the production of truth
• undecidability
• the identity of writing, categories and genres
• recognizing the identity of writing – reading and writing practices
• order, ordering and syntax

If you put all of the different kinds of writing you might produce using
the above points, what kind of writing would you be doing?

Example 4.10   Writing autobiography

General Considerations

- What form will the writing take?
- What genre?
- What kind of ordering or sequence will organize the writing?
- Where will it begin? At what different points could it begin?
- What different kinds of memories will it include?
- What different kinds of language will be used to write about different memories? What different sorts of discourse might be involved?
- What different kinds of data will be included? What will be the sources of the data included?
- From what position will the writing be done? Will it always remain the same?

Autobiographical Data

- What different kinds of data might you include in a conventional autobiography?
- What other kinds of data might be included in different kinds of autobiography? Think of examples of different kinds of auto-biography and identify the different kinds of data they might include.
- What would be the sources of the data in the different cases you have considered? How could an autobiography include writing about the sources of its data?
- If someone else wrote someone's biography or autobiography, could it change the status of the data?

Example 4.11   Autobiography and psychoanalysis

conscious	-	'ego'	-	'I'
unconscious	-	'id'	-	'it'
symbolic order	-	language	-	the identity of things

What might the idea of the unconscious contribute towards considering the writing of an autobiography?

Would it be possible to write elements of the unconscious into an autobiography?

What would the idea of the difference between the conscious and the unconscious suggest about identity? How might this be taken into account in relation to writing and autobiography?

What are the implications of the unconscious and conscious for the idea of the controlling author?

What are the implications of the unconscious and conscious for the idea of meaning – and the control of meaning?

What might be the effects of the symbolic order of writing of an autobiography? How does the symbolic order determine the identity of the writer of an autobiography?

Example 4.12   Autobiography and dreams

• Would writing about dreams in an autobiography be writing about the unconscious?
• How would you know the importance and meanings of the dreams?
• How would writing about dreams – or writing a description of dreams – be different from the dreams themselves?

Example 4.13   Autobiography and codes in the language of personality: interviews, statements and contexts

---

Take some of the statements you produced by doing interviews and writing reports on them.

Statements

She's got a very guilty conscience.
He definitely doesn't eat peanuts.
She is afraid of large spiders and fire.
Luminous jumpers annoy her.
She would like to change her parents ages and their dress sense.
She doesn't think that she has been loved or in love.
She gets annoyed with people who are always happy.
He thinks you go up to heaven when you die.
She hates boys who act macho.
She doesn't believe in reincarnation.
She's afraid of being buried alive.
She's never stolen anything.
Someone she loves dying would hurt her more than dying herself.
She has recurring dreams about elephants, seals and Sainsburys.
He doesn't want to be too unconventional.
She doesn't wish death on people but sometimes wishes that people had never been born.
She always reads the last page of a mystery novel first.

He thinks men are just lucky to have nipples.
She's always exaggerating.
She takes great pains to be liked and to be genuine.

These statements might be dealt with by looking at the following:

the truth/reality of each statment: is it decidable?
the grammar of each statement – and what it suggests
the context and discourse of personality at work

The initial analysis/discussion of these statements might be extended in relation to examples from:

* teenage, women's, sport magazines
* TV news reports
* soap operas
* novels
* school reports

going on to look at how different discourses of personality operate in different contexts and involving the possibilities of doing research into them.

WRITING AS COMMUNICATION? CONVENTIONAL AND ALTERNATIVE MODELS

The challenge of theory in relation to writing runs counter to the grain of common-sense understanding of language. Writing as communication of thoughts, feelings and ideas, for example, is not quite what it was thought to be. The effect of theory can be disturbing to complacent preconceptions of the subject, English. The nature of this disruption can be approached with school students of English. In response to the thoroughly philosophical question: 'What is writing?', the following ideas may be productive starting points for explicitly formulating a general alternative view. The alternative model of communication can be offered for consideration and debate.

Conventional model: experience → language/meaning → interpretation → writing

(and then in reverse for the reader?)

Alternative model: language/meanings → interpretations → experiences → writing

(and then in reverse for the reader?)

In the conventional account of language, experience is translated or transcribed into a form of expression which may capture the flavour or quality of the experience, to varying degrees, according to how 'good' or 'authentic' the writing is. The form of expression conveys the idea of the experience in a more or less neutral form – and can communicate its flavour, its feelings, its 'quality' in general.

In an obvious, though not necessarily often expressed, sense, writing and experience are two completely different things. It is not the case that they are directly related in the way that is often assumed in ways of talking about language – ways that might use terms like 'truth' or 'reality' and so on, any expression in fact of writing's authenticity in the sense of a fidelity to experience. Writing may record experience, but this is then transformed by the process of writing into a linguistic experience, a writing experience, and this is not the same as the experience 'itself'. The experience itself, in so far as it is past, does not exist, in its original form, as itself. It is gone. Memory is a kind of writing, recording in another form, a form that transforms experience into a kind of writing.

At the same time, and on the other hand, the deconstructive, alternative model inverts the conventional view and claims, in effect, that the nature of experience, its quality, is actually formed and structured by the language expressing it, or rather, the alternative model would claim (rooting out a false opposition) that the difference between language and experience cannot easily be made and sustained. For the forms and categories of language will determine the nature of the knowledge of the experience, and will even determine what that experience *is* according to the ordering of language within the structures of the symbolic order. The symbolic order being the system of networks holding meanings and identities in place, determining – through language in conjunction with social experience – ways of being, seeing and feeling.

The alternative account might claim that this is what writing *is* – and might go further in saying that this pre-structuring is what makes writing possible. According to the alternative model, the idea of individual expression is tenuous. The individual 'becomes' an 'I' in writing – a structural function of language – or a name in a system of named categories. The story of my life becomes shaped and constrained by the established structures of narrative expression – structures and conventions which may well exclude important features, operating a kind of secret censorship on me. Moreover, the demands of autobiography as a narrative form give a determining shape to how I see and feel my experience in writing it. The formal outline, offered as a guide, shown above, illustrates quite clearly how this structuring works as a positively determining force.

To take this topic further, practically, so that students may begin to think how their own writing of and/or about autobiography might take shape, some more considerations about the possible kinds of writing of autobiography – and its implications – might be simply addressed. The options could be laid out as shown in Example 4.14.

Example 4.14 Writing: on issues of autobiography, identity, writing, being, and memory

Narrative: but what kind could it be? A fairy tale, a detective story, a science-fiction narrative.

> How would the subject of this narrative be identified – 'I', 'me', 'he/ she', 'you', 'we', 'they'? How would this narrative be structured?
> What would it have to include? What would be necessarily excluded from it?

Or: a narrative of a different kind could be attempted – a reading autobiography; a dream autobiography; an autobiography of friend-ships, of films, of crises, of learning, of music . . . and so on.

Or: a self-conscious autobiography written in awareness of the issues and problems raised by the idea of autobiography, by the conventions of autobiographical writing, and addressing them explicitly.

Or: writing might be addressed to other forms that autobiography might take, forms utilizing different media: film, soap-opera, video, photos, clothes, 'personal' objects, and so on.

Or: an autobiography might be possible taking into account other people's memories and accounts, an autobiography having to take into account a number of different and specifically positioned perspectives.

If the considerations I've offered above are worth taking into account, then autobiography is not, as might be inferred from its usual pro-cedures in English, a simple and direct form of self-expression. It might, however, provide the occasion for many important textual issues, issues to do with writing – 'general writing' or grammatology – to be explored.

RETHINKING WRITING

The kind of theory used in relation to writing here aims to be deconstructively exploratory. It aims to offer a beginning, at least, for an examination of writing as a social practice, a conception of writing incorporating factors generally left out by established conventional and liberal practices. There are two main aspects to this kind of work with theory and writing. One concerns an examination of writing categories, of the different discourses that structure writing, of the institutions that writing operates within, and of the different forms of writing that get produced. On the other hand, there is the philosophical, deconstructive analysis of writing, examining ideas about writing in a critical way. This second aspect of the theory of writing seeks to ask fundamental questions about writing, how it works and what, in the end, it is. It entails looking at ideas about writing and eschewing the generally accepted notions that inform understanding of writing, in order to get new and different perspectives to bear on taken for granted assumptions.

It can be taught – in a number of ways, some implicit and some explicit – that writing is a very significant social practice taking many forms, inhabiting different contexts; that writing is mobile and that the categories of writing can be put into 'play', in theoretical and practical work. Different kinds of writing may be seen as ideologically loaded practices, reflecting ideas about a number of important social, cultural and, in the end, political issues. The importance of writing in shaping lives and in ordering different kinds of identity can be approached in this way.

It seems to me that this kind of movement, involving an expansion of the conception of the teaching of writing, is significantly more inclusive than the narrow round of writing activities, the narrow framework within which writing is taught to be understood at present.

5 Oral theory

TWO EXAMPLES OF PRACTICE

The identity of oral English – what it is both theoretically and in its established practices – is typified in its characteristic exercises. According to the historical conditions of its conception and growth, the 'classic' practice of oral English tends to be associated with more progressive models of the subject (though there are, of course, other kinds of oral work in English). The established, fundamental character of oral English – inscribed in syllabuses, endorsed by documents produced by various bodies claiming a stake in the identity of English and operating as routine practice – might be worth reconsidering, though, in the light of the critique and reconstruction that some kinds of theory can offer.

Role-play and small group discussion are two examples of the more liberal tradition of oral English at work in the classroom and these are briefly analysed in the following section. Innumerable citations could be given of texts and manuals of English teaching advocating, describing, analysing transcripts and so on – all dedicated to affirming their practical and theoretical justification. They constitute elements in what might be called the routine order of the subject.

ROLE-PLAY

The set-up for a role-play exercise might generally be represented as taking the following form: a situation is established, or a series of situations are established, and students in pairs or small groups improvise oral exchanges on the basis of assigned roles. The roles may be identified as part of the instructions of the exercise. Some consideration of how they are to operate might be given. There are classic examples including, at their most simple, family situations, meetings at bus stops, encounters in the work place, in a shop, for example – all of which have been associated with a fairly long tradition of role-play in English and in creative drama lessons. In the end, the students are left to improvise, having been given some degree of guidance. The function ultimately being to explore language in use, to gain experience, to try out different linguistic situations and different linguistic roles in an open context of 'play'. While all of all that might be fair enough, and may lead into some fruitful exercises, the full possibilities of role-play – of the potential of role-play in a more fully theorized, or considered form – are not, it seems to me, realized in the exercise conceived in that simply active convention.

The positive value of the characteristic role-play exercise can be questioned on the following grounds. In this conception oral English begins and ends in practice, as it were. There is no analysis. The exercise depends on a notion of teaching language through practice – which is fine as far as it goes, and better perhaps than some crudely instrumental versions of language learning according to a monolithic notion of, say, grammar and composition. The classic role-play exercise is at least based on the positive assumption that it allows students to explore their language competencies in different language contexts.

The role-play exercise is based on a notion of language development linked directly to 'practice'. It assumes that the conditions that are set up are necessarily enabling and productive – and that the context provided unambiguously offers opportunities for the exploration of linguistic identities. But without some explicit way of addressing issues of context and identity, it is by no means assured that any sense of their significance will be realized in the enactment of role-play activities. In addition to this, the role-play situation is, obviously, subject to its contextual limitations; it is not a free-floating and unconstrained activity. The language that operates remains enclosed within the institutional context. Not that you can ever devise activities in education that somehow completely escape institutional determination. But the classic formulation of role-play has no way of making this explicit, of addressing and dealing with it. It is certainly questionable whether the role-play situation actually corresponds to the way language development occurs. Questions about operative notions of language and development may well throw the idea of oral work signified by role-play activities into serious – but necessary – doubt.

The exercise is illustrative of a specific model of oral work and of oracy – a model that entails specific notions of language, how language works, how language development is best fostered within the school context. The model – though apparently simple, though presenting itself as being self-evident or purely common sense – is not entirely without problems, such as problems concerning the way that the relations between language and the social are conceived, or are not conceived. The extent to which these problems are critical, or are perceived as problems, though, very much depends on your position, on what sense of language and the social you're working from.

It's always worth asking, when looking at any particular aspect of educational and/or classroom practice, why the exercise is configured in a certain way. Why not start by asking about what might be necessary to begin to construct a conversation of the nature classically defined in oral role-play exercise? Why not begin the exercise by asking about the possibilities in terms of the social, linguistic contexts talk takes place in? The assumptions that underlie the routine form of the exercise are limited to the extent that they assume that language practices are not bounded by institutional factors. Consequently, they assume that language development can be engineered and monitored in the classroom by the well-intentioned teacher's good practices – in this case, setting the exercise in motion, allowing it to follow its own logic of progress, perhaps gently intervening now and then (though when, why and on what grounds?). This naivety characteristically ignores issues of language and identity that could well be profitably explored, issues that could be made explicit in the way that students are invited to engage in activities, or to consider the nature of the oral work they are involved in.

This critique, or questioning of the identity and meaning of role-play doesn't necessarily mean that the concept has to be ditched altogether. There are ways of redefining the activity that might address the problems identified here and that might, in practice, greatly enhance its scope. One way is to put a new kind of emphasis on knowledge and research – both largely absent from the practices of English. Knowledge about how language works in specific social situations, in specific institutions, could be usefully communicated, and students could be given the means to conduct their own research projects into matters like linguistic role-play.

SMALL GROUP DISCUSSION OF A POEM

Another classic oral exercise of the more progressively constituted English classroom is the discussion in small groups – often of a text, very often a poem. Again, all sorts of assumptions are at work in this kind of exercise – assumptions about poems, and about the way texts work, entwined with assumptions about appropriate kinds of oral work, mostly to do with the opportunities for 'free' responses that poetry or other texts may allow.

The text here is in one sense, at least, a *pre*text – the point of the exercise being to enable the free expression of the students' responses to the language of the poem, its content or to the issues raised by some text or other. The point is also to enable the free responses of individuals a space or context for interaction, dialogue and exchange. The small group context is designed to make the discussion more freely available to all – to do away with any constraints that operate in full class discussion, to initially, anyway, eliminate the authoritarian position of the teacher in classroom discourse – to get more participation for more participants, to generate good discussion in the sense of lots of activity, high levels of interaction. In spite-of its apparently generous aims, this exercise still begs the question: What for? We may, for example, simply ask: Why is it thought that high levels of discussion are valuable? What kinds of interchange actually take place? To what extent are they 'free'? What kinds of text or pretext tend to get used in small group discussions, and why those? What kinds of content characterize small group discussions, and why? The simple use of small group discussion – undertaken without any very clear consciousness of language models, of contexts, of different language identities, of the relations between language and the social generally – cannot in itself make any unambiguous claim to positive value.

GENERAL CRITIQUE OF ORAL ENGLISH

The explicit emphasis given to speech in the classroom and to the importance of oral work in English may to a large extent have been associated with more 'progressive' versions of the subject. The evolution of the oral component of English is now expressed in its established place in the English assessment, formally recognized in authorized exam syllabuses and official documents. In one sense, it might appear that the various languages of students in classrooms have been given recognition – in the authenticity of their diverse identities. It is still, however, possible to attend oral moderation meetings where students are downgraded on the grounds of accent and dialect. This means that even the questionable liberal models of oral work are subject in certain contexts to traditionalist interpretations and procedures. It seems to remain the case that standard English is the dominant form, more likely than other forms to receive certificated recognition.

The assessment of oral work depends on the idea that there could be a model of good speech. The model proposed would have to claim for itself that it was inclusive and universal, in the sense that it would be valid in all contexts and for all occasions. In the end, such a model is likely to discriminate against certain groups, or against certain types of speech, or against certain attitudes towards speech held by certain groups of people. Speech, like other language and textual phenomena, is embedded in social differences, differences of many kinds – regional, class and ethnic differences, for example. It is not possible to say in some universal and inclusive way what a good performance in speech would consist of, because different kinds of speech operate different criteria of performance in different contexts. But the official systems of grading oral work in the school context depend to a large degree on the assumption that oral performances can be graded according to general criteria that hold good in all contexts. This negates some important features of language, and whether intentionally or not, reasserts the centrality of standard forms of English speech, making them a kind of model from which other versions are often seen as deviations. The criteria which make a good performance in standard English do not necessarily apply to other forms of the language, forms which are just as capable of expressing a full range of meaning, but which may well utilize quite other linguistic features and forms.

The very idea that people can be graded according to the language they use – and in terms of education, schooling, the language they use in a specific context under many different kinds of constraint – is dubious, to say the least. But the continuation of assessment which differentiates, negatively, like the system of grading that operates in schooling is what the continuation of the subject as we know it depends on. Oral work seems to highlight this more than other things. This is at least partly because the subject – or student – is more clearly and more sensitively exposed as a language user in oral work. Recognition of different forms of language would imply, in the end, the impossibility of assessment.

The subject of language – the student in the case of English in education – is exposed also in the sense of the position of the subject within the institution. The position of the subject is determined by a configuration of power relations operating, among other things, according to differences in speech. The subject of English, for example, is a subject of the distinction in language based on an identity that is organized within a hierarchy of linguistic differences. The subject of science – the student of science – is defined by being in a condition of lack or deficit in relation to a language. This language is organized in certain specific ways. To attain recognition as an effective subject, the student has to strive to adopt this language or at least orient him- or herself positively in relation to this language. This means that the function of an oral exercise in English, for example, is not necessarily so simple or straightforward as it might at first appear. The idea of open discourse must be set against the discursive context, which has already, as it were, set things up and defined the languages and the linguistic possibilities, their recognition and validation.

It's well known that a significant feature of schooling is the domination of a language, a domination that, while it may recognize other languages, continues to place them according to a hierarchy of distinction. If the language of schooling tends to be the language of standard English, then other kinds of language are likely to be marginalized and may even be negatively defined. This means that whole groups of students are likely to arrive in a state of disadvantage in relation to language. It must be important therefore to question whether the practices of oral English confirm or counter this kind of linguistic disadvantage – not a disadvantage in terms of competence, but one based on (many) different kinds of social difference.

The centrality of standard English has consequences for schooling generally, but seems explicitly relevant in relation to the stated aims of oral work in English. It is – necessarily – assumed that the function of oral work in schools is entirely and simply positive. Accordingly, it is thought that the more oral work the better. This position is related to the idea that learning and development best take place in a context where there is discussion and exchange, and that the functions of oral work coincide with a model of language which emphasises its exploratory, dialogue aspect. It is also believed that the classroom can be the site of this kind of 'open' learning, that it can produce the conditions for exploratory learning through language use. Similar to ideas about writing and its positive benefits, the progressive model of oral work is founded on the assumption that *doing* is developing, independently of other restricting and defining factors. The consequence is that the other, defining, determining factors do not get addressed or adequately taken into account.

The concept of oracy has enjoyed a kind of currency over the past twenty years in education. It has informed practice and this is reflected in teaching methods, and to some extent in exam procedures. The meaning of this development would be difficult to fix for certain. It may be at least partly traced back to the general trend in liberal and avant-garde reformulations, reflected in Bullock and carried through in the aftermath of the expansion of comprehensive schools, and a general, though uneven move towards the refunctioning of education and of

English in education. It can be roughly traced back to the influence of new models of language being imported into English from certain branches or versions of linguistics and psychology, versions which were, on the whole, incorporated into a positivist, progressive and liberal model. This model may have had many virtues, one of which may have been an attempt to recognize the validity of different kinds of languages. The English classroom provided probably the most propitious site for a model of more participatory kinds of learning allowing space for students' different languages – given the very uncertain content of the subject. (Talk could be about anything you liked so long as there was plenty of it.) The lack of an adequately explicit sense of the operations of the institution helped to allow for the partial illusion that learners could simply and directly be makers of their own meanings in the context of classroom practice.

Oral work in English was generally founded on a concept of oracy lacking a social or political dimension, that tended, in the end, to see language as a more or less transparent means to achieving ends that could be generally agreed on and universally recognized. These ends would be conceived of as consonant with the general aims of the whole curriculum, admittedly conceived in a spirit of equal opportunities. Hence the currency enjoyed by the idea of language across the curriculum, an idea that sought to emphasize the importance of oracy, among other things, in all areas of learning, where learning was to be conceived of as exploratory and – in the end – as essentially productive. Without an awareness of the uneven distributions of power at work in discourses – and pretty obviously at work in educational discourses – the balance of any classroom dialogue, and its meaning within the institution and the larger system, was doomed to be uneven and already loaded.

That is not to deny the positive spirit of the enterprise altogether, nor to deny its positive force. It remains necessary, though, to look at the way oracy is likely to be configured within specific institutional structures – whatever its explicitly stated ideal and aims. Oracy allied with literacy produces a union that covers the field of linguistic being. The institutional functioning of the alliance as a means of organizing subject identities is perhaps obvious, though not often – in terms of the practices of institutions of education – recognized as so. According to the ideology of progressive English, the role of the English teacher in the celebratory model of oracy is various: to recognize positively the language skills in speech that learners possess as competent established language users; to provide the context within which speech can be allowed to 'be' – to flow freely, as it were – and to develop oracy through use (a tricky idea). However, as already may have been implied, the problems with these notions are related to cultural identity and social differences – as they are expressed and experienced linguisitically or sociolinguistically and institutionally. The school is highly likely to represent different cultural values from those experienced and held by the student. The different values embodied by the student, or subject of education, and the school, or the institution of education, will be expressed as differences of a linguistic nature, often, obviously, as differences in speech. The context of learning is then differentiated according to the extent that students, subjects are defined in relation to language uses that carry institutionalized authority and power. Because of the institutional context of the practice of English, the ideal of the free flow of speech is restricted. Implicated in the scene of English is the politics of power that may be defined in sociological terms, in terms, that is, of how the institution distributes power unevenly. In a context defined in these terms, the idea of free expression is clearly untenable. Expression, written or oral, must be structured and defined. It is most likely to be structured and defined in favour of those whose language most accords with the dominant forms of language endorsed by the institution. This means that subjects will be systematically, structurally disadvantaged in terms of the language they bear with them and its difference from the languages of the institutional practices of learning. This disadvantage may occur in spite of the intentions of the institution and the individual members of it.

A major problem here is the very tricky matter of intervention. By what right, under what authority, can the 'celebrating' teacher intervene in the language use of his or her students. Critical analysis of the notion of intervention produces a contradiction in terms of the position of the teacher who a) legitimately wants to celebrate the language of the student, and who b) legitimately wants to modify the language of the student in respect to the forms of language required by institutionalized learning processes. The most positive, 'celebratory' forms of oral work will have to face problems when confronting some aspects of schooling. (What about the silent student and the meaning of the silence? Or the generously open question that may – implicitly or explicitly – receive the terse and perhaps equally open response: 'Fuck off'.) Intervention is a difficult problem to negotiate. No such immediate resolution is, I believe, possible – given that any educational practice must depend to some extent on the notion. A more theoretical – or interrogative – approach to oral work in English, might, however, make it less possible to suppress this problem in the practice of daily classroom activity.

I'd propose as a kind of alternative, a classroom practice of oral

'English' work that addressed more explicitly the content of talk in the classroom: in other words, what gets legitimated as proper talk and what is marginalized, or excluded, as well as exploring the kinds of topics that form the content of talk in the classroom.

Generally speaking, the positive model of encouraging oral activity in the classroom, though no doubt founded more securely in sound theoretical grounds than many other more restrictive models, and though giving rise to much greater apparent degrees of participation in 'official' classroom discourses, remains naive in so far as it neglects the institutional constraints that operate powerfully to determine the effects of classroom practice. These institutional constraints are powerful not simply as additions which operate as well as, but as forces which enclose and redirect meanings. In so far as English concerns itself with meanings and how they operate, it seems necessary to produce some model of practice that will address the operations of oral language in the learning context more fully, directly and explicitly.

The only way of tackling institutional power in an attempt to transform practice seems to be to incorporate explicit awareness of it in relation to any activities which are undertaken. This means making explicit the purposes and functions of the activities you're engaged in and their relations to the power of the institution. On this model, at least, there's no pretending that any activity is simply worth doing in and for itself – since that's an untenable position. Nor is it possible to believe innocently that any classroom oral activity in English simply and directly enhances language development. Although to put a position in regard to oral work in those terms may seem entirely negative, I believe it is possible – necessary, even – to work from that position towards a much more expansive definition of oracy in education.

PROPOSALS FOR PRACTICE

The few suggestions that follow can only partly address the issues raised by the problematic identity of oral work in English. It would be rash to pretend that they could be resolved easily; but they can be taken much more fully into account in a practical sense than tends to be the case at present.

Here it is essential that the practical practice of the subject itself addresses the issues and brings them into some kind of explicit focus. The importance of this is the effect it has on changing the identity of the subject, so that the established, taken for granted procedures and foundations cannot remain unperturbed. A reflexive mode – a mode of practice which doesn't accept the activity in and for itself alone, a mode which makes explicit a number of important determinant features – seems to me to be as essential in this context as in any other. In the end this would imply radical changes in the assessment procedures of oral work in English – changes in the direction of an insistence on the necessary recognition of differences of language as positive.

How can oral work in English begin to address the institutional context, and the nexus of power and authority that functions in schools and other institutions? How could students begin to explore the forms of oral exchange that characterize so many linguistic encounters in the school context? How could students begin to get hold of some kind of analysis or definition of the constraints on oracy that operate in institutional contexts, and, conversely, to analyse or define the kinds of linguistic exchanges that are enabled, and produced by institutions? And would it really be possible for students themselves to undertake a general critical evaluation of orality as it is determined by characteristic definitions of work and productivity in institutions? In fact, to attempt that in the end might well require that students develop a whole sense of the construction and maintenance of meanings within institutions – a demanding and far-reaching theoretical enterprise.

On the other hand, what other approach is possible which doesn't pretend to be simply valuable and productive in itself?

ACTIVITIES – SOME PROPOSALS

An extended section of oral work – or a complete course – may be instigated taking examples from standard practice and giving them different emphases by introducing new elements into them, to give a theoretical emphasis to practical procedures.

1   Issues

The piece of work shown in Example 5.1 follows the standard form while including some consideration of the politics of public rhetoric and the politics of agendas of debate. Where possible, students may find out about access to different kinds of information from different sources, too, and this aspect can obviously be an important part of the work they're doing. The emphasis here can be given to exploring different positions taken in relation to topical issues and to some consideration of the different groups of people who might adopt or be in accord with different positions. Many other topics can be suggested by the students themselves.

Example 5.1   Oral work on contemporary issues

This is, initially, a piece of oral work that will involve a lot of preparation and will end with a final presentation. A piece of writing may emerge from the work you do on this topic.

You will be working mainly in a group of four or five.

These are some issues which people might think of as being 'controversial' or important in the world today:

abortion	peace
drugs	nuclear weapons
death penalty	education

There are many others, too. You should try to identify some of them. Try also – in your groups – to agree on 1) an order of importance, and 2) an order of interest to you.

When you have decided what issue you want to tackle you will need to discuss and define a few things:

1 what are the main aspects of the issue?
2 what different opinions / positions are there in relation to this issue?
3 how will different kinds and different groups of people regard this issue?

You will then need to consider how you can construct a presentation which takes into account all the above points. Your presentation could include:

speeches	explanations	writing
drama	dialogue	arguments

You should carefully consider the kind of language used to express different positions taken up by people in relation to the issue you're dealing with.

You should also consider what general beliefs about the world and society people have who take up particular positions in relation to the issue in question.

When you are preparing your presentation you should check through this sheet to ensure that you have followed the directions completely.

2   Role-play

The topic of role-play can be configured anew including some consideration of social class and dialect and role-play in real life social drama. This could mean examining the relations between role-play and the languages of social intercourse, involving consideration of languages in relation to power, the power of standard English and institutional power and social groupings. The complex relations between institutions, language and power can be formulated in an active approach which incorporates theoretical perspectives. This might include an analysis of how roles are acted out within institutional formations as shown in Example 5.2.

Example 5.2   An approach to language and role-play

For this exercise you will be working in groups of three or four.

For this exercise you are required to draw up your own role-play situations. You will need to define:

- the participants in the role-play
- the social identity of the different participants
- their roles
- the kind of language they speak and what special features it is characterized by
- the institutional context within which it takes place
- the topic, or topics of the role-play situation
- the perspective or perspectives taken by each participant
- the institutional context, or contexts, that have a bearing on the role-play situation and the contributions made by institutional context in defining the roles of the participants

You will need to examine at least three role-play situations in order to begin to explore different possible forms of encounter. Try to find examples in real contexts and draw some conclusions from them. You might then find it possible to more clearly construct a role-play situation of your own devising.

---

3   Small group discussions

Characteristically, small group discussions concern snippets of literature, to be worked on for decipherment or explication. The practice of small group discussion, though, is often conceived of as worthy of

pursuit in itself, and it is certainly the case that in much liberal/
progressive practice, whether explicitly or implicitly influenced by
certain kinds of reading of Vygotsky, a small group discussing a poem
is doing something worthy, irrespective of the poem and irrespective of
the kind of interpretation or orientation of the discussion.

Clearly, the possibilities of small group discussion are truly endless.
Anything could be the focus for talk of this kind. And it is generally
taken for granted that an element of good teaching involves the
dicussion of topics in small groups – whether or not that leads to a
larger discussion. It is useful, practically, for a number of reasons. And
it is perfectly easy to introduce into the general scenario of small group
talk in the classroom some indicators that might lend a useful theoretical perspective on the process. The following pointers – or some of
them – might provide a useful guideline for a reflexive approach to
small group talk.

What is the subject of the discussion? Can the subject be changed?
How and in what ways?
What do you think is expected of you by this conversation and the
way it has been set up? Why?
What kind of language is likely to be considered suitable for this
topic? Are there other kinds of language that might be used? What
might they be? What might be the effects of using them?
In what different contexts might discussions of this topic take place?
With what different participants? With what different effects?

Small group discussion could then be set up to consider important linguistic features, including the motivation and control of the subject; the
occasion of the exchange and the constraints it imposes; the rhetoric of
discussion and the determining effects of the context of the discussion.

4 Sociolinguistic analysis

The outline in Example 5.3, or something like it, could be used with
students, to encourage them to conduct their own analyses of oracy.

This could take the form of preliminary tools for investigations. It
could be applied to many different kinds of context, contexts that could
be discussed, and taxonomized, as part of an extensive project.

5 Projects in oral ethnography

This kind of analytic work could be developed in the form of specific
projects. A number of these would be relevant to an emphasis on

Example 5.3　Sociolinguistic analysis: a guide for the elementary analysis of speech acts/speech situations

---

Questions To Answer:

　What is the occasion of the conversation?
　What is the subject of the conversation?
　What is (are) the function(s) of the conversation?
　In what context is the conversation taking place?
　What roles are being taken by each of the participants?
　How many people are present at the conversation?
　Who is participating in the conversation?
　Who is talking most?
　What kinds of things are being said? With what vocabulary?
　What are the differences between speakers?

---

theoretical material and its implications for the productions of meanings in specific social contexts. The following topics could provide the grounds for a great deal of small group work – oral work both analytic and productive in kind:

Dialect and social class

Students could examine extracts from sociolinguistics or could simply be introduced to some of the main ideas. They could do active work looking at the ways in which dialects may deviate from standard English, for example. Interesting ethnographic work could then be done devising and using questionnaires to examine how dialect speakers experience their relations with standard English in the different contexts they move in.

The language of youth cultures – subcultural groups

Similar work could be done to examine the different kinds of language used by different youth subcultural groups – looking at variations in vocabulary, for example, and relating these to different sets of beliefs and ideological positions expressed by different groups.

6　Oral work and media analyses

Oral analysis might very usefully be applied to media products; and this could form the basis for what might be called a sociolinguistics of the media. This would offer a way of addressing media products, focusing on the way in which they represent spoken language, and language differences, for example.

Focusing on the way the media represent sociolinguistic phenomena could, clearly, provide the basis for a good deal of analytic and productive work. Analyses of media products – and the way they represent different kinds of language, the way they may 'stage' different kind of rhetoric, and the way they may linguistically represent different social groups of various kinds – could be very instructive and could provide the basis for looking at students' own productions, and for looking at alternative modes of representation to those that seem to be dominant. This kind of analysis could obviously add a necessary supplement to other forms of semiotic analysis of media products – and could easily be managed by students along the lines suggested below.

Soap operas – dialect and social class; the language of the family; the language of the representation of gender differences.

News broadcasts – the different kinds of language in play in news broadcasts.

Analyses of TV schedules – looking at different times taken up by different kinds of language.

Analysis of radio – for example, radio 4 and/or radio 1, going on to examine different audiences, audience responses to different kinds of languages.

Analyses of different forms of popular music – the different forms of language and the different vocabularies they utilize.

(Alternatively, students could define and examine texts using their own terms of reference, determining issues for themselves and organizing their own findings.) Any of the above could be addressed using the kind of relatively simple, interrogative forms of analysis, I have outlined. A teaching of language, though, which encouraged some – even rudimentary – awareness of issues of a sociolinguistic nature, could quite easily generate the possibilities for a different kind of oral work. The kind of oral work I've attempted to begin defining here is practically analytic and practically active, but also has some theoretical direction and some commitment to the idea that the social and the linguistic are closely linked. The significance of this differently conceived kind of oral work is that it goes beyond the simply active models that assume, perhaps too easily, that the classroom can itself be the site for the free development of oracy.

I would consider an important aim of any attempt to redefine oral work that it be applied to, or that it address, explicitly, institutional language practices. It would then be possible to give a more specific, theoretical focus to the connections between language and the social, to address more clearly the relations between institutional structures, different forms of language and institutional power. This might well engage debates about the issue of standard and non-standard English – but again with a more sharply theoretical edge and with the possibility of formulating a vocabulary beyond the limited scope of common-sense and established, habitual practice to deal with the issue. Even role-play, for example, an established favourite, can be redefined to take on extra dimensions and be much more ambitious in its scope; by enacting debates about issues in sociolinguistics, by framing established activities in a context of theorizing which gives them specific point and direction. Standard oral work practices may be specifically motivated and may provide a context for explicit, conscious and self-conscious understanding.

These suggestions are preliminary only. To address the issues of orality in relation to English in this manner – as though it could ever be a discrete entity anyway – is false. But given that English makes of oracy a separate – and not fully intrusive – component of the exam process, its worth considering how the practices of oral work might be transformed in the direction of theoretical awareness, in order to highlight the place of oracy and the idea of orality within the contexts of the institutions that have some fairly powerful determining force in deciding what it is, how it is to be officially described, defined and – in the end and rather crudely – judged.

So the kind of oral work described rather sketchily above is continuous with the suggestions for developing theoretical preoccupations of other kinds of work, other fundamental categories of the subject. Oral work can be undertaken in the form of a project that is specifically constructed to address issues of language and power in a general sense as with Example 5.4.

Example 5.4   Language and power

In relation to class discussions about language and power, you are asked to produce some kind of presentation dealing with issues relating to the following points:

- In what different ways are language and power related? Give specific examples.
- What different languages of power are there? Give some specific examples.
- Define some different contexts where language and power can be seen to operate. Describe specific examples.
- Does language of one kind remain powerful in all contexts? Consider the question in relation to specific examples.

- Describe/define two different kinds of language in terms of the style/ manner and vocabulary of the languages.
- Is any one kind of language better than another? How might judgements about that question get made? Consider the case of standard English and other kinds of English.

This investigative work could then lead into a more complex exercise along the lines shown in Example 5.5.

Example 5.5 Making a documentary or presentation on language and power

To make a documentary about language and power consider the following:

- an introduction – identifying the issues in relation to language and power that you are going to try to explore, and explaining something about how you intend to begin to look at those issues, explaining what different positions might be taken;
- an explanation of context or contexts – looking at different kinds of language and how they operate in different contexts; looking also at how different contexts position speakers;
- different language identities – looking at how different speakers will be given identities in relation to the language they speak and the way they speak it;
- people using languages in different contexts – bringing together both the previous sections, looking at how language identities of individuals may change in different contexts, but also considering how certain language identities will tend to be excluded from certain contexts or will be less powerful within them;
- institutions and languages of power – looking at the way particular institutions organize different identities for people and looking at how these different identities may be expressed in different kinds of language;

  a conclusion and concluding questions – looking at the implications of the various things you've been considering, the issues they've raised, considering what questions may be asked about language and power – and what conclusions you may want to draw.

You need to plan out the shape of your documentary production, considering the different elements you want to include, how you will present them and how they will be put into sequence.

CONCLUSION

Although some of the preceding drift of this chapter has been a critique of the *specific* practices of oral English, it is important from a theoretical point of view to consider oral practices as belonging to the whole enterprise of English. The daily conduct of the subject is theoretically understood in terms of its general assumptions – the principles that are consistent with the ideological bias of the subject. The history of oral English makes it a relative latecomer into the subject's constitution, as a part of a general liberalizing trend. Liberal models of the subject were partly developed in relation to various currents of linguistics that were identified as significant – while others, of course, were ignored or rejected. The writings of Vygotsky, for example, on psychology and linguistics, provide a characteristic example of the way the subject was being determined by a specific kind of liberal model. Certain strands of Vygotsky's thought were incorporated into English. Small group discussion work, especially, was given a theoretical basis in a reading of Vygotsky that adopted certain aspects of Vygotsky's ideas and rejected or ignored others, specifically those concerned with the political dimensions of language and speech. Oral English came into (official) being without any established way of addressing the political dimension of language and with no explicit aim to address it at all. Oral English was never introduced as an element of a theoretical revision of English; it was an addendum, and as such was unlikely, though ostensibly officially adding another very significant dimension to the subject, to effect any fundamental constitutional change of it.

The way that oral English was absorbed without effecting a significant, theoretical change has had important consequences and these may be seen as contradictions or difficulties that English has had to face – and which remain – in relation to the practice and the status of oral work. In the first place the liberal practice of the subject must confront the problem involved in the very *demand* for oral work from its students. The demand is of its nature anything but liberal. It necessarily involves constraint and – in the context of the school – implies assessment. The most liberal of liberal practices cannot shuffle off the determination of what it does by the nature of the institutional context in which it gets done. The explicit recognition of this is very much counter to the liberal declaration concerning oral work – where oral work, more than writing, is seen to implicate the very nature of the individual in a more immediate sense. Admittedly, this is a problem for all educational practices in schools, but liberal versions of English have no means of addressing the problematics of the institutional power of the subject. In the second place, the liberal model of the subject must also confront the recognition that, while it may itself have argued for a greater role for oral work in official, publicly institutionalized English – in the form of what gets examined as juridically present on the syllabus – the secondary, lesser role for the oral component is clearly and unequivocally expressed in the relative weighting given to oral and written work in assessment. If speaking is really central to English, why is its assessment constructed as an affair of supplementary significance? The liberal model of the subject may feel uneasy about all that, but again has no way of explicitly and directly addressing it – either in its debates with itself or in its favoured practices.

It remains the case that oral expression, though arguably of infinitely greater significance in general, everyday discourses, is relegated in the institutional discourse of English to supplementary significance. Oral English is somehow less official, less trustworthy than written English. This relegation of importance corresponds to a general suspicion or hesitancy about the assessment of oral English. It seems there remains a general feeling among English teachers that oral English is decidedly more difficult to examine than written English. The reasons for this are varied; though many possibilities come to mind. For example, many English teachers in oral assessment meetings will express great hesitancy in assessing oral performance, and will want to know a great deal about the context of the performance in relation to all sorts of parameters that they are generally uninterested in in relation to writing. The general hesitancy and uncertainty might be traced to the residual importance of two dominant factors. The first is the idea of objectivity in examining – the notion that criteria of assessment are established as objective measures of performance. The fallacy of this notion may be self-evident, but it remains central to the possibility of assessment in English. In oral work – perhaps because of its relative newness, perhaps because of its association with what is deemed to be subjective – the established procedures of assessment enjoy a much less secure foundation. The second factor concerns social class and forms of ethnicity that operate different kinds of English from the standard form. The liberal model of the subject – just like its more traditionalist associate – cannot afford to recognize the grounding and application of oral criteria in differences of social class. While the more liberal of the liberal advocates might suspect that the whole enterprise of oral assessment is dubious, it's unlikely that their suspicions will have been translated into practices addressing the problem. To do that would necessarily involve a critique of the whole foundation of the identity of the subject, and would necessitate a rejection of the liberal model.

So there is a mistrust of assessment in oral work. It's too slippery and too indefinite. Writing is fixed and available and the criteria are well-established. Writing can be judged according to criteria that are objective, and its conditions of production, its authenticity can be guaranteed. Oral work involves judging too many variable factors, factors that go beyond the proper jurisdiction of the subject: there's the nature of the exercise to consider, how it was set up, the personality of the speaker, the suitability of the assignment; there may be relative roles in a role-play of interlocutors to take into account – all factors, among others, that might well make teaching examiners hesitant in the face of assessment, but, nevertheless, factors which are always anyway in play in any language situation, oral or written.

Oral English has generally been conceived of as practical, but is rooted in notions of language that are quite specific and strictly limited. Theory is a necessary component in moving beyond the inertia of dominant models to realize new forms and possibilities. It is possible to begin to formulate a practice of oral work addressing theory in its activities, making explicit the issues involved in relation to the social dimensions of language in general and within the context of English and education specifically.

6 Literature, language, literacy and values

THE CONSTITUTION OF THE SUBJECT

Analysis of the subject's view of literacy indicates characteristic gaps and particular mystifications. Literacy in education has been closely associated, if not equated, with something called 'reading', although the idea of reading has not been extensively analysed in English. This fundamental concept still tends to be figured naively as the individual reader alone with her or his (innate?) skills and chosen text developing happily and more or less freely through a graduated – though probably not too schematized – sequence of worthy texts. Another, and complementary, way of representing the reading process in English is to imagine the class as a body guided by the reading skills of the teacher and enthralled by the teacher's chosen text. Literacy and literature – as in both cases mentioned – have been all too simply and naively linked, with a definition of literature that has been, curiously, both remarkably narrow on the one hand, and on the other hand very much undefined. Though the approaches broadly outlined above may seem unexceptionable, they arouse all sorts of questions. Their predominance effectively displaces alternative ways of understanding and teaching reading that might be offered by a different and more inclusive notion of literacy.

The peculiar domination of fiction and the idea of poetry are only examples of the anomalies that have operated, and still operate powerfully in this context. These peculiarities, or anomalies, have been allowed to stand because they have been perfectly in accord with a specific subject ideology – a set of well established, but not always very explicitly expressed or justified, beliefs and practices. In fact, many of these beliefs and practices have become so well entrenched as to appear to be beyond question. This has certainly been the case for dominant reading practices, dominant versions of English – the kind of English you might find expressed in any offical syllabus, in liberal accounts of the subject and in countless examples of daily practice. This loosely defined notion of the subject and of its equally ingenuous model of literacy has enjoyed an almost theological status in some quarters.

Alternative versions of the subject have hitherto lacked institutional power, and have often found themselves in the contradictory position of colluding with that which they oppose. Ideas defining literacy as socially governed and reading practices as determined by institutional contexts, have not been considered within the terms of reference of established English. Even the most cursory glance through a copy of examination assessment criteria indicates that literacy is represented as a matter of individual competence, not of social construction. A historical survey of examination documents tells the same story. In the face of the power of these unconsidered assumptions, it is important to assert, or reassert, that literacy is not a self-defining thing. Literacy is not something you get on your own, or that is given to you simply by the learning processes set up in schools. Literacy is not one stable thing which you simply have or don't have. Literacy is subject to change, to redefinition and to challenge. It is, really, a scandalous fact that generations of students in state education have been taught to believe themselves to be inadequate in relation to literacy, not because they are, but because the institutions they passed through operated a strictly limited model of literacy. The literacy competences of these people were not admissible within the scheme of things. They were not the competences required by the institution. The operative model of literacy was, and largely remains, punitive and exclusive.

It was partly in the name of literature that this process of discrimination was and is maintained. Some institutions may have gone boldly against the grain of things in an attempt to give their students literature as a kind of cultural capital, in the belief that it was somehow intrinsically good for them, and that they were worthy of it, independently of their social origins. These efforts, though, in so far as they were serious, determined and democratic, were few and far between and were constantly confronted with the problem of the power of the institution – the institution of English. Literature was not alone in the process of making literacy limited and exclusive. Approaches to writing were also bound up with similarly restricted ideas about what it means to be effectively literate. Language practices – whether thoroughly mechanistic or ostentatiously creative – were embedded in a strictly qualified notion of effective literacy, a notion that – whatever else it was – was denuded of history, sociology and cultural theory. In English, the operative models of the subject, lacking social theory, lacking comprehensive theories of language, lacking any critical grasp of the operations of institutions in education, could hardly fail to be closely tied to the most discriminatory practices of schooling. To simplify, but not to oversimplify: models of language determining practices of writing in English were broadly founded on notions of accuracy, lucidity, appropriateness and fullness of expression. It was as though these things were self-evident qualities that all intelligent people would recognize and value equally when they saw them. Failure to achieve competence in attaining these qualities could then be written off as attributable to innate deficits – either of intelligence or of inclination or of social background. At a later stage, a fully fledged idea of creativity – based on a belief in the creative intelligences of individuals, and the creative resources of language – became significant and influential in English. From this 'creative' perspective, the 'whole' person is to be engaged in writing. Writing, like reading, is a means of personal growth, a means by which the individual can explore and discover his or her own identity in the order of things. When elements of the creative English teaching fraternity discovered an (albeit partially) social reading of the meaning of the subject and saw that the models it operated were disadvantaging the already marginalized students whose class background or ethnic origin excluded them from educational success, aspects of both approaches were adopted in an attempt to equip disadvantaged students either with a purchase on standard forms and/or to grant them the freedom to freely express themselves in their own languages, unconstrained by false notions of the correct. The development of an emphasis on the value of oracy as an idea and as a kind of practice was continuous with the positive recognition of language differences – and the implicit, at least, realization of the domination of standard forms of English. The negotiation of this tricky territory, though, was never fully theorized nor effectively managed. It was partly the absence of coherent theories of the language, education and culture nexus that meant it was not possible to implement this position as a fully reformulated definition of the proper aims and objectives of English, nor of a substantially defined alternative practice. These absences ensured that broadly and structurally English remained unchanged. English was still dominated – at the level of ideas, and overwhelmingly at the level of practice – by a conceptual framework that consorted unhappily with social analysis and cultural critique.

The intentions of all the positions and projects outlined sketchily and simply above may well have been honourable. They may well have produced plenty of examples of 'good practice', and at least some had the positive virtue of beginning to address relations between the dominant institutionalized forms of the subject and its constituency.

They were, however, still purblind to the politics of the subject – to the politics of education, the politics inevitably implicit in all institutionalized practices of language and literacy. Lacking critical theories about the constitution of the academic discourses they were engaged with, lacking a critical sense of the identity of the 'subject' of education (and therefore unable to construct working alternative models of any power), they were lumbered with impossible contradictions.

THE GHOST OF LITERATURE: IDENTITY AND THE QUESTION OF VALUES

Although in some very significant senses the idea of literature may be dead, or slowly dying, the ghost of the intrinsic value of literature still haunts a great deal of English teaching. Historically embedded in the constitution of the subject, literature has been and remains a determinant characteristic of the subject's identity. The residual presence of literature belongs as much to popular conceptions of the subject as to the educational arena, implicated in popularly, professionally and institutionally cherished ideas of English. There are many reasons why the hegemony of literature in English should be considered an anachronism in need of change.

The idea of literature as a special category worthy of attention in itself, with its own special qualities and specific effects, and its very own modes of engagement is really a very dubious affair. This is a philosophical issue – in the sense that what literature is cannot be defined in terms of any essential features nor in terms of any unique qualities or effects it might have. Literature has to be maintained by specific groups in specific practices – and these tend to be minority affairs conducted in academic institutions, though often endorsed in many other contexts. In schools, the idea of literature has been generally maintained by professional English teachers whose professional identity relies on the maintenance of the special identity and special qualities of literature. Teachers of English have believed, in a necessary ideological move, that literature really does exist – *in itself*, somehow – and that it really does have intrinsic qualities that make it worthy of study in itself. They have maintained, one way or another, that literature is generally very good for you, if you're lucky enough – or sensitive enough – to appreciate it. If you're not able to appreciate it this is likely to be due to innate insensitivity or poor social conditioning, or maybe the general decline of culture into technological mindlessness and media intoxication. This position has been held as an act of faith, sometimes loosely as a more or less casual assumption, sometimes fervently as a messianic project. The question of literature, then, is clearly not just a philosophical issue. It engages questions about institutions and professional identities, about ideology and culture, and about the sociology and the history of education, too.

It may well seem, repetitious to rehearse the same old questions; but there remains a case to be answered. There are a number of vitally important issues at stake in asking: What is literature? Why is literature given a privileged position? What values does literature represent? Theoretical tunnel vision to the challenging force of questions about the problem of the identity of literature, and the problem of the value of literature, has been necessary to its very existence in English. One of the major snags with the valorization of the whole idea of literature – and the same applies to the more specific idea of English Literature – as is well known, is that what exactly it is has proven to be something of a problem. In terms of deciding what's in it and what's not, the identity of literature has never been clear and uncontested. Nobody can say definitively and authoritatively what it is. The so-called 'canon' has only ever been an idea of mutable substance. Without the defining body of a canon, the idea of literature threatens to spill over into complete formlessness. The insuperable problem of defining where the boundaries between English Literature and general literature might be drawn effectively deconstructs the very foundations of the identities of both. Literature can hardly operate, then, as a defining principle. Like Wittgenstein's beetle in the box; it's quite possible that everyone is referring to something quite different when they invoke it. It's consequently rather bizarre that the teaching of literature, though no-one really knows what it is, has been in places at times advocated with a missionary polemic, as though matters of theological importance were at stake. At the same time it's perfectly obvious – given the indefinite identity of the thing – that literature should be justified with various kinds of grandiose rhetoric.

English in schools – in its traditionalist or liberal versions – has never properly sorted out its attitude towards English Literature, nor ever really clarified its attitude towards literature, while pragmatically asserting the centrality of either or both these ideas. English remains, however, saddled with the idea of literature, one way or the other. The continuing significance of the idea of literature is evident in the general practice of the subject in schools and is confirmed in plenty of documents expressive of institutional power – from examination sylla-buses to government initiated reports. In spite of the contradictions and flaws of definition the idea is heir to, in spite of gestures made towards 'cultural studies' models of the subject, literature remains a pretty much universally acknowledged practice, as well as a dominant concept. In a recent edition of the *Times Educational Supplement* (June 14 1991) various luminaries are cited to justify and reaffirm literature:

> "The experience of literature is central to the English curriculum because it can illuminate the experiences, thoughts and feelings of students . . ."
> "Of course every child should study literature because it promises practical, intellectual and personal rewards . . ."
> "A nation's literature is a mirror in which its children learn to recognize themselves . . ."

Even though what's said here about literature could equally well be said about any number of things, there seems to be a general consensus at work. You can read about the 'essential' and 'central' nature of the experience of literature in official documents authorized by NATE – the body supposed to represent the interests and reflect the thinking of English teaching in a broad and general way. Claims of this kind are based on the assumption that literature exists in an unproblematic way, that it is clearly identifiable without contradiction. Actually, though, literature within the practices of English in secondary education has not really been sustained in any clear and unequivocal way. It has proven difficult to espouse the fully grown version of literature for the full range of the comprehensive constituency, anyway. English Literature 'proper' (though this has always been a changing and uncertain thing) has hardly been a category that English teachers in schools have really subscribed to – or rarely for *all* their students. Not being able to ditch the concept altogether and address a broad and inclusive textual field, English in schools has therefore had to live with an ersatz literature, the value of which has never been fully formulated, has never been very explicitly affirmed nor fully examined. What has been taught for examination at sixteen plus under the name English Literature has included many things ranging from Zeffirelli's film of *Romeo and Juliet*, to *Lord of the Flies*, *Zigger-Zagger*, *Of Mice and Men*, *Roll of Thunder, Hear My Cry* and Seamus Heaney's 'Digging' along with a host of other non-canonical, marginally canonical or pseudo-canonical texts. Whatever this literature has been, it has hardly ever been thoroughly and strictly English Literature. It has more probably been maintained because it has been necessary, for the maintenance of the identity of the subject, to hold onto the notion and practice of literature as distinct from absolutely *other* forms – of popular culture, for example. At least this has had the minimal virtue of giving the subject a content all of its own, even though the content may be pretty vaguely defined. The odd but well-established contradiction at work in all this has been central to the continuity of the identity of the subject.

In recent times, English in schools has tended to feel more comfortable with the idea of general literature. English has pragmatically, and perhaps cynically, maintained the generalized, but still very restricted idea of 'stories and poems' – ascribing (often in the form of ritual invocations of value) to these nebulous categories properties making the subject worthy of being. A host of texts – stories and poems unlikely to find themselves inscribed in *anyone*'s version of a canon – have constituted what is generally referred to and valued as literature, a substitute sub-canon without limits or definition. Justifications – and many of them have been hyperbolically grandiose – for exposure to this never defined body of texts have tended to be expressed in the terms of a vaguely liberal ideology, and are largely inscribed in established reading practices in English in schools, though not at all uniformly so. The guiding principles involved in this general nexus of ideas, attitudes and beliefs – expressed in terms like 'personal response', 'empathy', 'exploration' and so on – are drastically susceptible to serious contest by analysis of language and textuality as social and institutional practices.

The case of 'poetry' provides a classic illustration of how fundamental categories belonging to the idea of literature are bound up with mystification and confusion. Subjected to self-conscious reappraisal, the problems of definition and of value won't go away. The innumerable instances of the claim that poetry is of value rest on the assumption that the identity of poetry is a recognizable entity, for one thing, and that it is in some way bound to be worthwhile, once you can get it going. Like literature, though, the category of poetry has no beginning and no end. It can only exist as an institutionalized practice. The identity of poetry is very much a shifting one: current practices associated with the idea of poetry are very different from those now outmoded practices that had elementary school children, for instance, learning poems from *Palgrave's Treasury* by heart. The very identity of poetry has been changing ever since then, but it has never really settled into any distinctive body. What's more the special properties that might be ascribed to poetry might equally be claimed for a number of other things – such as popular music in various forms, though it has been important in the context of English to maintain a more or less clear distinction between them. What poetry is supposed to be and do, and its place in the curriculum has been completely uncertain and changing, but it rests in the end on specific and really ideological assumptions about texts, language and literacy, much of which ideology is not subject to critical appraisal. The same kind of uncritical thinking is implicated in the idea of writing poetry. There persists the idea that poetry is an activity that students of English should be engaged in by some kind of absolute imperative.

Equally uncertain and as potentially contentious as the identity of literature is the discourse of literary study, the established form of literary 'knowledge'. Although represented as the natural and proper way to study texts, the discourse of textual analysis in the study of literature is generally quite specific and certainly very limited. It's dominant species operates an amalgam of ideas, like personal response, and yet it structures responses according to a set of quite fixed assumptions about how texts and reading processes operate. This set of notions about texts and reading gives credence to the idea that texts have intrinsic meanings, though personal response promises the adventure of thoroughly individual meanings. Personal response, though, can't really ever be personal. Responses to texts are conditioned by all sorts of impersonal factors, and responses in English are conditioned by the habits of thought that are legitimated by the order determined by the subject's institutionalized identity. Other examples of ideas that dominate are to do with things like the author's intentions, the reading of proper names as 'character', with narrative continuity, with textual integrity and many other highly questionable things. Without the dubious notions of textual integrity, though, and of intrinsic meaning, there can't really be any reason why the favoured texts of English – whether English Literature or stories and poems – should continue to hold any kind of privileged position or status. There are, after all, countless other texts and signifying practices that a subject concerned with those things might address.

The values literature represents really belong to a specific social and ethnic group. It is not necessarily within the cultural value systems of all. Its identity is quite clearly set against the identity of popular culture; and for many people, including students in schools, is therefore alienating. This can be experienced as a form of social discrimination. The culturally valued artefacts of one group are given higher status and accorded greater significance than those of other groups, who see the cultural products they value being systematically excluded as insignificant, meaningless or trivial. This is a blatant case of cultural domination. It's also unquestionably, and troublingly, the case that the idea of English Literature has been closely associated with a conception of national identity – and to a large extent this continues to be the case. There has been a great deal of writing in recent times demonstrating how the subject as part of national state education was founded on the idea that English Literature constituted a vital element in our general cultural heritage. The idea of a specifically English culture, though, and of a literature bearing its values, is, pretty obviously, contentious. It presupposes and ignores a number of important factors. It presupposes, for one thing, some kind of commonly grounded national identity with generally common cultural experience and values. This is not necessarily the case, though. It reflects only one limited perspective on the nature of national identity, a narrow definition of culture and one quite specific notion of social structure.

To represent English as a project invoking the idea of a common cultural heritage must involve some notion of a homogeneous culture which all members benefit from and share in equally. Culture in this sense might generally be conceived of as a positive force representing the finer things, the more elevated expressions of general truths. Or it might represent the expressions of the common identity, purposes, beliefs and values of a people. These positions are bound to run into difficulties if we consider, for instance, that general truths must always be culturally specific, that the very identity of things is *not* universal, but is a culturally produced ordering, a set of symbolic meanings belonging to a particular cultural perspective. It's hardly possible, though, on any kind of modernist or post-modernist understanding to think of culture in this homogeneous sense. Culture in a modern state, in a modern society, is not something that belongs to everyone equally and always in the same way. Culture is splintered among different groups. Cultural differences are manifested by groups whose difference might be expressed in terms of age, gender, class, ethnicity, locality, employment, religion, political beliefs and so on. It's difficult to think of a cultural phenomenon that might erase all those differences in one unifying movement. Although that is what has been claimed at times on behalf of English literature – a cultural phenomenon that can hardly be said to speak for all those differences equally.

Literature has certainly not ever been something that has been enjoyed or attained or aspired to equally by all. Cultural differences may well represent positions that are likely to conflict with one another and be in a state of contest rather than of harmony. The thoroughly functionalist view of culture, represented by the idea of communicating a common cultural heritage, is the product of a specific perspective that claims its own version of culture to be culture *itself*. This is a thoroughly unsound notion, philosophically speaking. In the end, it indicates a will to promote one set of cultural experiences, values and beliefs over others – of no less merit but of considerably less established power. What's more, it's increasingly difficult to see how the notion of a specifically national cultural identity can be maintained when so much cultural experience is transnational – when the media of cultural experience have tended to intermingle things in a post-modern frenzy of intertextual activity. The transnational, transcultural character of much of modern cultural experience has only been minimally recognized in the idea of a multicultural approach to literature.

Multiculturalism, though, may have a neatly deconstructive impact on the idea of English Literature and its predominance. If, for example, the Bengali novel might be included in English, what about other kinds of novel and what about other kinds of cultural product. The idea of a specifically and specially *English* literature breaks down. But multi-culturalism remains, in its present general condition, tied to the notion of literature. The assumption, again speaking generally, is that cultural difference is explored most effectively in the form of imaginative fictions of one kind or another. The idea that there are complexities in terms of how cultures adopt other alien and perhaps dominant cultural forms is rarely explored in this context. Also the problem of how to teach multicultural literature where a culture may not have a literature in the commonly accepted sense is not confronted. Another problem in relation to multiculturalism concerns how conventional reading prac-tices determine the kinds of reading that texts assumed to be speaking from a different cultural perspective might be given. All of this – all these difficulties – will remain unaddressed for just as long as the subject lacks a proper social theory of culture in relation to a general conception of signifying practices. Multicultural literature remains within the limited confines of the ideas and practices of literature. A more expansive concept of textuality and language might make more effective use of the varied perspectives on things that multiculturalism potentially offers. At least in its present forms it challenges the idea of a predominantly English literature.

Literature has tended to express and reflect the interests of dominant groups in the social structure; whatever its intentions to the contrary, the notion of literature has depended on a sense of textual hierarchy. The study of English Literature has tended – in the context of state school education – to represent the interests of certain groups while failing to address the interests and concerns of other groups. The modes and values of literature have been seen as being set in opposition to the values and modes of popular culture. Popular culture has frequently in the past been denigrated at the expense of a high culture that has embraced literature as an important aspect of itself. It has been one of the defining features claimed for literature that it is more subtle, more rich and complex, less crude and manipulative, less riddled with cliché and free from the taint of commercial interests. None of these features belong especially to literature in any absolute sense. The clear opposition between literature and popular culture is only really maintained from one particular and very limited notion of what culture is – and it depends on a very partial sense of cultural identity.

The fear of the cultural melting pot is never very far away from the cry for the reassertion of common cultural values or for a reassertion of traditional literature. The very identity of Shakespeare as an idea is bound up with a sense of the national identity. The project of a specifically *English* literature at the centre of a specifically *English* schooling might be seen as the desire to sustain an ethnocentric and mythological national identity against the threatened incursions of an alien other – whether this other is the alien within, in the form of an inferior popular or mass culture, or whether it is the alien without, in the form of texts or cultural forms that express ethnic difference.

The idea of the intrinsic value of literature weighs on English, and the question about why it should remain privileged over other forms of text or language use that it isn't clearly distinguished from anyway, remains practically unaddressed, though visible in a number of forms. The values that literature and its teaching represent haven't been critically analysed. In spite of all its problems of definition and identity, literature grinds on, an odd assortment of texts loosely held together, never inscribed in any defining taxonomy, nor defined in terms of essential features. In this sense, at least, there's more hanky-panky in English than there is in Madonna.

Where does all this leave English Literature and English in schooling? If literature is merely chimerical, a nebulous category without definition, and if the rationales for its continued existence are thin, unconvincing and radically questionable, shouldn't the practice and the rhetoric of literature have done the decent thing and retired discreetly from the scene. Perhaps this is a reasonable, if not popular, proposition. For many practitioners of English, there's no doubt that a thoroughgoing deconstruction of literature does cause anxiety and concern, because the effect of such a deconstruction is to radically problematize the nature of the subject. For what groups of people does the deconstruction of the idea of literature represent a threat? In many quarters, it has would be seen as a negative thing, but there is no need to view a complete and thoroughly critical revaluation of the special place of literature as destructive. The deconstruction of the idea of literature suggests new and multiplied possibilities, rather than the reduction involved in persisting with the limitations of literature.

POPULAR CULTURE

One important function of English Literature has been to make a clear distinction between, for example, Madonna and itself. English has hitherto been organized around a segregation between its texts and texts of the order of popular culture. Popular culture has been denigrated explicitly and implicitly in the process. The case of Madonna, though, might provide an instance of an arguably complex and important cultural phenomenon, belonging to a complex and richly rewarding cultural form – popular music – and evidently capable of being addressed as a rich and rewarding intertext, as many feminist writers, for example, have chosen to do. Plenty of other examples of popular culture might be construed as capable of raising complex issues about a range of textual and intertextual phenomena. As an example of a mode of signifying practice, Madonna may well constitute a text, or series of intertexts, worth attending to, worth looking at from a number of different perspectives, worth thinking about and exploring. Consideration might, for example, be given to examples of videos and how they work, to the way Madonna is defined in the press, is produced and reproduced in countless different accounts. Attention might be given to different ways of reading Madonna, different reading techniques that might be applied and to different kinds of interpretation that might be made. Attention might also be given to audiences of Madonna and in what different ways Madonna might be received. Madonna might be examined in relation to complementary and contrasting kinds of texts or intertexts, connected by issues that could be interesting to define. A variety of media would need to be addressed to undertake work of this kind – and the relations between different media could be explored. A host of challenging and engaging possibilities could be constructed, dealing with texts and textual fields in a number of different ways.

In the present organization of the subject, it isn't really conceivable for Madonna to belong to English or to be part of English in the same way that Dickens is or reading a novel of your own choice might be. How come Madonna is not set on A level syllabuses, though, and is unlikely to be an examination set text? The mode of address that Madonna might get within English is likely to be very different from the special texts of English Literature. Any controversy that might be aroused by proposing Madonna as suitable as an A level set text depends on the assumption that there is a clear distinction in kind between literature and media texts. This distinction has been seen as more or less crucial in debates about literature in the public arena –

whether concerning Madonna and Marvell or Chaucer and Chuck Berry. These public representations, found recently in all sections of the press, echo institutionally critical points. The Madonna issue raises fundamental questions about the nature of literacy in education, questions about identities and values, questions about, for example, literature and gender. Look at many popular cultural forms and the issue of femininity, the question of gender roles, ideas about masculinity, significant matters of identity, are often dynamically represented, often far more likely to engage the interest and critical attention of students, frequently in forms that are more interesting and more challenging than their high cultural counterparts from the realms of literature. These judgements of value, though, are not, in the end, what is most crucially at stake. What is at stake is the restriction and limitation of a field, as well as the restriction and limitation on ideas that may be put to use addressing textual phenomena.

Cultural forms, such as rap music, tabloid newspapers, game shows and video films, constitute a significant portion of most people's cultural experiences, yet they don't figure in any kind of systematic way in the official constitution, nor in the widespread definitions of the subject in practice. This seems strange in a subject that claims to be dealing, in some fundamental and essential way, with linguistic and textual experience. To deconstruct the opposition between the category of literature and the category of popular culture in order to demonstrate that neither is self-sustaining and neither has special qualities peculiar to itself, may well be an important move in a radical review of what has hitherto been assumed to be the uncontested identity of the subject. Exorcising the ghost of that distinction may enable an approach to culture of a much more inclusive, theoretically rigorous and powerful sense. This may well entail shedding time-honoured inhibitions about dealing with cultural forms that have traditionally been denigrated by the habits of thought of the subject English.

The whole business of looking at individual texts taken out of their specific social contexts of reading, out of their various institutional sitings, though, is highly questionable. Of course, pursuing the philosophical and social implications of decontextualized reading is unthinkable in terms of the idea of literature, personal response 'theory' and all its associated practices. These practices actually depend on the suppression of the social as it bears on educational practices in the field of literacy. This is a direct consequence of the reign of the ideology of 'liberalism', of individualism with its critically limiting suppression of the social – the consequences of which are far from liberal. The failure to centralize critical issues such as race, class, and gender – their decentralization or marginalization, in effect – means that conservative values dominate the subject's ideological constitution and its practice, even at its most apparently liberal.

There may be a danger that the substitution of the study of media texts from popular culture simply displaces one set of texts for another, without considering fully the implications of a deconstructive revision of the field as a totality. There is a point in addressing texts that would otherwise be kept away by an exclusion process that devalues the cultural experiences of so many people. The restriction of meanings to texts is a danger here and one that can be avoided by looking at language practices, signifying processes, reading practices and values and meanings as they circulate, become ensconced, get changed or contested in their many and varied contexts.

Cultural experiences do not merely reside in either literary or popular forms and texts: they inhabit many cultural practices. It's important to radically expand the notion of what a text is, to look beyond the limits of what's conventionally understood as the textual. The thoroughly intertextual nature of signifying practices in a more inclusive arena may then be contemplated and practically addressed. This implies that it is necessary to forge a model of ('popular') culture which takes into account not just the media texts that have been in some cases identified as being popular culture themselves, for that is a limited and limiting model, too, but a conception that takes into account and realizes the languages of general cultural experience, the positions of subjects, the forms of thinking, seeing and feeling in their many different contexts. It may well be as important to deconstruct the purely textual view of popular culture as it is to pretend that culture is some kind of recognized body of valued experiences caught in aesthetic forms that speak a universal language to all forever and that bear our true and common cultural heritage.

MODELS OF LANGUAGE

The idea that language should be 'taught' within the context of state education hardly seems strange, though the whole project can be seen as questionable. It certainly seems worth reassessing the models that inform the practice of language teaching in English, the ideas that structure it. It might be as well to ask afresh what motivates this teaching of language, what its explicit and stated aims are and how these match up with an analysis of its practices and its effects. The idea that language should be assessed is particularly subject to question. The assessment of language is implicated at all levels of English teaching. It seems important to ask: What is the motivating force driving this assessment? What are the established criteria based on? What assumptions maintain them? According to many intellectually respectable positions, the models of language and ideas about language that have informed the assessment of the subject have theoretically deficient and, in the end, discriminatory. Rather like literature, the idea of standard English has imposed its restricted version of language on the subjects of English whose languages have been excluded by this monologic domination. What would happen if the well established critiques of language in education were written into the constitution of the subject English? The favourite practices and forms of assessment would need to be thoroughly revised, at the very least.

A critique of both traditionalist and liberal models of language entails a practical re-examination of the processes of education – at the level of daily classroom practice and of the social significance and effects of the curriculum. These two most dominant notions of language remain influential and cannot be strictly separated from one another. Both dominant models – traditionalist and liberal – have tended systematically to negate language as social practice, both being content to operate within a framework of assessment criteria that might be subject to radical critique from sociolinguistics, for example – or in fact, from any theory or set of theories engaging with language as social practice. Liberal and traditionalist forms of English still remain implicated in what ought to be recognized as the brutal and unacceptable discrimination against people based on misreadings of the meanings of language differences.

Any English which doesn't recognize and theorize its very specific social functions within its institutional context is always subject to determination by conservative forces, even when they are masked as liberal ideology. Deeply rooted prejudices about good and effective language practices are implicated in liberal and traditionalist models, because they lack – by choice or by blindness – the capacity to address, self-reflexively, how they work. The critical absence or gap in these models of language is the social, the relations between social differences and differences in language. Writing, reading and speaking subjects of English are constantly being defined by discriminatory models posing as common sense. A method of English teaching wanting to address the discrimination of dominant models would need to develop a different kind of theory and practice.

How *does* English explain different levels of language achievement under its formalized grading procedures? (And how do English teachers negotiate their own positions in relation to the procedures of assessment?) If the criteria of assessment can claim – as they must, and do by implication – some kind of universal validity, how come a very significant proportion of students fail to achieve the critical grade C or above? Are different levels of achievement equal to different capabilities in some generally applicable, absolute and universal sense? Are different levels of achievement in English examinations indicative of different levels of language? Are some people's language competences, in a general way, inferior to others – less worthy of positive recognition, less close to the ideal represented by grade A? The implication of the assessment system in English is that some forms of language, belonging to specific social groups, are superior to others – and this is very obviously suspect.

The grading system can only really work if some general notion of levels of performance, distinguished by a hierarchical system of ordering, is in operation. The grading system depends on *ideas* about language, ideas informing its assessment, and the central idea that language – in its individual usage – *can* be assessed according to criteria that are objective and universal. This position may seem obvious and unexceptionable. On the other hand, it may appear outrageously presumptuous and unjust. It can only appear as common sense within a specific context of ideas about language – the ideas of English – that are determined to repress and exclude sociolinguistic critique. Other ideas that don't come within the compass of established English challenge the validity of all the assumptions implicated in the position.

To take grading into account means addressing the institution of English. It means, also, that English is about things other and more than creative self-expression and personal response. The institution of English – that self-avowedly delights in the wonders of human creativity expressed in poems and stories, and in the free individual responses they engender – also supervises the universal, and largely punitive, grading system that grants status to certain forms of language – the ideal at grade A, and the far from ideal at grade G. These grades, as everyone knows, carry weight in other contexts, too – beyond English and beyond the school.

The institution of English, in its present condition has no real place for sociolinguistics, or a sociolinguistic analysis of its ideas and practices. It is, in fact, necessary to keep sociolinguistics away from the central being and identity of English. Sociolinguistics is thoroughly incompatible with grading in English, in a way that individual creativity and personal response are not. Sociolinguistics operates in accordance with a principle of linguistic relativity – looking at different forms of language in an analytic way rather than, as with English, in a hierarchical and judgemental way. Sociolinguistics looks at how some favoured forms of language may carry more power and status, in certain contexts, than others – and examines why that's the case. English blankly accepts linguistic status distinctions and construes them as universal, and somehow, as natural. Sociolinguistics is interested in examining and defining the operations of language in different contexts, whereas English tends to deny the significance of context – and denies its own very specific institutional context.

There is no reason, in an absolute sense, why sociolinguistics should not figure centrally in a redefinition of English. The implications for the grading system would be drastic; but it's perfectly possible for sociolinguistic practice of the subject to be developed. Such a practice might involve, for example, looking at ideas about different kinds of language, different kinds of language contexts and how these relate to specific social groups and specific social practices. Teaching might deal explicitly with different kinds and styles of reading, writing and speaking. Ethnographic projects could address a range of language institutions and differences. A practice of a subject conceived of in this way would be far removed from what English has been.

Ideas associated with the term post-structuralism could also furnish a basis for the production of models and practices in relation to language, undercutting the false certainties that hold English together. A post-structuralist reading of language can be envisaged as directed towards an emphasis on culture, on the social and the political aspects of linguistic practices. All of these are currently banished by official and dominant models of English. A post-structuralist practice could involve looking at sign systems of different kinds, how they operate general cultural meanings, how general cultural meanings circulate, hold power, are contested and how they operate differently in different contexts. Deconstructive ideas about mobility of meanings are likely to mean that the ideas keeping English in place can no longer pretend to their innocent neutrality. Psychoanalysis, for example, proposes a completely different model of the relations between language and the individual – incorporating phenomena conventional English cannot address.

In all of this are a host of productive possibilities. In the end, the precise source of ideas hardly matters. It is important to retain the idea of theory as being the kind of self-conscious awareness that brings into the field of the subject's sense of itself – and into its practices, into its rhetoric and into its very constitution – an explicit awareness of the social dimension of language.

LEARNING TO BE LITERATE

Definitions of literacy in English are frequently laconic, as though the word 'literacy' always referred unwaveringly to the same thing. It seems symptomatic of English that it should lack any coherent theory of what literacy is, or might be. English blithely eschews theoretical definitions of literacy, relying on the authority of the subject, rather than on the arguments for particular models or positions. The implicit definition of literacy at work in English is consequently exclusive and limited. It practically denies different ideas of literacy. Different literacies, different kinds of competences framed by different practices, operating within different arenas are barred from current definitions and practices.

Different notions of literacy are produced by different conceptions of culture. Dominant notions of literacy are, historically, at least, associated with ideas of national identity – as may witness the literature surrounding the foundation of the subject and the frequent attempts to increase its emphasis in state education. Numerous publications in the public sphere – in newspapers of all casts, for example – testify to the conflation of literacy with culture and national identity. The tendency of the association of literacy with national identity is narrowing, moving towards exclusivity rather than inclusiveness. Dominant cultural forms are likely to predominate, and are likely to exclude or marginalize those that are different and less powerful. Liberal versions of English, versions that might feel uneasy about its association with notions of national identity, are still unlikely to address the politics of this issue, being unequipped to deal conceptually with the politics of literacy.

There is a politics of literacy, a politics constantly at work institutionally and ideologically in the daily practices of schools. Literacy is not a space that can claim to be free from the operations of power. In English the ascendancy of certain ideas ensures that certain groups are identified positively, and others negatively on the basis of language differences. This is the politics of literacy at work, organizing the identities of it's subjects into a hierarchy of differences defined on the basis of a dominant conception of literacy.

The national grading systems of English might be represented as the agreed criteria for assessing levels of literacy. And yet it would be difficult to indicate how and where and by what processes agreement about what literacy is was ever achieved. In the end, it would have to be conceded that whatever the process involved in defining dominant, institutionally powerful definitions of literacy, it never had anything to do with democracy, and it produced a definition that has been sure to exclude the majority of its subjects – subjects who, with or without a national curriculum, must pass through its filtering system.

In public debates the question of standards of literacy frequently arises, though how it would be possible to measure standards of literacy is difficult to imagine, except by reference to the most banal conceptions of the idea of literacy imaginable. What kinds of questions would have to be formulated to address the matter? Are standards of literacy rising or falling? How could you tell? Would more people reading more Wordsworth, in their places of work or in their front rooms, indicate greater levels of literacy than before? What would be the meaning of literacy in this case, and what positive inflection could it be given? What about people who might display an addiction to the writings of John Wilmot, The Earl of Rochester? Are they more literate than readers of Jackie Collins novels? Is there more or less computer literacy now than before? Do more people spell more words right when they write Christmas cards than previously? Is the general populace any less sloppy than before in its command of grammar and pronunciation, or are the kinds of errors English teachers have traditionally enjoyed mocking as howlers just as common as before? Are there more people with bigger vocabularies deploying a greater range of complex sentences than in the old days? Or are people these days making sharper use of smaller vocabularies, cultivating an un-Shakespearian economy in their choice of words? Is there now more or less media literacy? Are people developing more canny ways of reading media texts? Is there generally more deconstruction of common cultural stereotypes going on? And so on.

Of course, different groups of people and people engaged in different kinds of activity may well construe literacy quite differently. English has continued under the assumption that literacy is one thing, albeit vaguely defined, but in the end reducible to sentence structures, vocabularies, accuracy of spelling and punctuation – all in relation to a quite restricted model – and to a few limited kinds of responses to a few limited kinds of text. The notion of different – let alone conflicting – literacies is not allowed, an exclusivity that can hardly be consonant with the idea of a democratic society. What conception of a democracy is operative where the notion of conflicting interests is suppressed? A large and complex issue is opened in relation to this question about the identity of literacy. It is an issue of great importance in so far as it reflects gaps in the constitution of the curriculum and in so far as it represents possibilities for a different conception of educational processes.

VALUES

The issue of values can't be avoided by any subject dealing with language and textuality. Any pretensions of English to have been or to be neutral or value-free are untenable. The grading system clearly expresses values concerning reading, writing and speaking. No self respecting theory or model of language would deny that all language is always already value-laden. It's a condition of language to be loaded with values. The values of English have been either entirely unspecific or, rather, concealed. In the obvious case of examination assessment criteria and exam syllabuses they have exposed themselves as being implicitly laden with all sorts of assumptions that most models of language and culture would find objectionable. In the context of a society claiming to be democratic, English and the values it represents seem to be a glaring anomaly. English, at the heart of state education, is fundamentally anti-democratic in its values and practical application of them.

Race, class and gender are issues deconstructive of the subject's founding principles. Race, class and gender are centrally relevant to any conception of English in relation to the idea of democracy. (It must be said that the issues of race, class and gender make the idea of democracy problematic and suggest that the idea be aligned with a more deconstructive theory of what it might be.) They're issues that do not currently have a fundamental and centrally informative role in the constitution of the subject. They appear, when they do appear, as other facets in a structure whose main interests are elsewhere. This means that, within the structure of English, issues concerning race, class, gender and questions that might raise the problematics of democracy are marginalized. English does not, as it might, address issues of race, class and gender as part of its fundamental and central structure – nor are concerns of democracy written into the fundamental and central constitution of the subject. Most attempts to address these critical issues in English have systematically marginalized them. Liberal practices of English, for instance, have been systematically and essentially de-politicizing, and therefore aligned with conservative values and position, associated with ideas about the individual and the personal.

A conception of literacy is required which recognizes differences, different conceptions of literacy, and the different forms of literacy people live by. To begin to attempt to understand how different literacies may be organized within communities might mean to begin to operate against the systematic discrimination which, in the name of English, officially denigrates what it doesn't recognize as identical with itself – the punitive grading system, for example, that depends on the domination of a monologic conception of literacy. To deconstruct the dominant conceptions and the practices that go with them might well enable other literacies to enter the field of address, other possibilities to be written into the constitution of the subject.

7 Aspects of English

The subject – English or any other – is not just what gets taught in classrooms or what's written down in syllabuses. The identity of English is caught up in a network of aspects, some of them briefly addressed below, all of them of significance in any attempt to theorize the subject in its institutional and social contexts.

THE SOCIOLOGY OF EDUCATION

Sociology offers a salutary challenge to simplistically positive claims of liberal education. The sociology of education represents a very different view from liberal versions of English – with their emphasis on the development of the individual – addressing matters that English has largely chosen to ignore: the structural effects of educational practices. Taking a general, analytic position, the sociology of education has far-reaching implications for English, having a critical effect on any claims, including the present one, to offer a transformative subject content – whether transformative of the person, as in the liberal model, or transformative of the identity and orientation of the subject generally, as with the model proposed by this book.

The sociology of education would generally tend to suggest that schooling is designed – and very effectively organized – to reproduce particular patterns of social organization. To put it another way, the function of schooling is to produce and reproduce particular forms of subjectivity useful to current forms of social ordering and maintaining social difference. Some sociological studies take a special interest in examining how groups of students in schools are – by culture, inclination or class – disbarred from effectively participating in the education system. The general trend of the case established is that school culture – in its official versions – effectively operates in favour of established values and powerful groups, that it effectively operates against alternatives. It's not difficult to see how the perspective of the sociology of education, then, presents a harshly uncompromising critique of liberal pretensions. If the system systematically discriminates against *groups*, addressing individual cases and allowing class distinctions to continue to operate, this can only be regarded as tinkering with structural effects.

The sociology of education has suggested that one important structural function of schooling is to inculcate the acceptance of hierarchy. It's easy to see how the workings of any school – with their necessary emphases on certain kinds of discipline and self-discipline with reference to different hierarchies of attainment and different powers assigned to subjects – are implicated in the process. It's also easy to see how the acceptance of grading practices might have similar effects. The legitimation of inequality is another dominant theme announced by the sociology of education. On this kind of sociological reading, schooling is concerned to establish, and actually to *construct*, certain kinds of inequality – academic inequality for instance – and to make inequality seem to be a function of the qualities of the individual concerned. Students who fail, therefore, may be categorized as being of low ability or of poor inclination to take full advantage of the opportunities for academic success ostensibly open to all. The illusion of equality of opportunity is conceived by the sociology of education as one of the central myths of education in the kind of society characterized as western liberal democratic. Students confronted with an establishment culture ensconced in the academic curriculum, established in its languages and procedures, feel alienated. Already in a state of cultural exclusion, they cannot effectively partake of school culture without having to renounce important elements of their own, different, cultural experiences. Within the context of the school this may produce a counter-culture operating a value system at odds with the value system of the school. While groups resisting dominant values may well be expressing their own rights to maintain a voice, in terms of the social prestige granted to educational attainment they will lose out.

The sociology of education has sought to explain different kinds of attainment in education by using other criteria than the difficult notion of intelligence. It has sought to describe the relations between culture, class and educational attainment. It has also put language into the centre of discussions about matters like the effects of pre-school socialization and speech patterns on educational attainment, looking critically at ideas like cultural deprivation and compensatory education. Some versions of the sociology of education have maintained that what education has to offer is a kind of cultural 'capital'; they suggest that differential achievement depends on how much capital you already have to invest in the system. Schools are seen as sites of cultural reproduction, where dominant cultural values are established, maintained and replicated within the identities of individuals and groups. Sociological accounts of education based on this kind of model might emphasize the social function of elimination, identifying as important elements in educational processes typing, labelling and the general production and reproduction of social roles and identities. Centrally important in many sociological studies of educational attainment and in the study of structural inequalities are issues of gender difference and ethnicity. Studies of educational attainment, educational values and practices have indicated clearly that schooling is implicated in fundamental inequalities associated with these issues. In terms of the dominant language and culture of education in schools, it has been possible to identify inherent racism naturalized as knowledge. The sociology of education has explored the idea that knowledge and power – including the kind of knowledge purveyed as the curriculum – are not strictly distinguishable. Knowledge represents and colludes with power – replicates and produces differences in power – in the institution of the school in the processes of schooling. This critique extends from the academic curriculum to educational vocationalism.

As far as the teaching of English in schools is explicitly concerned, the most strikingly significant areas of the sociological analysis of education concern language. Whichever way you look at it, at the very centre of educational practice is language. Although English teachers may have seen their functions more positively, sociologists have suggested that language assessment criteria are related to social stratification, equating language teaching and assessment with the operations of power and discrimination. While many different positions have been taken in relation to language and the sociology of education, there has never been any doubt that the language of schooling is central to its operations – that language is very much an issue of cultural difference and identity. To continue to pretend that the criteria of assessment in English examinations and the way that they are characteristically interpreted, for example, represent some natural and inevitable order of things, represent a proper and objective framework for assessment, is either to ignore or to deny that there *is* a sociology of education.

The role and function of English can be reinterpreted in the light of this social analysis – furnishing a critique of the established beliefs and practices. Sociology is a very powerful form of theoretical critique. Other elements of theory might provide the means to pursue the critique in relation to fundamental concepts and particular practices, giving a means by which these can be viewed afresh, from a different – and more inclusive – vantage point. An important aspect of any attempt to instigate a more conscious and self-conscious theory of English teaching would need to address the sociology of the education, re-examining the functions and identity of English in relation to it.

HISTORIES OF ENGLISH

The history of English has received attention in recent times. Academic studies have appeared charting the progress of the subject through various phases of its changing identity. One thing these studies have in common is the idea that English has always been – and was founded as – a kind of ideological project, crucially bound up with ideas about culture and society. Since its, relatively recent, origins English as a school subject has been represented as significantly related to the cultural well-being of its subjects. Accounts of this history have concentrated their different kinds of interest on public documents and 'debates' that have been taken to represent the significant trends in the history of the teaching of English. Tracing the development of the idea of English, and its inception in state education, from the ideas of Arnold, through the Newbolt Report (1921) and beyond, these studies indicate how certain individuals and institutions sought to determine the identity of English. The development of the identity of English is clearly aligned in these accounts with the imperative of social cohesion. English is represented as a technology for the management of the personal development of the individual subject – intellectually, emotionally, ethically and spiritually. Following the story of the birth and growth of English, language and literature became the grounds for creativity and self-expression, but were also understood as the grounds for forging a common idea of a culture allied with national identity for the masses coming under the authority of state education. Both personal growth and moral management are identified as features of the publicly formulated purposes of English in schools. The history of the subject is seen as the development and refinement of these processes, with the tendency of the personal growth model to gain ascendancy in its later phases. This development is perfectly compatible with the development of an ideology of individualism, but an individualism that still wants to appeal to a sense of common cultural interests, common cultural heritage and identity.

There exists no full account of the history of English in schools as a history of specific practices. These specific practices are unlikely to have followed the clear and even development figured in most histories of English. The differences represented by different practices, differences that have fissured the subject remain – in various forms – operative even now, though their particular forms of expression may have altered. Any serious effort to challenge the hegemony of the subject's dominant modes and forms must address these other aspects too, because they are essentially implicated in the subject's composition as part of its effective working identity. They belong to the archaeology of the identity of the subject as unwritten elements in its history. It would be difficult, of course, to define all of these things and impossible to survey the various movements of the past in detail. The difficulty of the project, though, doesn't discount the significance of the recognition that any account of the history of English in schools that regards only published materials, government sponsored reports, and so on, must be partial to the extent that it doesn't take into account the majority of the practice of the subject.

It's probable that a great deal of the unwritten practices of English have been and remain deeply conservative in their ideological bent and in their effects. Unquestionably, the majority of the subjects of English have, historically, been defined negatively by the subject. It's significant that this aspect of the history of the subject remains unwritten – and remains unwritable by conventional histories and by post-Foucauldian genealogies alike.

English has characteristically tended to take an ahistorical view of things, representing values as transcending historical time. But there *is* a history of meanings, a history of changing identities for things linguistic and textual, and a history of a subject fissured and changing in its ideas, practices and effects. This history itself might profitably be addressed by a redefined subject, aware of its own history and changing identity, conscious of its orientation into the future. If history – deconstructively speaking – is a rewriting of the past, then it might also be a rewriting of the present moving into the future. What this implies is a conscious appropriation of a redefinition of the history of English – one that necessarily projects a different kind of future for the subject, one that opens the institutional space for the possibility of such a future.

THE PROFESSIONAL IDENTITY OF ENGLISH TEACHERS

For English to function effectively as a social practice engaging ideas about language, literature, other cultural forms and the nature of society, particular kinds of professional identity have been called for. It would be important – for any account of what English has been, is, and is to be – to examine how the teachers of English have seen their roles and functions. It would no doubt be useful and revealing to examine particular ideas of English teachers concerning language, literature and other cultural issues. Questions could be asked about these ideas and the professional practices they've informed. How have professional educators explained to themselves the significance, or otherwise, of what they have been doing as teachers of English? Other questions might be very revealing – about, for example, how English teachers have seen their professional role more generally, what contradictions as English teachers they may have had to negotiate, as well as questions concerning their sense of what the subject is, what its purposes and effects are and should be. Teachers of English are subjects of its institutional being just as much as students are, though in different ways. Any serious attempt to investigate the identity of the subject, to explore the history of the subject, or to project a redefinition of the subject, would need to take this crucial factor into account.

SPECIFIC INSTITUTIONS

There are obviously both general trends and the play of differences at work in the way particular institutions of education operate. Schools that follow general trends in terms of ideology and practice may differ considerably in many particular respects. An account of the identity of English, or a history of the subject, would need to explore the localized situations of the subject, the nature of similarities, general trends and differences in the way schools have operated and in the way they have thought themselves to be operating. This kind of investigation could include, for example, a consideration of management systems, attitudes towards classroom management, staffroom identity and staffroom culture.

An investigation into the particular institutional identity of any school might also include some analysis of financing, the policies of the local authority, the location of the school and the social character of its constituency. The history of the school and its changing culture as an institution would also be factors influencing its particular identity. An approach to the identities of the school as mediator of cultural experiences would need, then, to take into account the common structural characteristics and its particular, specific configuration. Staffroom culture, ideas and ideals, details of curriculum and constituency would all come into play.

CHANGING DEFINITIONS OF SCHOOLS

Schools have had their own history. Various reorganizations of secondary education have impinged significantly on the identity of the institution of the school. Grammar, secondary modern schools and technical schools stood for a different notion of the purposes of education from comprehensive schools. In more recent times LMS (local management of schools), GMS (grant maintained status) and a host of other measures have made their different impacts on the way that education and schooling been defined and practised. The deconstructive effects wrought by these initiatives on hitherto dominant notions of the purposes and functions of comprehensive schools are very much in progress. Other changes have been effected by evolving ideas and practices of management, by developments in attitudes towards processes of learning and by the pressures of the various initiatives of central control.

The definition and delivery of the curriculum have not been unaffected by these changes. A history of the identity and meaning of any subject would need to take into account how changes in the organization and definition of schools had determined the nature of the specific educational practices within them.

DEFINITIONS OF THE CURRICULUM

If the National Curriculum was instigated as an attempt to make uniform all the thinking and all the practices of English in all schools across the nation, it can hardly be reckoned to have been a success. If the intention was ever there at the outset it was certainly foiled by the published materials. The statements concerning the nature of English, for example, in the official documents allow for considerable variation. The prescriptive elements in the National Curriculum concern only assessment in relation to the notion of stages of development and achievement. The tone and manner of the documentation of the National Curriculum in relation to English suggested proposals for consideration rather than prescription – allowing for different attitudes and practices. The English curriculum has always tended to allow for a good deal of variety; its definitions have always been characterized by degrees of variation. Given the nebulous content of the subject and given the way that it has been differently interpreted by practitioners, the meaning of English within the general curriculum – from the level of the individual schools to the national level – must have been similarly fractured and inconsistent.

Though no doubt important general trends will have prevailed, the curriculum in operation is not simply what it is claimed to be in official publications, nor what its more vocal representatives have described it as. The shifting nature of the curriculum and of the way that English has been configured within it – in other words its history – demand a clear conception and exploration of how the English curriculum has operated at all levels, and demand also an understanding of the identity of English within the curriculum as implicated in more than simply its avowed tenets. In other words, English needs to more consciously and fully theorize its particular forms in relation to the forces determining its meaning within the curriculum; if, that is, it is to be a meaningful practice at all distinguished from the general processes of schooling. Although the criteria of assessment have remained largely unchanged by recent curriculum developments – both in their form and in the way they get interpreted – the subject's gaps and vagaries offer the potential for radically different practices, and in the end, for radically different attitudes towards assessment, towards the purposes and the meaning of the subject generally.

POPULAR CONCEPTIONS OF ENGLISH

Popular conceptions of the subject are clearly appealed to in countless press articles, dealing, for example, with so-called debates and differences about the proper contents and direction of the subject. Canny ministerial moves have been made to address public concerns over issues like standards and notions of cultural heritage. Television programmes are broadcast to present the issues and to represent the various positions that are thought to exist. English is the subject of concern for that rhetorically, politically significant body referred to as parents. English must be the subject of innumerable 'popular' discourses on the subject taking place in a diversity of contexts. As a central, core element of the curriculum in state education, English is a topic engaging attitudes that reflect significant perceptions about the nature and functions of education. In popular discourse a range of different attitudes are bound to be expressed. Most English teachers are familiar with the attitude expressed as the unease that can come over people when they discover what you do for a living. This unease reflects how English places and has placed its subjects.

An account of popular attitudes towards, notions and representations of English would be more than simply interesting for whoever has a stake in the identity of the subject. It could reveal a great deal about the perceptions different groups of people have of their educational experiences. It could indicate important things about the varied practices of English, about the sense of people's relations with their own languages and the official language of schooling and certification. It could follow through the development of national consciousness of ideas about culture and language, the national literature and other kinds of cultural experience which continue – whatever position is being expressed – to be perceived as significant.

ATTITUDES EXPRESSED IN EXAMINING PROCEDURES

Public examinations in English have changed through the subject's history. English was an important component in the eleven plus exam, and was implicated in the academic and social divisions it enacted. Although the eleven plus no longer exists, the kind of task it was set to do may now be carried out by tests undertaken in the name of the National Curriculum. This will certainly have a determining effect on the nature and direction of the subject, English, just as the definition of GCSE English, supervised by the controlling body, SEAC, has affected the practices of the subject at that level.

Clearly the subject English in schools has been partly determined by exam processes, and these have had a history of their own. The kinds of questions set for formal exam papers, the criteria of assessment in operation and the ideology of the subject embodied in teachers of English exams and examiners – have all had a bearing on the identity of the subject. Lists of set texts studied at A level now and the kinds of paper on offer will differ markedly from the lists and papers of previous times. What is the meaning of this difference and what is the meaning of the shifting trends it may represent? What are the implications of the changing identity of the subject on the idea of the subject's integrity? Obviously, detailed work – examining documents precisely and also taking account of less tangible and theoretical considerations – would need to be done to find answers to these questions.

In the case of exam syllabuses, for instance, the kind of writing submitted for coursework during the history of the exam's progress is likely to indicate trends, persistent tendencies and shifts in the identity of the subject. It might be revealing to have some account of its variations and some account of its generally conformist trends. Questions about different and similar positions that get expressed in coursework topics might indicate the static and the changing features in an ever shifting configuration. Exam papers might be analysed also in terms of their contents and how they get marked, how the markers understand the processes of assessment. This kind of account of the identity of the subject may be related to larger movements and features of the education system.

The meaning and 'results' of exams in English might also be viewed in relation to changes in ideas and social patterns outside the immediate context of education – changes in the larger political and social context.

THE HISTORY OF NATIONAL IDENTITY

An important correlation might be made by examining the idea of English in relation to larger notions of Englishness. This would probably entail some kind of study of national identity as perceived by different groups positioned differently by the idea.

The centrality of the ongoing and current debates about the nature of English are closely connected to ideas about Englishness in the larger sense. The connection, in fact, is frequently made explicitly. The significance of the subject is frequently figured as a kind of national cultural practice – engaging fundamental aspects of cultural identity, partly embodied in national literature. The maintenance of 'proper' standards of language, the maintenance of the idea of the English Language in some pure and absolute form is also significant in this context. Nostalgia for a time when standards were high and the language was robust and fundamentally *English* obviously reflects other kinds of national nostalgias about a more properly and robustly English past.

Both the national language and the national literature have been represented in various – thoroughly reactionary – contexts as under threat from dangerous tendencies. At the present time English remains very much the focus of media coverage that often attempts to reaffirm the cultural centrality of English as a national pursuit, a pursuit engaging very significant questions of national identity, often attempting to resuscitate the debilitated and discredited notion of cultural heritage. From other quarters other pressures and voices can be felt and heard, challenging the most precious and favoured assumptions of the subject, including its affiliation with ideas associated with the nation and national identity.

THE CONSTITUENCY OF THE SCHOOLS

Significant social changes have determined the nature of both the organization and the constituency of schools. Demographic shifts, some seismic and obvious, others more gradual and subtle, must have affected the nature of the constituency of schools, and of the subjects of English. English – what it is and does – can't be understood without some reference to its constituency. The impact of the subject – its reception, its meaning – is bound to be affected by the ideas, aspirations and attitudes of its subjects. This constituency is, obviously, different according to many factors, including local social and demographic conditions.

The orientation of any community towards education must shift in relation to economic changes. The nature of any community might also be affected by ideas and processes of education implemented by the institutions of education. To examine the necessarily complex relations between these factors could indicate important facets of the conditions in which English is doing its work, the kinds of receptions and meanings being made of it, and its various effects. The meaning of English can be understood, at least partly, by reference to how it addresses and defines an audience. Some awareness of the audience and its various receptions of English might be of great theoretical interest and significance. Examining how contentious issues in English may or may not have implications for the subjects of English must be of considerable significance in any attempt to understand, define or redefine the subject.

THE SPECIAL SPACE OF ENGLISH

The *idea* of English has been an especially potent force in the liberal and more progressive conceptions of education. This is to do with the way that English has been conceived of as a liberal discipline within the general curriculum. This kind of perception of English – as pre-eminently representing certain values and modes of operating in schools – has worked in collusion with what might be called the self-conscious identity of the subject. English has – at certain times and in certain contexts – been represented as *the* liberal discipline, pre-eminently humane and humanizing.

It is important, though, to reconsider the role of English within the curriculum as a whole. It might be reasonable to claim that for the past thirty years or so there has been a general tendency, in many institutions, to associate English, especially after Bullock (1975), with creativity, with the arts, with production. A self-avowedly creative, workshop model of English taking shape in Mode Three coursework schemes has strongly influenced its specific identity within the range of curriculum subjects. English has, albeit unevenly and disparately, been associated with having quite special functions, being seen as especially distinct from other areas of the curriculum. The notion of the special space of English belongs to a specifically liberal set of assumptions. Associated with this notion would be the idea of language as self-expression: entailing the encouragement of the individual's use of language in many (or any, really) situations, but might especially belong to the "expressive" forms – story writing, poems, descriptions, personal experiences, personal opinions. (Though why these should been deemed to be more expressive than others is not certain, except as a function of the domination of a certain model of language and identity.)

Another main strand of this – probably still dominant – general model of English would make special claims for the role of literature in the shaping of the individual consciousness. At the core of this privileging of literature lies the idea that education – at its best and most humane – is the ground for personal growth, and the idea that literature can play a crucially determining role in the process of the development of the individual. Literature does these things as an element in the curriculum, founded on notions of development and progression, but also, of course, constantly assessing and defining its constituents in a strict hierarchy of value.

English has at the same time been held to represent traditional values – sometimes this conception of English has been at odds with the more liberal versions, and sometimes it has been in alliance with them. In some of its various forms English has represented an amalgam of traditional and liberal, progressive values – with the general function of maintaining itself as a focus for a humane and enlightening experience of language and of literature, being at once free and open and, at the same time, ordered and ordering. The chaotic nature of personal experience, for example, has been seen as subject to the precise orderings of language, and the education of the emotions and of attitudes has been part of this. Literature has provided the means for the inchoate individual to discover an identity reflected in its universal themes and interests, and has been the grounds for the discovery of others' experiences of the world – thus empathetically ordering the individual's own.

This general idea – of the special place and functions of English – is highly contestable. In the first place the idea of English as language development fails to take into account a number of important considerations about the place of language within the institution of the school, and of the subject within the school, and about the regulatory function of schooling. Literature, of course, does not exist on its own, and its effects belong to a narrow conception of culture that really excludes large groups of people from its special humanizing qualities.

THE POLITICS OF THE SUBJECT IN THE PRESENT SITUATION

At no time in history has there been more active political concern over education. Among the most crucial issues of debate are many closely related to the identity of English. Successive reports have been authorized by the government. Innumerable articles and features have appeared in all sections of the press. The concern these various texts express with issues such as traditional literature versus popular culture touch upon very significant issues to do with public values and the proper functions of education. They touch upon vital matters of definition – concerning not just the classroom habits of English teachers, but the nature of society, and the particular kind of ordering we live in. Formalized, centralized statements on education, some produced by officially appointed bodies, some produced by government ministers, have proliferated in recent times. DES reports, many contradicting one another, have represented many different positions. These texts all belong to a discourse of considerable political significance.

In all sectors of the press, in TV and radio programmes both national and local, English has been given a thorough airing. All this media activity might be seen as the textual manifestations of general public concern about the proper scope of a subject felt to be central to the well-being of the nation's education system. On the other hand, it may be seen as part of the production of a discourse concerned to promote certain kinds of values, to promote a particular ideological position in regard to things educational and other things, too. The idea of a debate itself indicates a crisis of confidence in the functioning of education in the social order. It speaks of a kind of crisis of values, loss of a centrality and purpose that was probably never there. The idea of a golden age of universally high standards, nevertheless, motivates certain powerful positions in the ideology of education.

With a tendency in some quarters to emphasise vocational educational projects, there is likely to be a consequent emphasis on the harder elements of the subject's content, as is reflected in Keystage Four documents – documents, incidentally, that would be laughable for their simple-mindedness, if it weren't for the crude institutional power they also represent. In times of uncertainty and in a context of political reaction, a utilitarian model of English is more likely to emerge as dominant, a model based on naive notions of order and discipline in the field of language and of mythical, traditional values dressed in the dangerous idea of cultural heritage in the field of literature. The utilitarian and the idealistic go curiously together in this peculiar concoction at the centre of the new National Curriculum.

The present public concerns with identity reflect what has, rather politely, I believe, been referred to as a 'crisis' in English. Issues discussed in relation to the ideology of English teaching are part and parcel of other concerns and interests. Arguments about Chaucer and Chuck Berry are about more than those things. They may serve as useful reminders that education is an ideologically loaded field, a site for the exertion of influences, struggles for power and control – struggles implicated in the very nature of society.

All the aspects mentioned above are elements in the identity of English. English is not reducible to its apparent content, to its visible rhetorics or to its officially stated purposes. English is not reducible, either, to the terms of public debates that set one limited vision of the subject against another. What English is reaches into many domains. Any attempt to understand English to change it, or to displace it – needs to be aware of the various locations of its being.

8 New bearings

QUESTIONS FOR ENGLISH

This book has attempted to explore and question the identity of English. It's attempted to take an interrogative approach to how English works and what it is by applying a certain kind of reading of post-structuralist theory and comparative sociolinguistics to fundamental ideas of English. Looking also at practical classroom activities, the book has attempted to offer some initial moves towards transforming the practical identity and meaning of the subject. The general argument has been that the identity of English is untenable, that English has, in fact, been founded and remains dependent on quite deeply contentious premises, posing as enlightened common sense or as culturally enduring obvious truth. The upshot of this is that the subject is open to complete redefinition.

To go back to a point of beginning, these are some of the questions that might be posed by a revaluation of the subject, English, attempting to operate a theoretical self-consciousness about its constitution, attitudes and practices:

- How are criteria of assessment constructed? What notions of language do they operate? Who are they written by? Who maintains them, in what institutional contexts, and by what procedures? How might they be changed?
- How is a grade A student different from a grade F student? What different kinds of 'subjects' does English claim and in what different ways does it identify and speak to them?
- Why does English give unequal recognition to the languages of its subjects – the students who are subject to its systematic processes of ordering? On what authority is the ordering done? What ideas about language are at work in the process? Are those ideas based on universal truths?

- What aspects of sociolinguistics are there in English? What might English look like given a more central interest in sociolinguistics?
- To what extent is literacy a self-defining thing? How does literacy get defined in schools? What *is* literacy? What notice has English taken of changing ideas of literacy?
- Why is English so preoccupied with reading and writing stories? Are stories *really* a category in themselves?
- What *is* poetry? What special qualities does poetry possess? What special benefits does poetry confer? How is poetry distinguished from popular music lyrics, for example, or from TV advert texts? What is the special value of reading poetry, or of writing responses to it?
- What is the greatness of *King Lear* founded on? Would it be possible, in the context of English, to challenge the greatness of *King Lear*? What about any other texts classed as literature? What about *all* other texts classed as literature?
- Is *The Color Purple* as good as *Boyz n the hood*? Is *Romeo and Juliet* better than *Thelma and Louise*? Is Marvell better than Madonna or the *Daily Mirror*? In what ways are any of these things the same as or different from one another?
- Is studying *The Tempest* more useful than studying *Twinkle*? What might be the criteria of usefulness that operate in relation to this question? Are texts ever really studied on their own? Is it ever possible to address single texts in isolation from their (various) cultural contexts?
- What *values* does English Literature support? How were they established and by whom? How are the values of English maintained – by whom, in what institutional contexts? Do the values of English Literature depend on a body of texts or a body of ideas? Do the values of literature address different groups of people in different ways?
- What ideas about culture are promoted by the values and practices of English? Does English explicitly acknowledge its position in relation to ideas about culture? How might cultural differences be addressed in schooling?
- Where does English stand in relation to questions of race, class and gender? Could those issues be central to English in its present forms? What ideas and practices might make those issues central?
- What different positions could all these questions be approached from? What explicit allowance does English – in present forms – make for different positions? What kind of institutional power is granted to different positions regarding the identity and practice of English?

- What possible futures are there for English in schooling? How might any future for the subject be constructed? What would need to be addressed to intervene in the history of the subject to construct a different future for the subject – based on democracy and equality? What would these things – democracy and equality – mean, though, and how would they operate? What specific kinds of institutions and institutional practices might they entail?

The questions, general and specific, clearly don't come within the well established constitution of the subject. Taken seriously, their implications threaten to sink its confident assumptions.

THE MEANING OF THEORY

The identity of theory has, conventionally, tended to be associated with *academic* discourses about language, writing, culture and society. It has been considered remote and inaccessible, arcane and irrelevant. What's more, theory is also, so the story goes, foreign, radically un-English. Deconstruction – the writings of Jacques Derrida, for example – operates a language far exceeding the limits of common sense. The comprehensive secondary school hardly seems the most likely context for the introduction of theory – given its commonly perceived identity.

If theory, the questions it poses and the issues it's capable of raising, seem far removed from the everyday concerns of English teachers, it is also partly because the routine practices of schools and regular habits of thought – the general culture of secondary education – have tended to displace theoretical reflexivity, the kind that demands self-conscious reappraisal. The process of reappraisal and redefinition is not generally what liberal educational reform has aimed at – teachers of English becoming more active in the constitution of their own practices, the meaning, direction and assessment of their work, in relation to values they've consciously considered and configured within a general understanding of the social processes of education, educational institutions and discourses of learning.

Theory, though, represents potentially a powerful body of ideas and practices, capable of disturbing the foundations of English and the special kind of complacency English has been founded on. Theory puts the authority of the subject in question: its ideas, its practices and its institutional definitions are all subject to serious and powerful critique. But theory, is no more than a kind of self-consciousness – an awareness of the ideas informing what you do and the way you do it. Theory makes alternative positions explicit. But theory has also come to mean a certain *kind* of theory, associated broadly in the context of English with post-structuralism. Post-structuralism itself is a loosely defined thing and might include many different kinds of writing and different ideas. It's possible, though, to identify particular ideas and trends of thought in post-structuralism that provide the basis for an unqualified critique of English, at the same time proposing more powerfully explanatory models of language and textuality. Post-structuralism itself, however, doesn't propose a coherent social theory of meanings to complement its powerfully deconstructive ideas. Social theories of meaning might be usefully provided by sociolinguistics and other elements of sociology, social theory and cultural theory. (They certainly won't be provided by English.)

Semiotics and post-Saussurian linguistics, for example, can be made to take the familiar stuff of English beyond the level of assumption and assertion. Semiotics and linguistics provide theoretical groundings for understanding basic and complex operations of language. Semiotics is capable of addressing the changing nature of languages within specific historical and social conditions. The kinds of ideas expressed in, for example, English examination assessment criteria, or in liberal practices of English, are hardly able to even begin to address these issues or take them into account. Loosely formed notions of the individual and the individual's relations to language inform characteristic English practice. Psychoanalysis, on the other hand, as a general theory of meaning and culture, commands powerful ideas of subjectivity and language. Practices of English as we know it have no way of addressing the structural relations of language and consciousness. Nor do they have any way of examining the relations between cultural norms and the individual's perceptions of the world – and the way these are implicated in conscious and unconscious aspects of language.

A crucial effect of deconstruction has been to address our most fundamental habits of thought at the level of familiar and deeply rooted ideas embedded in forms of expression. Deconstruction has suggested, and demonstrated, that these forms of thought and expression are not in any absolute sense identical with the truth of things; that all forms of thinking, all forms of expression are bound up with and determined by specific ways of perceiving the world, particular ways of thinking about the world. Deconstruction suggests that, in the case of our own experiences, we see the world and construct meanings within the limits of a general system of thought and perception that is culturally dominant, that tends to be patriarchal and ethnocentric. Writing, according to a deconstructive position, is perceived as a general system of meanings and ideas – a system of established forms and constraints that organizes thought and perception. Writing extends, in this sense, well beyond its common-sense definition.

A deconstructive position would also suggest that all meanings and systems of reference are ultimately relative. Historical shifts bring new discourses of knowledge into being, and new forms of social organization related to new and different forms of knowledge. Discourses, in this sense, do not simply provide a means for understanding different aspects of the world. Discourses bring new ideas, terms and ways of perceiving things into existence – organizing their subjects differently too. Discourses construct identities and manoeuvre meanings – but not in a neutral way. Discourses are always caught up in contexts of power and ideology. If deconstruction is a relativist theory, denying the claims of any discourse to the absolute authority of truth, it means that the confrontation with ideology and power is unavoidable. Ideas, meanings and ways of seeing are caught up in networks of power and constructed ideologically. As teachers, perhaps uncomfortable choices – ethical choices, political choices – are involved in all our attitudes and actions. To rely on the notion of the simply practical is to allow powerful institutional forces to determine choices. Theory is a necessary component of choice: you can't choose if you're blind to alternatives, if you're locked into one monologic, monolithic – or common-sense – view of things

Theory is not merely abstractly concerned with general issues of language, subjects and discourses. It has in recent times, in academic and non-academic contexts, explicitly addressed particular social issues. Feminism, for example, has operated at the level of high theory, but has also addressed specific social contexts and practices. Not surprisingly, feminism has had a great deal to say about language, discourses and the operation of patriarchal power. Feminism has sought to conduct specific cultural analyses of the representations and positions of women in society. Feminism has been political in a very broad sense, examining signifying practices and cultural experiences as they determine people's daily lives. Feminism has also attempted to theorize and realize challenges to existing conditions. Much modern feminism has drawn on ideas from post-structuralism, from psychoanalysis, for example, but has also maintained a steady regard for the politics of daily life. It hasn't seen the two – theory and the real world – as distinct realms, mainly because they are not.

Theory potentially proposes redefinitions by examining existing ideas and practices. Theory has the power to challenge the authority of discourses – examining practices and institutions where discursive authorities are maintained, identifying institutional systems of difference and authority. Theory – in a newly-defined context – is the proper process of questioning, of calling to account, of re-examining; a process essential to the health of any cultural practice. This interrogative function has the effect always of sharpening awareness, refusing to be content with what is established simply because it is established, or because it works. Essential to the process of theoretical enquiry, is the examination, re-examination and representation of values. Questions about what English is, for example, are also questions about authority and about institutions. Questions of literacy clearly relate to questions of social identity. Within the field of education, it isn't really possible simply to theorize the academic subject, whether English or anything else, without also theorizing the institutions of education. In this sense, theory is about moving beyond the apparent limits of the subject, beyond the limits of the school, in order to get a perspective on both subject and school within the social formations enmeshing them.

Theory often deploys a language alien to the established vocabulary of English, often offends by addressing notions characteristically left alone. Of course, everyone knows the difference between literature and popular culture: it's obvious, common sense. It's silly to treat popular entertainments, trivial as they are, with the serious and overloaded vocabularies of semiotics, or psychoanalysis, or deconstruction, for example. This commonly expressed attitude is deeply conservative, thoroughly anti-intellectual and anti-theoretical. It avoids asking questions of the familiar and established. If the vocabulary of poststructuralist theory, for example, is thought to be alien and long-worded, it's no more alien and difficult to get hold of to the general constituency of students than the vocabulary of established response to literature, or the vocabulary of geography, or of nineteenth century novels, or of maths and chemistry. The reason for the acceptance of one set of vocabularies and the hostility to the other is that everyone has a stake in popular culture and in literature, too. This is particularly the case for English teachers, of course. It's assumed that these identities are self-evident. Their relative value is placed and fixed. It's assumed that popular culture – and other kinds of everyday discourses – clearly don't belong to the arena of academic discourses with their distinctive vocabularies. Ideas about metonymy, for example, might well prove illuminatingly useful in relation to forms of representation and generally current cultural meanings; students are often likely to be more receptive to ideas like metonymy, though, than English teachers who might feel their professional being is undermined, or who have been trained to exclude unfamiliar ideas from the limits of their thought.

The identity of English on the curriculum is – theoretically at least – eradicated by awareness of the social, political and cultural nexus. English, as it has been predominantly, can survive only as a kind of blindness, suppressing, excluding, censoring and denigrating the theory and the innumerable social, signifying practices that don't come within its very limited scope and forms of thought. This must be a thoroughly anomalous position for a subject still claiming in some contexts to be empowering or liberating.

A redefinition of the discourse and culture of English in schooling implies a redefinition of many things, including, among others, the general idea of what schooling is for, the relation between subjects and institutions, authority and social constitution. Theory, of one kind or another, is the only way of making and understanding these connections.

A MORE INCLUSIVE CONCEPTION

There is more to the identity of English than its definition as a curriculum subject. Historical and sociological factors, for example, are also implicated in what it is; beyond the notion of a discrete and self-contained English, may be placed the subject, its ideas and practices with and against a larger, more inclusive understanding of education and society.

To pretend that English is simply about learning particular kinds of skills, or that it is simply about what happens within classroom walls is either to be naive about the identity of the subject and the discourse of education in society, or to choose a position that is content with the anomalies, gaps and contradictions of the conventional and dominant modes of the subject. To continue to teach literature, for example, without challenging the idea of literature, to continue to promote stories and poems without reflecting on what these are and why they should be done in English, seems to be merely cynical. To continue also with the established practices of teaching language in English seems thoroughly compromised, too, once you've applied a theoretical – social, political, cultural – analysis to it all.

Both sociolinguistics and post-structuralism dislodge the limited ideas of language promoted by English with powerful and more inclusive alternatives. Theory is likely to promote a very much more inclusive conception of language and textuality – capable of addressing history, discourses, culture and society, a range of social practices and institutional contexts – than English. The dominant practices of English are limited; applying theory to the field of the subject's concerns is likely to open up many more possibilities, to be much more inclusive both in terms of texts addressed and ideas utilized – as well as in terms of modes of assessment and attitudes towards the jurisdiction of the subject.

NEW BEARINGS

Conceptions of literature and language in English have masked the importance of the general field of culture – and the functions and effects of signifying practices within them. A subject addressing general textuality and language cannot remain separated from media studies, for example, cannot continue to ignore issues of culture and politics, and cannot continue to marginalize questions about language, texts and values in the way that English has. The significance of signifying practices in general cultural and linguistic life needs to be realized in definitions and practices of a subject redefined. Discourses in social contexts, the forms they take and how they operate – daily life conversations, for example – all these things might be brought within the scope of the subject, and all are things that oral work in English has never really examined. Different kinds of linguistic rhetoric – at work in many fields in many ways – might be brought within the scope of a differently conceived and defined subject.

Literature and its modes of thinking have operated according to ideas about reading, meaning and interpretation remarkable for their narrowness. English Literature has been a kind of textual extremism, powerfully and ideologically exclusive, and remarkably restricting. Personal response and associated attitudes to things textual have been similarly narrow and exclusive. English generally has neglected all modern thinking associated with linguistics, sociolinguistics, theories of discourses, semiotics and its deconstructive offshoots. The social, ideological and political dimensions of language and textuality have been excluded, if not negated by English. English cannot plausibly remain simply what it has been. New dimensions must come into play, new bearings must be found. Gender, race and class as issues express a powerful critique of English, but also provide a basis for considerable extension of its scope. New modes of thinking are required to address the problematic relation between subject English and democracy and equality. A deconstructive approach to these issues would be quite different from, and necessarily more mobile and productive than, the present failure to approach them at all.

I've proposed changes: different directions and different fields in a general redefinition. This need for redefinition comes not simply and not only from realization of flaws, but also emerges from the awareness afforded by the kinds of theory I've been advocating, by theory as a necessary self-consciousness of purposes and practices opening up social, cultural and political dimensions of language and textuality. Opening up necessarily involves the redirection of attention to much more general and significant cultural phenomena than English has been prepared to address. If this means that the subject of English is no longer recognizable as itself, then so be it.

Bibliography

The main direct sources of post-structuralist theory in general are the following:

Althusser, Louis (1977) *Lenin and Philosophy and Other Essays*, London: New Left Books.

Derrida, Jacques (1976), *Of Grammatology*, translated by Gayatri Spivak, Baltimore: Johns Hopkins University Press.

—— (1978) *Writing and Difference*, translated by Alan Bass, London: Routledge and Kegan Paul.

—— (1981) *Positions*, translated by Alan Bass, Chicago: Athlone Press.

—— (1982) *Margins Of Philosophy*, translated by Alan Bass, Chicago: Harvester Press.

Foucault, Michel (1972) *Archaeology Of Knowledge*, London: Routledge.

—— (1977) *Discipline And Punish*, translated by Alan Sheridan, London: Allen Lane.

Lacan, Jacques (1977) *Ecrits: A Selection* translated by Alan Sheridan, London: Tavistock.

—— (1979) *The Four Fundamental Concepts of Psychoanalysis*, translated by Alan Sheridan, London: Harmondsworth.

Lyotard, Jean Francois (1984) *The Postmodern Condition*, translated by Geoff Bennington and Brian Massumi, Manchester: Manchester University Press.

Although not generally cited as a post-structuralist, like Nietzsche, Wittgenstein is sometimes associated with post-structuralist theory:

Wittgenstein, L. (1953) *Philosophical Investigations*, translated by G.E.M. Anscombe, Oxford: Basil Blackwell.

—— (1967) *Zettel*, translated by G.E.M. Anscombe, Oxford: Basil Blackwell.

For general introductions to post-structuralist theory I'd recommend:

Harland, Richard (1987) *Superstructuralism: The Philosophy of Post-Structuralism and Structuralism*, London: Methuen.

Weedon, Chris (1987) *Feminist Practice And Post-Structuralist Theory*, Oxford: Basil Blackwell.

For the history of English the most frequently cited books are probably:

Baldick, C. (1983) *The Social Mission of English Criticism: 1848–1932*, Oxford: Clarendon Press.

Doyle, B. (1989) *English and Englishness*, London: Routledge.

Hunter, I. (1988) *Culture and Government: The Emergence of Literary Education*, London: Macmillan.

Mathieson, M. (1975) *The Preachers of Culture: A Study of English and its Teachers*, London: Allen and Unwin.

For theories of social context, culture and meanings:

Ang, Ien (1985) *Watching Dallas*, London: Methuen.

Bourdieu, Pierre (1986) *Distinction: A Social Critique of the Judgement of Taste*, translated by R. Nice, London: Routledge and Kegan Paul.

Fiske, John (1989) *Understanding Popular Culture* London: Unwin Hyman.

Tomlinson, John (1991) *Cultural Imperialism*, London: Pinter Publishers.

Key texts in the sociology of education:

Bourdieu, P. and Passerson, J. (1977) *Reproduction in Education, Society and Culture*, London: Sage Publications.

Bowles, S. and Gintis, H. (1976) *Schooling In Capitalist America*, London: Routledge and Kegan Paul.

Willis, Paul (1977) *Learning To Labour*, Farnborough: Saxon House.

For recent, and classic, statements on the identity of English (official versions):

Department of Education and Science (1975) *A Language For Life: Report of the Committee of Inquiry appointed by the Secretary of State for Education and Science*, Chaired by Sir Alan Bullock ('The Bullock Report') London: HMSO.

—— (1985) *English 5–16: Curriculum Matters 1*, HMI Report, London: HMSO.

—— (1989) *English 5–16* ('The Cox Reports' (1988 & 1989): 5–11; 5–16), proposals of the Secretary of State for Education and Science and the Secretary of State for Wales, Chaired by Professor B. Cox, London: HMSO.

—— Kingman Inquiry (1988) *Committee Of Inquiry into the Teaching of English Language*, Chaired by Sir J. Kingman, London: HMSO.

For introductions to sociolinguistics and critical language study:

Bourdieu, Pierre (1991) *Language and Symbolic Power*, edited and introduced by John B. Thompson, translated by Gino Raymond and Matthew Anderson, Oxford: Polity Press in association with Blackwell.

Fairclough, N (1989) *Language And Power*, Harlow: Longman.

Trudgill, P. (1974) *Sociolinguistics*, Harmondsworth: Penguin Books.

For an exemplary collection of teaching materials, illustrating alternative reading practices in detailed work on fiction:

Mellor, B., Patterson, A., and O'Neill, M. (1991) *Reading Fictions*, Perth: Chalkface Press.

Works cited:

The End of Something by Ernest Hemingway appears in *The Essential Hemingway*, (1977), London: HarperCollins.
Shane by Jack Schaefer (1957) is published in Oxford by Heinemann.

Index